Containing Iran

Strategies for Addressing the Iranian Nuclear Challenge

Robert J. Reardon

Supported by the Stanton Foundation

RAND CORPORATION

The research described in this report was supported by the Stanton Foundation.

Library of Congress Cataloging-in-Publication Data is available for this publication.
ISBN: 978-0-8330-7631-1

Published 2012 by the RAND Corporation
1776 Main Street, P.O. Box 2138, Santa Monica, CA 90407-2138
1200 South Hayes Street, Arlington, VA 22202-5050
4570 Fifth Avenue, Suite 600, Pittsburgh, PA 15213-2665
RAND URL: http://www.rand.org/
To order RAND documents or to obtain additional information, contact
Distribution Services: Telephone: (310) 451-7002;
Fax: (310) 451-6915; Email: order@rand.org

Preface

Iran's development of the nuclear fuel cycle, and its continuing progress toward the ability to produce a nuclear weapons arsenal, is one of the most pressing foreign policy issues for the United States. An Iranian nuclear arsenal could further destabilize an already unsettled region and put a number of important U.S. interests at risk. The United States has a strong interest in preventing such an outcome.

Yet it is an open question whether the United States and its allies are able to prevent Iran from developing nuclear weapons at an acceptable cost. After almost a decade of concerted effort involving economic, diplomatic, and military sources of leverage, there has been little progress toward reversing or substantially slowing Iran's nuclear progress. When the United States first began to seek UN Security Council action against Iran in 2003, the country had no stockpiles of enriched uranium, and lacked an industrial-scale enrichment capability. Today, despite all U.S. efforts, Iran has an extensive enrichment program and likely possesses the technical capacity to produce at least one nuclear weapon should it choose to do so. Sanctions, air strikes, or negotiations are unlikely to convince Iran to change course.

The objective of this study is to assess current U.S. policy options on the Iranian nuclear question and to identify a way forward. It addresses two important questions. First, how can the United States prevent Iran from developing nuclear weapons? Second, failing this, how can the United States best mitigate the negative international effects of a nuclear-armed Iran? The research presented here indicates that although both of these goals are challenging, they can be met through patient and forward-looking policymaking. Success will depend on the United States' ability to account for a variety of competing interests and policy constraints, including technical factors, Iranian domestic politics, regional alliances, and the international nonproliferation regime. No "silver bullet" solution is offered. If U.S. policy is to succeed, it must take the long view. Specifically, the United States can begin to lay the groundwork for an effective containment policy as it continues its efforts to forestall Iranian weaponization. A successful containment policy will promote long-term positive political change in Iran while avoiding counterproductive provocation.

The research for this book was concluded as the momentous events of the Arab Spring continued to unfurl across the Middle East, and the region's political future remained in flux. At the time of this writing, the implications these changes will have for Iran and its nuclear program are highly uncertain. At the same time, Iran's own political system is in flux. Rifts that were exacerbated in the aftermath of the 2009 election have continued to grow. Mahmoud Ahmadinejad, whose political fortunes have drastically declined, has ultimately failed in his efforts to challenge the political supremacy of the Supreme Leader and the clerical establishment. This study has sought to take these dynamics into account in its analysis. However, a fuller understanding will have to wait for future studies.

This research should be of interest to members of the U.S. security policy community, and to scholars interested in the politics of the Iranian nuclear program. The work should be helpful to military strategists, diplomats, and scholars. It can serve as a useful primer on the Iranian nuclear question, and as a reference that can be consulted for specific information or for finding source materials. Instructors may find this book useful in courses on U.S. foreign policy, conflict resolution, and nuclear proliferation.

Significant debates remain among the policy community over the most appropriate course of action with Iran, and there are legitimate disagreements on a number of the issues addressed in this monograph, including the costs and benefits of using military force, internal Iranian decisionmaking, the speed with which Iran could create a bomb, and the viability of a containment strategy.

Stanton Nuclear Security Fellows Program

The research reported here was prepared as part of the Stanton Nuclear Security Fellows program at the RAND Corporation. Research is conducted during a one-year fellowship at RAND under the guidance and supervision of a RAND mentor. This fellowship is financed by the Stanton Foundation. The author of this report thanks the input of colleagues and reviewers for improvements to the report, but any remaining errors or omissions are the sole responsibility of the author.

Comments are welcome and may be addressed to Robert_Reardon@hks.harvard.edu.

Contents

Figures

Table

Summary

The Iranian nuclear program is one of the new century's principal foreign policy challenges to the United States. An Iranian nuclear weapons capability could further destabilize an already precarious security situation in a key region of the world. It could also upset the existing military balance between an adversarial Iran on the one hand and the United States and its regional allies on the other. This could have important negative consequences for U.S. and world unfettered access to the region's energy resources, a prerequisite for economic growth and stability in a world only just recovering from a major financial catastrophe. It could also put U.S. interests and U.S. military forces at risk in Iraq, Afghanistan, and throughout the Middle East. Finally, it could trigger a regional nuclear arms race, prompt Israel to declare its opaque nuclear arsenal, or even risk nuclear conflict.

An accounting of worst cases, however, should not lead to inattention to what is actually likely, or how the United States' substantial military, economic, and diplomatic tools of statecraft can shape outcomes, even if Iran were to cross the nuclear threshold. This project seeks to provide a forthright and objective assessment of U.S. policy options, their potential costs and benefits, and the most appropriate strategies to achieve realistic goals. It seeks to avoid the Scylla and Charybdis of alarmism and Pollyannaism. In doing so, it adopts a long-term view of the Iranian nuclear crisis, and seeks to identify promising U.S. policy choices that can maximize security and promote U.S. regional and global interests while avoiding unnecessary costs and risks.

The central finding of this study is that negotiations with Iran and offers of *positive inducements* in return for Iranian concessions on their nuclear program have real value *even if they fail to convince Iran to agree to concessions in the near term*. In other words, the United States and its allies ought to continue to negotiate with Iran whether or not there is a realistic chance of producing a settlement. Much of the current policy debate on the Iranian nuclear crisis centers on the prospects for such a settlement. This study finds that, although such a settlement would be very welcome, the potential for reaching it is not a necessary justification for diplomacy. In this sense, the debate misses an essential point. Continued efforts to negotiate offer strategic benefits beyond the possibility of reaching a deal. The continued offer of positive inducements can instead be viewed as an integral part of an overall containment strategy: it helps build international support for U.S. nonproliferation efforts, undermines the position of the Iranian hardliners that currently dominate the regime while strengthening domestic political opponents, lowers Iran's incentives to weaponize, and helps to further isolate Iran.

At the same time, it carries little cost. As long as the United States does not have any clear alternative options such as "crippling" sanctions or preventive military force, negotiations cannot be used by Iran to stall for time. Similarly, other important elements of an overall containment strategy such as the enforcement of existing sanctions and the development of regional military capabilities and alliances can be pursued simultaneously. Finally, the study finds that the claim that negotiations undermine U.S. credibility and signal weakness is unsupported.

The most appropriate frame in which to consider the United States' Iran policy is one of *containment*. Importantly, this does not refer exclusively, or even mostly, to a military strategy, but an overarching policy framework that incorporates the broad spectrum of U.S. statecraft, including military, economic, and diplomatic instruments. All of these tools can be used effectively to craft a multilateral strategy that successfully denies Iran any political or military gain from its nuclear program, maintains regional stability and upholds the international nonproliferation regime, and applies pressure on Iran that encourages positive domestic political change over the long term.

The study does not find a single, clear "silver bullet" policy for dealing with Iran's nuclear ambitions. The United States likely does not have any viable policy options that can eliminate the Iranian threat in the near term at acceptable cost, and without inviting substantial risks. Preventive military strikes against Iran's nuclear infrastructure are unattractive and unpromising. They could trigger retaliation, upset alliances, destabilize regional states, and cost the United States multilateral support for its nonproliferation policies, all without succeeding in eliminating Iran's nuclear program over the long term. Preventive military force will likely only lead Iran to redouble its efforts and reconstitute its program.

Economic sanctions in the near term also are unlikely to convince Iran to give up its nuclear ambitions. The current leadership in Tehran places little value on international legitimacy or integration with the international political economy. It instead values self-sufficiency and autonomy, and derives domestic legitimacy from U.S., Western, and Israeli hostility by portraying itself as the only legitimate guardian of the Islamic Republic's core principles. It also views its interactions with the United States and its allies in zero-sum terms, and will likely view any concession to coercion as an unacceptable signal of weakness that would only invite further coercive demands. The regime has repeatedly signaled its resolve to withstand tight sanctions, and has staked its domestic and international reputation on it.

At the same time, the United States has likely exhausted its ability to achieve tougher sanctions through the UN Security Council. Washington has successfully won Moscow's and Beijing's support for four successively tighter sanctions resolutions, which have imposed important restrictions on Iran's finances, access to conventional weapons, and ability to acquire materials and technology for its nuclear program. However, it is not likely that the United States will be able to convince Russia and China, or its European allies, to support stricter sanctions that impose serious restrictions on Iran's oil and gas sectors. The issue is not whether the United States can successfully continue to horse trade with Russia and China to win greater support. Russia and China both have important security considerations in the balance in their relations with Iran that could be threatened by much tougher and more comprehensive sanctions. It is unlikely that either country will jeopardize these interests for any price the United States is willing or able to provide, especially considering the substantial doubts that both states have over the efficacy of economic sanctions and their ability to achieve a meaningful solution to the crisis.

Negotiations with Iran, and the offer of positive inducements in return for nuclear concessions, are unlikely to produce an acceptable compromise that resolves the nuclear issue. Iran has committed itself to possession of the nuclear fuel cycle, and it is unlikely that the United States and the other members of the P5+1 (the five permanent members of the UN Security Council—China, Russia, France, Britain, and the United States—plus Germany) will be able to offer incentives to convince the Iranians to back down from this position. Regime hardliners see any deal that sacrifices enrichment as a non-starter, and fear that the United States and its allies will use any bargaining success as a wedge toward increasingly intrusive demands. At the same time, factional discord in Tehran provides each group with an incentive to deny its rivals the gain in domestic legitimacy that could come from forging a deal.

The poor prospects for sanctions, military force, and positive inducements for resolving the nuclear crisis in the foreseeable future suggest that the United States will likely be unable to prevent Iran from improving its "breakout" capability. Iran will likely continue to improve its mastery of the nuclear fuel cycle, shorten the time it would take to build one or more bombs, increase the potential size of its arsenal, improve its delivery systems, and improve the defenses and survivability of its nuclear infrastructure. It will also continue to harden and disperse its nuclear sites and to pursue redundant paths to the production of fissile material. All of these activities can be undertaken while continuing to allow International Atomic Energy Agency (IAEA) inspections, maintaining Nuclear Nonproliferation Treaty (NPT) membership, and sustaining the pretense that the program is purely civilian in nature and consistent with Iran's international treaty obligations.

Nonetheless, it is not a foregone conclusion that Iran will develop nuclear weapons. The United States has already demonstrated that economic sanctions, export controls, and covert operations can delay Iran's progress and raise the costs of the program. The revelation of the secret Fordow enrichment complex also demonstrated that the United States has a potent intelligence capability, and the Iranians cannot be safe in the assumption that they can conduct clandestine nuclear activities undiscovered by the United States and its allies. Although safeguards and inspections in Iran are relatively weak, they also complicate Iran's ability to act in secret and make it difficult for Iran to make a dash for a weapon without the United States knowing it. Thus, although Iran can improve its breakout capability, it would be difficult for it to weaponize without the risk of triggering a military attack.

As a result, the United States and its allies should focus their efforts on developing an effective containment strategy against Iran. Similar to the original containment strategy proposed by George Kennan in the early Cold War, it should incorporate the broader spectrum of U.S. instruments of power, focus on denying Iran not only military but also *political* gain in the region, and consider positive domestic political change in Tehran as a long-term goal. The success of U.S. nonproliferation efforts will depend at least as much on influencing these long-term political dynamics as it will on denying or degrading material capabilities. Containment should be aimed at delaying any decision to weaponize and denying Iran political gain in the region while furthering these long-term domestic political trends.

Acknowledgments

The Stanton Foundation and the RAND Corporation provided generous support for the research and writing of this report. The author is grateful to the numerous colleagues who provided their assistance and helped to improve the quality of this report. Mark Fitzpatrick and Brian Chow generously took the time to provide formal reviews of the manuscript, and Dalia Dassa Kaye thoughtfully provided an informal review. Markus Schiller and Robert English helpfully reviewed sections of the report. Paula Thornhill, Andy Hoehn, David Kearn, Lynn Davis, and Bruce Bennett offered significant feedback and advice, as did Graham Allison, Al Carnesale, and the participants at the 2011 Stanton Nuclear Security Conference in Washington, D.C. Lt. Gen. Richard Y. Newton III, U.S. Air Force, generously took the time to discuss many of the arguments and ideas contained in this report. Roger Molander, Ryan Henry, Tom McNaugher, David Thaler, Steve Miller, Matt Bunn, Jim Walsh, Jim Quinlivan, Paul Davis, Forrest Morgan, Ali Nader, Melanie Sisson, and Jeff Martini all provided important and useful insights and assistance. Sarah Harting provided critical help on this report throughout the entire research project. The author is especially indebted to Stanton fellows David Kearn and Markus Schiller for the invaluable help and support they gave throughout the project, to Mark Fitzpatrick for his thorough and detailed review, and to Howard Shatz for his guidance and support. Although many helped with the creation of this report, the author bears sole responsibility for its contents. The substance and conclusions of this report in no way reflect the positions of RAND, RAND reviewers, or any RAND employees or affiliates. They are the author's alone.

Abbreviations

AEOI	Atomic Energy Organization of Iran
AP	IAEA Model Additional Protocol Safeguards Agreement
CISADA	Comprehensive Iran Sanctions, Accountability, and Divestment Act
E-3	The three European states negotiating with Iran 2002–2006: Germany, France, and the United Kingdom
FEP	fuel enrichment plant (Natanz)
FFEP	Fordow Fuel Enrichment Plant
FFL	fuel fabrication laboratory
FMP	fuel manufacturing plant (Isfahan)
GCC	Gulf Cooperative Council (Saudi Arabia, Bahrain, Oman, UAE, Qatar, and Kuwait)
HEU	highly enriched uranium (at least 20% U-235; 90% for weapons grade)
HEUF6	highly enriched uranium hexafluoride
HWPP	heavy water production plant (Arak)
HWR	heavy water reactor

IAEA	International Atomic Energy Agency
ICBM	intercontinental ballistic missile
IDF	Israel Defense Forces
ILSA	Iran and Libya Sanctions Act
INTC	Isfahan Nuclear Technology Center
IR-40	Iran's HWR at Arak
IRBM	intermediate-range ballistic missile
IRGC	Iranian Revolutionary Guards Corps (*Sepah e Pasdaran*)
LEU	low enriched uranium (<20% U-235)
LEUF6	low enriched uranium hexafluoride
LWR	light water reactor
MRBM	medium-range ballistic missile
MWe	megawatts (electric)
MWt	megawatts (thermal)
NAM	Non-Aligned Movement
NATUF6	natural uranium hexafluoride
NCRI	National Council of Resistance in Iran
NIE	National Intelligence Estimate
NIKIET	major Russian nuclear research and design institute in Moscow
NNWS	non-nuclear weapon state
NOC	national oil company
NPT	Treaty on the Non-Proliferation of Nuclear Weapons

NWFZ	nuclear weapon–free zone
P5+1	the five permanent members of the UNSC (United States, Russia, China, United Kingdom, France) plus Germany
PFEP	pilot fuel enrichment plant (Natanz)
PHRC	Physics Research Center (Tehran)
PLC	programmable logic controller
Pu-239	plutonium isotope used in weapons
Pu-240	plutonium isotope unsuitable for weapons
RBMK	Russian LWR design (*Reaktor Bolshoy Moshchnosti Kanalniy*)
SRBM	short-range ballistic missile
SWU	separative work units
TNRC	Tehran Nuclear Research Center
TNRR	Tehran Nuclear Research Reactor
U-235	fissile uranium isotope
U-238	non-fissile uranium isotope
UAE	United Arab Emirates
UCF	uranium conversion facility
UCL	uranium chemistry laboratory
UF4	uranium tetrafluoride
UF6	uranium hexafluoride
UNSC	United Nations Security Council
UNSCR	UN Security Council Resolution
UO2	uranium dioxide

URENCO	uranium enrichment company based in the United Kingdom
VVER-1000	Russian LWR design (*Vodo-Vodyanoi Energetichesky Reaktor*)

CHAPTER ONE

Introduction

Can the United States prevent Iran from developing nuclear weapons? Can it do so at an acceptable cost? What policies are most appropriate for the United States to address Iran's nuclear efforts?

The future of the Iranian nuclear program will ultimately be determined by the country's technical and material capabilities and the decisionmaking process of its leadership. Iran faces a number of constraints on its ability to produce a nuclear weapons arsenal, including access to necessary resources, technical hurdles, and financial limitations. It is also likely that the regime has not yet made a decision on whether or not to try to develop nuclear weapons, and is instead seeking to acquire the necessary components to do so quickly, should it so choose.[1]

---

[1] This finding is consistent with those of the U.S. Intelligence Community. In March 2011, summarizing the findings of the 2011 National Intelligence Estimate on Iran's nuclear program, Director of National Intelligence James Clapper stated, "We continue to assess Iran is keeping open the option to develop nuclear weapons in part by developing various nuclear capabilities that better position it to produce such weapons, should it choose to do so. We do not know, however, if Iran will eventually decide to build nuclear weapons." Later in his testimony, DNI Clapper was pressed to clarify this statement by Senator Carl Levin in the following exchange:

"Chairman LEVIN. Now, relative to Iran, Director Clapper, you mentioned in your statement that you do not, we do not know, talking about the Intelligence Community, if Iran will eventually decide to build nuclear weapons. I read into that that Iran has not made a decision as of this point to restart its nuclear weapons program. Is that correct?

Mr. CLAPPER. Yes, sir. I would like, though, to defer a more fulsome response to a closed session.

Current and future U.S. policy choices can strongly influence both Iran's material ability to produce a bomb and its nuclear decisionmaking. The United States possesses military and economic policy instruments it can use to delay Iran's nuclear progress, raise the program's costs, deny it necessary resources, or destroy many of its key facilities. The United States can influence Iranian decisionmaking by using coercive sanctions and offers of positive inducements to alter the calculus of Iran's leadership. To a large degree, success will depend on building and maintaining international support for multilateral policies.

U.S. Interests and Policy Challenges

A nuclear-armed Iran could present a number of challenges to U.S. interests. An effective containment strategy must address the following concerns:

Nuclear weapons may embolden Iran to become more aggressive regionally. This concern reflects the "stability/instability paradox": while nuclear weapons may create stable *nuclear* deterrence, paradoxically, this may actually encourage greater *conventional* adventurousness.[2] A nuclear Iran may believe that its arsenal will deter the United States and its regional allies from retaliating should Tehran engage in regional provocations. These provocations could take several forms. Iran may invade a neighbor, use conventional forces to challenge shipping in the Persian Gulf, engage in subversive activities in regional

---

Chairman LEVIN. Okay. But, what is level of confidence that you have that as of this time they have not decided to restart that program? Is that a high level of confidence?

Mr. CLAPPER. Yes, it is."

DNI James Clapper, Testimony Before the Senate Committee on Armed Services, "Hearing to Receive Testimony on the Current and Future Worldwide Threat to the National Security of the United States," March 10, 2011.

[2] See Glenn H. Snyder, *The Balance of Power and the Balance of Terror*, San Francisco: Chandler, 1965. Also see Robert Jervis, *The Illogic of American Nuclear Strategy*, Ithaca, N.Y.: Cornell University Press, 1984. Jervis (p. 31) describes the stability/instability paradox as "To the extent that the military balance is stable at the level of all-out nuclear war, it will become less stable at lower levels of violence."

states or support insurgencies, increase its material support for terrorist organizations such as Hezbollah, or encourage terrorist attacks.

Iran may provide nuclear weapons or fissile material to others. Iran may, either for strategic motives or economic profit, decide to transfer nuclear technology to other states, or to terrorists. On the low end of the threat spectrum, this includes the transfer of equipment or technical assistance to other states to help them develop an indigenous nuclear program. This could be a civilian program with the potential of being adapted for weapons production, or it could include the transfer of warhead designs and other technologies solely related to the construction of a bomb. The likeliest candidate for Iran would be Syria; however, if the motive is simply profit, Iran could find any number of global buyers.[3] On the high end of the threat spectrum, Iran could provide nuclear weapons to terrorists who could then use them against Israel, the United States, or other targets in an act of nuclear terrorism.

Iran could lose control over one or more of its weapons. Iran's command and control system could be inadequate and the stewardship of its nuclear arsenal insecure. A weapon or fissile material could be diverted or stolen, or an individual or group within Iran with access to nuclear weapons or materials could transfer them to a foreign state, or to terrorists. Diversion, sale, or theft of nuclear material is a significant concern in states such as Russia and Pakistan, and could be an even greater concern in a nuclear Iran, which may lack the ability to maintain control over a weapons arsenal, particularly if the arsenal is dispersed and hidden to reduce vulnerability to preemption.

Iran could attack U.S. allies or U.S. forces in the region with nuclear weapons. U.S. (and Israeli) nuclear forces would likely deter Iran from launching a preemptive nuclear strike. In particular, it is unlikely that Iran would conduct a nuclear attack on U.S. or allied interests unless the regime believed that it faced an imminent threat of attack. However, misperception and miscommunication could lead to Iranian nuclear use during a conventional crisis or conflict if it erroneously

---

[3] Current domestic instability in Syria, as well as Syria's recent referral to the UN Security Council for past NPT violations, however, cast doubt on whether it would be the most likely candidate to be a recipient for Iranian nuclear assistance in the future.

believed such a threat to the regime were manifest. The danger of an Iranian nuclear attack also would be greater if centralized command and control over the country's nuclear arsenal were degraded or disrupted. Although deterrence can never be perfect, the United States and its regional allies could reduce the risk of an Iranian nuclear attack through effective conflict management and avoidance, and by maintaining clear and effective lines of direct communication with Tehran, especially during times of crisis.

U.S. regional allies might bandwagon—or at least hedge—with a nuclear Iran.[4] U.S. regional partners such as the Gulf Cooperative Council (GCC) states or Iraq could become reluctant to maintain their alliances with the United States for fear of provoking a nuclear-armed Iran. These states could either more greatly align themselves with Iran, or hedge by refusing to grant basing or overflight privileges to the United States.

Iran's development of a nuclear-weapons capability could lead other states in the region to pursue their own nuclear arsenals—i.e., *Iran could trigger the falling of nuclear "dominoes."* There are several states in the region that could—should they have sufficient resolve, time, and foreign assistance—mount a successful nuclear weapons program. Members of the Saudi leadership, for example, have already suggested that they would pursue a nuclear capability should Iran acquire weapons.[5]

An Iranian nuclear capability could convince Israel that it must publicly declare its own nuclear capability in order to deter Iran. An Israeli declaration could raise tensions with Iran, contribute to the further spread of nuclear weapons in the region, and lend legitimacy to Iran's own nuclear weapons activities while undermining international support for U.S. nonproliferation efforts.

---

4 The term "bandwagon" refers here to the tendency of minor powers to align with threatening greater powers. It stands in contrast to "balancing," which refers to efforts to increase one's military capabilities or to seek out powerful allies in order to protect oneself from threatening states. For a discussion of balancing and bandwagon tendencies by minor powers, see Stephen M. Walt, *The Origins of Alliances*, Ithaca, N.Y.: Cornell University Press, 1987.

5 Ray Moseley, "Saudi Prince Warns Iran on Nuclear Weapons," *al Arabiya*, June 30, 2011.

Iranian weaponization could undermine U.S. credibility and the legitimacy of the international nonproliferation regime.[6] Iran's development of nuclear weapons could undermine the reputation of the United States, and lead allies to question its commitment to their defense. This is particularly the case given the United States' repeated statements that it will not accept an Iranian nuclear arsenal. Because Iran is a signatory of the Nuclear Nonproliferation Treaty (NPT), its development of weapons could undermine the legitimacy of the treaty and complicate multilateral nonproliferation efforts.

Iran's development of nuclear weapons, or the initiation of a breakout dash toward weaponization, could trigger regional armed conflict. If Iran were to build or test a weapon, or if it were to begin to produce weapons-grade highly enriched uranium (HEU)—i.e., breakout—it could trigger a military response from Israel, the United States, or other concerned states in the region. An attack on Iran could provoke Iranian retaliation and could escalate to a wider conflict.

Objective of the Study

The objective of this study is to evaluate the United States' ability to address these challenges, assess available policy options, and identify important vulnerabilities and weaknesses the United States or its regional allies may have. This requires frank assessments of the threat posed by the Iranian nuclear program, policy tools available to the United States, and constraints on U.S. policy choices. A sober appraisal of the Iranian nuclear program and an assessment of Iran's future choices must be careful to avoid both over- and underestimation of the threat. Similarly, U.S. policy tools—military, economic, and dip-

---

[6] The term "weaponization" is used in this text to mean the physical production of all of the necessary components of a deliverable weapon, including the possession of a delivery vehicle. The weapon need not be assembled, tested, or mated to a delivery system to meet this definition, however, all of the weapon components, including the physics package, must be built. This is distinct from the possession of a "virtual" capability, in which case Iran would possess all of the necessary elements required to rapidly weaponize without having actually done so. These distinctions are covered in greater detail later in the text.

lomatic—vary in their potency and effectiveness according to a complex set of factors, including the specifics of a policy's design, regional strategic realities, degree of international support, and domestic political dynamics in Iran. By their very nature, all of these policy choices involve significant uncertainties and risk.

U.S. policy toward Iran is not chosen in a vacuum. American policy choices are sharply constrained by how they may affect a wide set of interconnected interests, such as U.S. relations with regional allies, ongoing military operations in Afghanistan, the stability of Iraq, and—not least—U.S. domestic politics. A full evaluation of U.S. policy options must take all of these considerations into account.

Organization of the Text

The text is organized as follows. Chapter Two considers the past, present, and future of the Iranian nuclear program and lays the substantive groundwork for the analysis. It provides an overview of the nuclear fuel cycle program in Iran and considers the possible pathways available to Iran to produce nuclear weapons should it choose to do so.

Chapter Three examines the political aspects of the nuclear program. It surveys the internal and external motivations for Iran's nuclear decisions, including security threats, regime legitimacy, ideology, and prestige. This chapter concludes with a section that details the domestic political actors and processes that shape the nuclear decisionmaking process.

Chapter Four identifies a number of important factors that will influence and constrain U.S. policy choices on the Iranian nuclear issue. The United States will need to reconcile its pursuit of counterproliferation goals in Iran with the interests of regional allies, existing military balance in the Middle East, uncertain social and political dynamics in the region, and interests of key global partners. This chapter considers in detail the most important of these actors, including the Gulf States, Israel, Russia, and China. It also examines the potential trade-offs involved in pursuing U.S. policy goals in Iran with the international nonproliferation regime as a whole.

Chapter Five examines U.S. policy options and offers a conceptual framework that allows for an improved policy analysis. This framework highlights the ways that military, economic, and diplomatic tools of statecraft can be used to both influence Iran's decisionmaking process and directly affect Iran's available policy choices by degrading capabilities or starving the nuclear program of necessary resources. This framework is then used to guide an assessment of specific policy options. The chapter evaluates the costs, risks, and likely consequences of different policy choices, and highlights important trade-offs that U.S. policymakers must face. These insights are then used to describe the contours of an effect containment strategy that focuses on two U.S. objectives: (1) preventing Iran from developing nuclear weapons; and (2) failing this, mitigating the negative effects of a nuclear-armed Iran both regionally and globally.

Chapter Six, the conclusion, summarizes the study's findings and lays out a specific set of policy recommendations for the United States. Although the study does not identify a single "silver bullet" likely to quickly and definitively solve the nuclear crisis, it does offer a coherent set of policy recommendations that can contain the negative effects of Iran's nuclear program, reduce the chances of Iranian weaponization, and promote long-term positive political change.

CHAPTER TWO

Iran's Nuclear Program: Past, Present, and Future

Iran's nuclear program has made impressive progress, particularly considering the efforts taken by others—most importantly the United States—to deny Iran access to outside resources and assistance. At the same time, it is important to recognize that Iran's existing nuclear capabilities are the product of decades of effort. Iran also has benefited greatly from past foreign assistance, especially the A.Q. Khan network, which provided Iran with many of the essential elements of its enrichment program.

Iran's nuclear program is not without its problems. Some result from U.S. and Israeli sabotage and multilateral sanctions. Much of it, though, comes from technical problems and resource scarcity within the country. These problems may prevent Iran from ever successfully completing full-scale and indigenously constructed nuclear energy infrastructure that can reliably provide the country with electricity. However, Iran is well capable of meeting the less demanding goal of producing the fissile material required for nuclear weapons.

It is unlikely that Iran will produce nuclear weapons within the next year, and it could be years—if ever—before it does so. At present, although Iran likely possesses the technical ability to make at least one deliverable nuclear weapon, it would be very difficult for it to do so without accepting serious risk. If Iran were to use its declared facilities for a breakout dash, it would likely require at least one year, and potentially more than two years, to build a bomb. Iran would find it extremely difficult to carry out a breakout dash using these facilities without alerting the United States and its allies, providing them with several months to consider a response. A potentially more attractive option for Iran would be to use a covert facility for HEU enrichment. However, this route would require the clandestine construction and operation of a facility, which would also carry significant risks. It is likely that Iran instead intends to focus its efforts over the near term on improving its breakout options, and to do so in ways that are unlikely to trigger a serious response, such as air strikes. Such a goal would be consistent with what has thus far been observed in Iran.

History of Iran's Nuclear Program

Nuclear Program Under the Shah

Iran's nuclear program has a long history, beginning with U.S.–Iranian civilian nuclear cooperation at a time when Iran was ruled by the shah, and was a close U.S. ally. The United States and Iran signed a civilian nuclear cooperation agreement in 1957, and a 5 MWt research reactor was completed by the American firm AMF in 1967. The reactor (the Tehran Nuclear Research Reactor, or TNRR), and a set of related research laboratories, became part of the Tehran Nuclear Research Center (TNRC).[1] As a condition of American nuclear cooperation, Iran signed the NPT in 1968, and ratified the treaty in 1970. In 1974, Iran signed a Safeguards Agreement with the International Atomic Energy Agency (IAEA), putting all of the country's nuclear facilities under the IAEA's inspection and monitoring regime.

The Atomic Energy Organization of Iran (AEOI) was established in 1974 and charged with fulfilling the ambitious goal of producing 23,000 MWe by 1995. Included in these plans was the development of the full nuclear fuel cycle and, specifically, the ability to enrich uranium.[2] Iran developed plans to construct 22 nuclear reactors over the coming decades, to be supplied by European and American contrac-

---

1 Nuclear Threat Initiative, "Iran: Nuclear Overview," www.nti.org/e_research/profiles/iran/Nuclear/index.html.

2 International Institute for Strategic Studies, *Iran's Nuclear, Chemical and Biological Capabilities: A Net Assessment*, London: IISS, 2011, pp. 8–9.

tors. Also, in 1974, the country extended a $1 billion loan to the European nuclear fuel manufacturer Eurodif, in return for the supply of 10% of the company's fuel production.[3] In 1976, Tehran signed a contract with the German joint venture Kraftwerk Union to construct two 1,300 MWe light water reactors (LWRs) at Bushehr. The same year, the Iranians contracted with Framatome to construct two 900 MWe LWRs at Darkhovin. Iran also signed letters of intent with French, German, and American suppliers for an additional 18 reactors.

India's first nuclear test explosion in 1974 sparked reconsideration in Washington of nuclear export policies and greater scrutiny of foreign nuclear programs, including Iran's. In 1977, the Carter administration decided to withhold nuclear fuel cycle assistance from Iran, and required that Tehran accede to IAEA comprehensive safeguards in order to receive continued civilian nuclear assistance from the United States.[4] Although there is no evidence of an Iranian nuclear weapons program under the shah, U.S. concerns were well founded, as the Iranians did view their civilian program as a means of acquiring a nuclear "breakout" capability (i.e., the ability to quickly produce a bomb once such a decision is made), and there is evidence that Iranian scientists secretly conducted experiments related to the nuclear fuel cycle.[5]

Revolution, Rejection, and Revival: 1979–2002

The Iranian Revolution dealt a setback to the country's nuclear program. Ayatollah Khomeini was skeptical of the nuclear effort, which he viewed as "Western" and contrary to the teachings of Islam. Iran also lost many of its top nuclear scientists and engineers as a result of the revolution, which triggered the flight of educated Iranians from the country. Foreign nuclear suppliers became reluctant to trade with

---

[3] Oliver Meier, "Iran and Foreign Enrichment: A Troubled Model," *Arms Control Today*, Vol. 36, No. 1, 2006.

[4] The new U.S. policy was codified in the March 1978 Nonproliferation Act. See William Burr, "A Brief History of U.S.-Iranian Nuclear Negotiations," *Bulletin of the Atomic Scientists*, Vol. 65, No. 1, January/February 2009.

[5] David Albright and Andrea Stricker, "Iran's Nuclear Program," in Robin Wright, ed., *Iran Primer: Power, Politics, and U.S. Policy*, Washington, D.C.: United States Institute of Peace, 2010, pp. 77–81.

the new Iranian regime, particularly after the United States began a campaign to bar civilian nuclear cooperation with Iran. The nuclear program was left without funding, talent, international assistance, or initiative.[6] Tehran quickly canceled pending nuclear contracts that were initiated under the shah's ambitious program, and withdrew from Eurodif. As a result of financial disputes and pressure from the United States, Kraftwerk Union suspended its work on the Bushehr nuclear facility, leaving the two reactors at the site only partially completed. The Bushehr facility was also repeatedly damaged by air raids during the Iran-Iraq War.

Despite these setbacks, the country's nuclear program was not abandoned during the 1980s and, in fact, several important steps to advance it were taken during this period. In 1985, with French assistance, Iran completed laboratory-scale uranium conversion and fuel fabrication facilities at Isfahan.[7] Most significantly, the AEOI initiated fuel-cycle research at the TNRC in the mid-1980s, and began to purchase designs and components for uranium enrichment from the A.Q. Khan network in 1987. Iran has argued that it turned to the black market in search of fuel-cycle technology after being rebuffed by legitimate nuclear suppliers.[8]

The Iraqi use of chemical weapons against Iran during the Iran-Iraq War, and the international community's failure to respond to it, may have triggered a renewed interest among the Iranian leadership in the country's nuclear program.[9] The death of Ayatollah Khomeini in

---

[6] IISS, 2011, pp. 10–12. Among other things, Iran's relationship with Eurodif was severed, the Germans canceled their contract for Bushehr, and the Americans stopped supplying fuel for the TNRR (a contract was later signed with the Argentines).

[7] Iran contracted with a French supplier to purchase a uranium chemistry laboratory (UCL) and fuel fabrication laboratory (FFL) for the Isfahan Nuclear Technology Center (INTC). Between 1985 and 1993, Iran conducted laboratory-scale experiments in uranium conversion and fuel fabrication. These activities were not declared to the IAEA until 1998 (IAEA, GOV/2003/75, November 10, 2003).

[8] IAEA, GOV/2007/75, November 15, 2007.

[9] There is little direct information available on Iran's nuclear decisionmaking. Iran's nuclear program was revitalized during the Iran-Iraq War. However, the program not only continued after the war, but grew in importance even as the Iraq threat was greatly reduced by

1989 also contributed to the rekindling of Iran's nuclear efforts. In the early 1990s, Iran advanced its uranium enrichment efforts and conducted research on plutonium reprocessing.[10] Tehran also began to more actively pursue foreign suppliers of nuclear technology. In early 1995, the Russian firm Zarubezhatomenergostroi signed a contract with the AEOI to complete the Bushehr plant. The $1 billion contract provided for the construction of a 900 MWe LWR, and was intended as only the initial step for Iranian-Russian nuclear cooperation.

During this period, the United States began a diplomatic initiative to put pressure on potential suppliers. The United States was particularly concerned with assistance from Moscow. Washington discovered that in a secret protocol to the Russian-Iranian 1992 nuclear agreement, the Russians had agreed to provide Iran with more sensitive nuclear technologies such as plutonium reprocessing and uranium enrichment facilities.[11] The protocol was nullified in response to U.S. pressure, but the plans for Russian-built reactors at Bushehr went forward in spite of strenuous objections from Washington.

China also became a principal supplier for Tehran. In the early 1990s, China agreed to provide Iran with research reactors, laser enrichment equipment, and an industrial-scale uranium conversion facility (UCF), as well as uranium fluorides and oxide. In 1992, China and Iran signed a contract for the sale of a 300 MWe LWR and a large research reactor capable of producing plutonium for a nuclear weapon.

---

the Gulf War and subsequent efforts to destroy Baghdad's nuclear, chemical, and biological weapons programs. This suggests that while near-term security threats may have initially served as the impetus for a renewal of the nuclear program, other motivations are required to explain later nuclear policies. See Shahram Chubin, *Iran's Nuclear Ambitions*, Washington, D.C.: Carnegie Endowment for International Peace, 2006, pp. 7–10.

[10] Iran admitted to irradiating 7 kg of UO2 pellets in the TNRR and then separating plutonium from 3 kg of the pellets in hot cells, yielding trace amounts of plutonium. These experiments took place between 1988 and 1992. The hot cells were reportedly dismantled and put into storage at Esfahan in 1992. IAEA, GOV/2003/75.

[11] Steven Greenhouse, "US Says Russia Promised Nuclear Gear to Iran," *New York Times*, April 29, 1995; "Ministry 'Engineered' Parts of Iranian Nuclear Deal—Russian Ambassador to US," Interfax, May 10, 1995 (BBC Monitoring); Robert J. Einhorn and Gary Samore, "Ending Russian Assistance to Iran's Nuclear Bomb," *Survival*, Vol. 44, No. 2, Summer 2002.

The Chinese, too, eventually yielded to U.S. pressure, and agreed to sever their nuclear ties with Iran in 1997 in return for a "123" nuclear cooperation agreement with the United States. Many of the projects promised by the Chinese, such as the two large reactors, were never delivered. However, the Chinese-initiated UCF at Isfahan was sufficiently complete for the Iranians to finish the work themselves.[12]

Iran received substantial assistance for its enrichment program from the A.Q. Khan network. Although Iran began to receive help from the Pakistani network as early as the mid-1980s, its efforts were more limited than they later became. It was not until after the death of Khomeini in 1989 that Iran pursued more extensive assistance from A.Q. Khan. In the mid-1990s, the Khan network provided designs for both the P-1 and the more advanced P-2 centrifuges, necessary parts for their assembly, and hundreds of used centrifuges from Pakistan. The network also gave the Iranians important technical advice.[13] This assistance was critical to the success of the Iranian program, and served as the basis of Iran's eventual ability to produce highly enriched uranium (HEU) that could fuel a weapon.

Over the course of the 1990s, the Iranian enrichment program grew rapidly. By the end of the decade, Iran had achieved the ability to enrich uranium to 1% U-235 using a small centrifuge cascade at the Kalaye Electric Company's facilities outside Tehran. In 2000, construction began on both the Pilot Fuel Enrichment Plant (PFEP) and the industrial-scale Fuel Enrichment Plant (FEP) at Natanz. Iran planned to equip the PFEP with 1,000 high-speed centrifuges, and the FEP with 50,000 centrifuges.

Revelation and E-3 Negotiations: 2002–2006

In 2002, the exiled opposition group National Council of Resistance of Iran (NCRI) publicly revealed the existence of secret nuclear facilities in Iran, including the Natanz facilities and a heavy water production

---

[12] Shirley A. Kan, *China and Proliferation of Weapons of Mass Destruction: Policy Issues*, Washington, D.C.: Congressional Research Service, RL31555, May 26, 2011, pp. 9–21.

[13] Adrian Levy and Cathy Scott-Clark, *Deception: Pakistan, the United States, and the Secret Trade in Nuclear Weapons*, New York: Walker, 2007.

facility at Arak. Iran confirmed the presence of these facilities when IAEA Director General Mohamed ElBaradei visited Iran in February 2003. By then, Iran had installed a single 100-centrifuge cascade at Natanz, and had assembled—but not yet installed—many more. IAEA inspections conducted over the course of 2003 also uncovered evidence of past enrichment activity, and information about Iran's ties to the A.Q. Khan network.[14]

While the United States preferred an immediate referral of Iran to the UN Security Council (UNSC), its European allies favored a negotiating strategy. Under pressure from the IAEA and the West, Tehran struck a deal with the United Kingdom, France, and Germany (the "E-3") in October 2003 to sign the Additional Protocol (AP) to the NPT, which provided for expanded safeguards and inspections by the IAEA. Iran also agreed to suspend its uranium enrichment activities and to be forthcoming about its past nuclear efforts. In return, the E-3 agreed to enter into negotiations with Iran.[15] This agreement was later formalized in the 2004 Paris Agreement. In March 2005, the United States agreed to support the E-3 initiative, provided that if negotiations with Iran were to fail, the Europeans would support referral to the Security Council.[16]

The E-3 negotiating position was to offer a package of positive inducements that included security guarantees, assistance with civil-

---

[14] IAEA, GOV/2003/40, June 6, 2003; IAEA, GOV/2004/83, November 15, 2004, pp. 7–9.

[15] Iran and the E-3 originally agreed to an enrichment suspension in the Tehran Agreement of 2003. However, sources of contention between the IAEA and Iran arose almost immediately, as Iran disputed the IAEA's definition of what constituted a suspension, and continued to make progress in some areas of its nuclear program. Iran insisted that activities such as fuel conversion and the manufacture of centrifuge parts ought not to be considered violations of the agreement. Thus in mid-2004, once Iran completed the UCF at Isfahan, it announced that it would begin producing UF6 and that it would initiate construction of an HWR at Arak. In the November 2004 Paris Agreement, Iran finally agreed to suspend all enrichment-related activities, including uranium conversion and centrifuge assembly, but by then the UCF had already become operational. Also by then, Iran had stockpiled 2 metric tons of UF6. IAEA, GOV/2004/83.

[16] David E. Sanger and Steven R. Weisman, "U.S. and European Allies Agree on Steps in Iran Dispute," *New York Times*, March 11, 2005.

ian nuclear technology, and the lifting of economic sanctions. In return, Iran would need to give up its enrichment program, stick to an enhanced IAEA inspections and safeguards regime, and answer outstanding questions about past behavior.[17] However, negotiations between Iran and the E-3 foundered as the two sides stuck to mutually exclusive positions on enrichment. The E-3 (and the United States) insisted that any deal include the full cessation of uranium enrichment. The Iranians insisted that their nuclear program was peaceful, and vowed never to give up the fuel cycle, arguing they had a "right" to an enrichment program.[18]

Failing to reach a negotiated settlement with the E-3, and with its presidential elections approaching, Iran announced its intention to restart enrichment activities in 2005, and began producing UF6 at Isfahan immediately after the election of Mahmoud Ahmadinejad.[19] In early 2006, Iran broke the IAEA seals at Natanz and other facilities to begin research with its centrifuge program. In February, Iran began to feed natural uranium UF6 feedstock (NATUF6) into centrifuges in the PFEP, and that April announced that it had successfully enriched

[17] IAEA, INFCIRC/637, November 26, 2004; Elaine Sciolino, "Europeans Say Iran Agrees to Freeze Uranium Enrichment," *New York Times*, November 16, 2004.

[18] Reuters, "Iran Vows to Resist Pressure to Drop Nuclear Fuel Program," March 13, 2005. The E-3 did not fully share the U.S.'s commitment to no enrichment. When Iran proposed a deal in March 2005 that would allow it to keep a pilot enrichment program, the Europeans agreed to "consider" the proposal. However, the Europeans also were aware that for any agreement with Iran to work, it would require the support of the United States. "Europe 'Rock-Solid' That Iran Cease Enrichment Ahead of New Talks," Agence France Presse, April 16, 2005.

[19] Molly Moore, "Iran Restarts Uranium Program," *Washington Post*, February 15, 2006. A last-minute E-3 offer was rejected by Ahmadinejad as "absurd," again on the grounds that it demanded full cessation of enrichment. Iran also rejected a Russian proposal in which Iran's uranium fluoride feedstock would be shipped to Russia for enrichment. Iran was willing to agree to the proposal in principal, but only if it did not involve giving up its indigenous enrichment program. "Iran Rejects 'Unacceptable' EU Nuclear Offer," Agence France Presse, August 5, 2005; Ed Johnson, "Europe Offers Iran Civilian Nuke Support," Associated Press, August 5, 2005; Lionel Beehner, "Russia's Nuclear Deal with Iran," *Council on Foreign Relations Backgrounder*, February 28, 2006.

uranium to 3.5% U-235.[20] Tehran also announced that it would no longer implement the AP or any other "voluntary" cooperative arrangements with the IAEA. The IAEA Board of Governors voted to report the matter to the UNSC.

The P5+1, Ahmadinejad, and UN Sanctions: 2006–2008

In 2006, with Russia and China opposing sanctions in the UNSC, the United States agreed to join with the other four permanent members of the Security Council, plus Germany (the "P5+1"), to offer a new package of positive inducements to Iran. The P5+1 offered a package of inducements similar to the earlier E-3 proposals, but demanded that enrichment suspension be a precondition for any negotiations. Washington also dropped its insistence that enrichment be forgone completely, and allowed that some limited enrichment capability could be acceptable at a future date. This date, however, was not specified, and could only come after Iran had restored confidence in its peaceful nuclear intentions, something unlikely to occur in the foreseeable future. In July, the UNSC passed Resolution 1696, which set an October deadline for negotiations before sanctions would be considered.[21]

A breakthrough nearly came in September 2006, when the Europeans successfully brokered a tentative deal with Ali Larijani, Iran's chief negotiator. Under the deal, Larijani would meet at the UN in New York with E-3 representatives and agree to a suspension of enrichment in return for removal of Iran's nuclear dossier from UNSC deliberation. As soon as that was accomplished, Larijani would then enter direct negotiations with U.S. Secretary of State Condoleezza Rice. Rice was prepared to agree to a token Iranian enrichment program that was

---

[20] The process of uranium enrichment involves increasing the concentration of the uranium isotope U-235. This is discussed in greater detail later in this chapter.

[21] Glenn Kessler, "Early October New Deadline for Iran," *Washington Post*, September 21, 2006; Paul Kerr, "U.S., Allies Await Iran's Response to Nuclear Offer," *Arms Control Today*, Vol. 36, No. 6, July/August 2006; "China, Russia On Board in Sweetened Offer to Iran," CNN, June 5, 2006.

limited to research. This deal was killed, however, when Larijani failed to win approval from Supreme Leader Khamenei.[22]

After the October deadline elapsed, UN Security Council Resolution (UNSCR) 1737—the UNSC's first sanctions resolution against Iran—passed. Much weaker than the United States had hoped, 1737 imposed a ban on many forms of civilian nuclear and ballistic-missile cooperation with Iran, and placed financial sanctions on a number of Iranian entities tied to the nuclear program.[23] The Bushehr reactor project was exempted from the resolution, and Moscow continued to reaffirm its commitment to finish the reactor and supply low enriched uranium (LEU) fuel for its operation. UNSCR 1737 also set a new deadline—in late February 2007—for Iranian suspension of all enrichment-related activities. Iran responded to the sanctions by announcing that it would begin installing centrifuges at the FEP, and banned 38 IAEA inspectors from Natanz.

After the February 2007 deadline set by UNSCR 1737, the UNSC quickly passed Resolution 1747.[24] The new resolution extended financial sanctions to more Iranian entities linked to the nuclear program and banned Iranian arms exports (imports were unaffected). A new deadline was set for 60 days after passage. Iran responded to 1747 with further restrictions on inspections and safeguards. It announced that it would no longer adhere to the revised Code 3.1 of the Subsidiary Agreements, and instead would provide notice of new facilities only 180 days before nuclear materials would be introduced.[25] April 2007

---

[22] "Iran and the West, Part 3: Nuclear Confrontation," BBC News, first broadcast February 21, 2009. Cited by IISS, 2011, p. 32. The Supreme Leader reportedly saw Iran as having the upper hand in negotiations in light of the deteriorating situation in Iraq at this time.

[23] United Nations Security Council Resolution 1737 (2006), S/RES/1737(2006), adopted December 23, 2006.

[24] United Nations Security Council Resolution 1747 (2007), S/RES/1747(2007), adopted March 24, 2007.

[25] The revised Code 3.1 of the Subsidiary Agreements requires member states to declare new nuclear facilities to the IAEA while they are at the design stage. The Subsidiary Agreements specify the procedures for implementing the Safeguards Agreement. Code 3.1 originally provided for notification of new facilities 180 days before they would receive nuclear materials. The IAEA later modified this to stipulate that member states should notify the IAEA once a

marked a critical turning point, as Iran began industrial-scale enrichment to 3.5% at the FEP, using more than 1,000 centrifuges.[26] The May 2007 deadline passed without any Iranian concessions.

In summer 2007, the EU and Iran began to discuss the possibility of a deal focused on a "freeze-for-freeze," in which the UNSC would cease deliberations over further sanctions in return for an Iranian agreement not to further expand its enrichment program. This deal reportedly had the support of Ali Larijani, Iran's nuclear negotiator, but was opposed by both the United States and President Ahmadinejad, who ultimately killed the proposal.

In December, the Bush administration's push for tougher coercive measures was set back by the release of an unclassified summary of the 2007 National Intelligence Estimate (NIE) on Iran's nuclear program. The 2007 NIE concluded that although Iran had a nuclear weapons program up until fall 2003, this work was likely discontinued. It also found that while Iran was continuing toward a breakout capability, it had likely not yet decided to weaponize.[27] These findings were seized by both domestic advocates of restraint and by states such as Russia and China to argue that there was no urgent need for further sanctions (or military force).

---

decision has been made to construct a new facility. Iran accepted this modification in 2003, then unilaterally reversed this agreement in 2007. Iran argued that it was not legally held to the revised code, as it was only following it on a voluntary basis—a position the IAEA does not accept. IAEA, GOV/2007/22, May 23, 2007, para. 14.

[26] Iran began feeding UF6 into centrifuge cascades at the FEP in April 2007. As of May 13, 2007, Iran was feeding UF6 into eight 164-centrifuge cascades, producing LEU at an enrichment level of roughly 3.5%. David Albright, Jacqueline Shire, and Paul Brannan, "IAEA Safeguards Report on Iran: Iran Making Progress but Not Yet Reliably Operating an Enrichment Plant," ISIS, May 25, 2007.

[27] The report's findings were more nuanced and tempered than they were often portrayed. It stated with "high confidence" that Iran had had a nuclear weapons program before fall 2003. It also found with "moderate confidence" that this work had been suspended in 2003, and that the available data was insufficient to determine whether or not that work had been resumed. The report's conclusions were challenged by allies such as France and Israel. Office of the Director of National Intelligence, *Iran: Nuclear Intentions and Capabilities*, National Intelligence Estimate, November 2007.

In an effort to restore momentum to its push for tighter sanctions and to counteract the political effects of the 2007 NIE, in February 2008 the Bush administration turned over to the IAEA the U.S. intelligence findings on Iran's nuclear weaponization work from a laptop obtained from an Iranian defector in 2004. The laptop allegedly contained thousands of documents related to a secret Iranian nuclear weapons program. The IAEA later presented this evidence to member states (Iran refused to examine it or offer any explanation beyond blanket denials).

Buoyed by this intelligence, lingering questions about Iran's past activities, and Iran's continued progress on its nuclear program, in March 2008 the UNSC voted in favor of a third sanctions resolution, UNSCR 1803.[28] These sanctions, too, fell far short of what the United States had preferred. Resolution 1803 again expanded the list of Iranian entities subject to sanctions, authorized the inspection of Iranian cargo, and banned the trade of more dual-use technologies. But Iran's vast energy sector was left largely unaffected. The new sanctions did little to slow Iran's progress. Benefitting from high oil prices, the Iranians remained defiant. Reaffirming Iran's refusal to give up its enrichment program, in May 2008, Ayatollah Khamenei declared, "No threat can hinder the Iranian nation from its path. We will forcefully continue on our path and will not allow the oppressors to step on our rights."[29]

In June 2008, the P5+1 presented Iran with a new incentives package, which included the incentives offered in 2006 and several added sweeteners. The deal built on the earlier freeze-for-freeze plan, under which Iran would continue to enrich uranium but freeze any expansion of its program. This would provide a "pause" during which negotiations could take place. For the first time, a U.S. representative attended the talks with Iran, when the Bush administration elected to

---

[28] Kenneth Katzman, *Iran Sanctions*, Washington, D.C.: Congressional Research Service, RS20871, March 1, 2011. The United States also had to agree to another offer of positive inducements in order to win support for sanctions.

[29] "Iran Vows Not to Halt Its Nuclear Program Despite Western Pressure," Associated Press, May 5, 2008.

send Under Secretary of State William Burns to the P5+1 meeting in Tehran in July 2008.

Yet despite several mixed and confusing messages from Iran, which may have reflected divisions within the regime, Tehran remained firm in its insistence that it would not suspend enrichment, even temporarily, to allow for negotiations. Only days after the July meetings, Ahmadinejad announced that Iran would not "retreat one iota" in its nuclear efforts. Supreme Leader Khamenei later stated that Iran would "continue with its path."[30] With the inducements package rejected, the P5+1 returned to the sanctions track.

A New Administration: 2009–Present

Upon taking office, President Obama signaled a willingness to pursue an engagement strategy with Iran. The President expressed his desire for diplomacy and compromise in an interview with al Arabiya television, a Nowruz address to the Iranian people in which he specifically referred to the "Islamic Republic of Iran," and a landmark June 2009 speech in Cairo. The administration also announced that the United States would directly participate in all P5+1 negotiations.[31]

Despite a professed greater willingness to negotiate, however, the new administration's Iran policy retained many elements of the previous administration's approach. Overall, the new administration continued to follow a dual-track policy that sought to use coercive pressure to force Iran to negotiate on more favorable terms. The administration also did not take the military option off the table. In April 2009, Secretary of State Clinton told the House Committee on Foreign Relations that the United States would pursue "crippling sanctions" should

---

[30] Alan Cowell, "Iran Won't Retreat on Nuclear Program," *New York Times*, July 24, 2008; Graham Bowley, "Despite Call to Halt, Iran Says It Will Continue Its Nuclear Program," *New York Times*, July 31, 2008.

[31] "Obama Reaches Out to Muslim World," BBC News, January 27, 2009; Ewen MacAskill and Robert Tait, "TV Diplomacy: Obama's Video Message to Iranians," *Guardian*, March 21, 2009; President Barack Obama, Prepared Remarks at Cairo University, June 4, 2009; Mark Landler and Nazila Fathi, "United States to Join Nuclear Talks with Iran," *New York Times*, April 9, 2009.

diplomacy fail, and reiterated the Bush administration's position that the United States would not accept a nuclear-armed Iran.[32]

The administration's plans for an engagement strategy were also soon upset by the 2009 Iranian elections, the resulting protests, and rise of the Green Movement. Washington was forced to adopt a wait-and-see attitude toward the uprisings, fearing that diplomatic outreach could provide the regime with additional legitimacy. The new administration also faced a number of other outside pressures. Most important was Iran's continuing progress with its nuclear program. Iran crossed the symbolic threshold of stockpiling enough 3.5% LEU for one nuclear bomb in 2009. In April 2009, Ahmadinejad announced that Iran had acquired the "entire nuclear fuel cycle" when he unveiled a fuel fabrication plant near Isfahan.[33] Israel's impatience with Iran also put pressure on Washington. With Benjamin Netanyahu assuming the premiership in 2009, Israel's position toward Iran hardened. In his visit to Washington in May, Netanyahu pushed Washington to accept an end-of-the-year deadline for progress with negotiations before switching to a coercive track.[34]

In September 2009, in a move to put greater pressure on Tehran, the United States revealed the existence of a secret uranium enrichment facility at Fordow, near Qom. The following month, in talks with Iran held in Geneva, the United States presented a "fuel-swap" proposal: a confidence-building measure under which the Iranians would agree to ship 1.2 metric tons of 3.5% low enriched UF6 (LEUF6) to Russia in return for completed fuel assemblies for the TNRR. Iran was running out of the 20% LEU fuel for its Tehran reactor, which it used to produce medical isotopes, and had asked the IAEA for help procuring replacement fuel in summer 2009.[35] Under the fuel-swap proposal, Iran would be given the necessary fuel, but only after most of its own

---

[32] "U.S.: Iran Faces 'Crippling' Sanctions If Nuclear Talks Fail," Reuters, April 22, 2009.

[33] IAEA, GOV/2009/8, February 18, 2009.

[34] "Obama Prods Netanyahu, Iran in Mideast Foray," Associated Press, May 19, 2009.

[35] In 2009, Iran asked the IAEA for assistance in finding an international seller for 20% LEU fuel for the TNRR. Iran claimed its existing supply of fuel, purchased from Argentina in the 1992, would soon run out, an assessment supported by the United States, Britain, and

stocks of enriched uranium (about 1.6 metric tons of 3.5% LEUF6 at the time) had been shipped out of the country. The swap would do little to resolve the outstanding dispute over enrichment, but could buy time for negotiations to make progress. In the October meetings in Geneva, the Iranian representatives agreed to the deal in principal. In further talks held later that month in Vienna with the United States, Russia, France, and the IAEA (the "Vienna Group") to discuss the plan in greater detail, the Iranians said they considered a proposal sponsored by the IAEA in a "favorable light," but would need time to provide a definitive response.[36]

The fuel-swap deal came apart, however, after Ahmadinejad encountered political resistance in Tehran from all sides. Even reformists, eager to deny Ahmadinejad any political victory, criticized the deal. Most objectionable to the deal's opponents was the stipulation that LEU be shipped abroad before fuel for the TNRR would be produced. It would therefore require a year after the shipment before reactor fuel could be provided, raising the concern that the West would find an excuse to renege and leave Iran without either the fuel or its own LEU stockpile. After Khamenei took the side of critics, Ahmadinejad was forced to renege.

With the collapse of the fuel-swap plan, the P5+1 began to focus again on sanctions.[37] The cautious optimism of October 2009 quickly gave way to renewed pessimism as Iran responded with increased defiance. In December, Ahmadinejad announced that Iran would begin

---

France. Peter Grier, "Why Does Iran Need More Potent Uranium? Medical Care," *Christian Science Monitor*, October 21, 2009.

[36] Mark Fitzpatrick, "Iran: The Fragile Promise of the Fuel-Swap Plan," *Survival*, Vol. 52, No. 3, June/July 2010.

[37] As members of the P5+1 prepared a draft of a new sanctions resolution, in May 2010, Iran signed a joined declaration with Brazil and Turkey in which Iran agreed to send 1.2 tons of LEU to Turkey in return for fuel for the TNRR within one year. The eleventh-hour agreement, coming one day before the finalization of the sanctions resolution draft, was rejected by the P5+1 as a stalling tactic. Although the Brazil-Turkey deal was largely the same as the fuel-swap plan proposed the previous October, in the intervening seven months, Iran had greatly increased its stocks of LEU, and had begun enriching to 20%, negating the original intention of the proposal.

enriching its 3.5% LEU stocks to 20% in order to fuel the TNRR on its own. Enriching uranium to 20% also would bring Iran much closer to being able to produce fuel for a bomb. Iran further announced its intention to build ten more enrichment sites similar to the one at Fordow, and threatened to again reduce its cooperation with the IAEA. After rejecting a last-ditch offer from the West to help Iran purchase medical isotopes on the open market, Iran announced in February 2010 that it had begun enriching to 20% at the PFEP at Natanz.[38]

In June, the UNSC passed Resolution 1929. Again, China and Russia blocked any inclusion of sanctions against the country's oil and gas sector. Resolution 1929 did, however, impose a ban on most arms imports, provide for (voluntary) restrictions on financial activities related to the IRGC, and open the door for the United States and its Western allies to enact tough new unilateral sanctions. Significantly, Russia used the passage of Resolution 1929 as justification to cancel its deal to provide Iran with the S-300 air defense system, a move not strictly required according to the resolution's language.

The P5+1 has made little progress with Iran since the breakdown of the fuel-swap plan in 2009. Although talks were held between the P5+1 states and Iran in late 2010 and early 2011, these yielded no positive results, because Iran insisted that all economic sanctions be lifted as a precondition for substantive negotiations on its nuclear program. Tehran has, however, signaled a willingness to end its enrichment to 20% in a deal that provides Iran with fuel for the TNRR.[39] The United States also has continued to work with Russia in its effort to craft a step-by-step plan under which Iran would provide improved assurances about its nuclear program in return for an easing of sanctions. However, the U.S. response to the plan has been lukewarm.[40]

---

[38] IAEA, GOV/2010/10, February 18, 2010; Alan Cowell, "Iran to Build More Enrichment Plants," *New York Times*, February 22, 2010.

[39] Ali Vaez and Charles D. Ferguson, "An Iranian Offer Worth Considering," *New York Times*, September 29, 2011.

[40] Steve Gutterman and Lidia Kelly, "Russia Hopes Its Proposal Can Revive Iran Nuclear Talk," Reuters, August 17, 2011.

Iran's relations with the West entered a period of greater tension in November 2011 after the IAEA released a report providing an unprecedented level of detail about Iran's past nuclear weapon-related activities. Although nearly all of these activities had previously been publicly known or suspected, the IAEA's report gave them greater significance and credibility, and offered new evidence to support previous claims. The report came shortly after U.S. accusations of Iranian involvement in a plot to assassinate a top Saudi diplomat had already soured Iran's relations with the United States and its allies.

Although the November 2011 IAEA report did little to facilitate additional sanctions resolutions in the UN Security Council—China and Russia remained opposed to further sanctions—it did lead to tougher unilateral sanctions by the United States and some of its allies.[41] The Obama administration tightened U.S. sanctions against Iran via executive order in November 2011. Britain and Canada also imposed new sanctions on Iran, including a British ban on all financial ties to Iran. The move triggered an Iranian escalatory response: Iran expelled British diplomats and, days later, a mob—possibly with complicity of the Iranian government—raided the British Embassy in Tehran.

In December 2011, the United States approved new sanctions that would deny access to the U.S. financial system by foreign firms that do business with the Iranian Central Bank. Because Iran's Central Bank processes the lion's share of Iran's international oil sales, these sanctions could impose a heavy blow on the country's oil exports, its lifeblood. The United States also began to successfully rally support among key allies for an oil embargo against Iran. Iran has responded by threatening to close the Strait of Hormuz in retaliation to an oil embargo, but also has signaled its willingness to engage with the West, although it

---

[41] Russia, in particular, took a strong stand against further UN sanctions. The Russian reaction may have been influenced by Moscow's opposition to NATO military operations in Libya at the time. Ellen Barry, "Russia Dismisses Calls for New U.N. Sanctions," *New York Times*, November 9, 2011. In the end, Russia and China would only support a rebuke from the IAEA, but no punitive measures or referral to the Security Council. The IAEA resolution expressed "deep and increasing concern" about Iran's nuclear activities. IAEA, GOV/2011/69, November 18, 2011, p. 2.

has not suggested it is prepared to make any significant concessions over its nuclear program.[42] As of January 2012, tensions between Iran and the United States, and between Iran and U.S. regional allies, remained high, and the outcome uncertain.

Program Elements and Status

The Fuel Cycle

The core of Iran's nuclear program is the nuclear fuel cycle, which is based on the enrichment of natural uranium to a concentration of U-235 suitable for reactor fuel. The same technology used to produce reactor fuel also can be used to further enrich uranium to a concentration (weapons grade, generally considered to be above 90% U-235) suitable for a nuclear weapon. Because the fuel cycle can be used for both purposes, the United States has long opposed Iran's possession of it, and has focused its efforts on denying Iran this capability.

Iran's goal is to indigenously acquire all of the necessary elements of the fuel cycle. This would include the mining and milling of uranium ore, the conversion of yellowcake (the milled product) into UF6, the enrichment of NATUF6 to LEUF6 using high-speed centrifuges, the reduction of LEUF6 to uranium metal, and the fabrication of reactor fuel assemblies from that metal. These assemblies would then be used in commercial-scale nuclear reactors for the production of electricity. The fuel cycle is represented in Figure 2.1. As discussed below, however, there are significant reasons to believe that Iran's intentions for its nuclear program are not restricted to the production of electricity and that, at a minimum, Tehran wishes to make available the option of quickly producing nuclear weapons.

Iran maintains uranium mining facilities at two locations: the Gchine mine near Bandar Abbas, and Saghand. Iran's uranium reserves are quite small, and mining operations at the two sites are far from

---

42 "Iran Says Turkey Best Place for Future Talks with World Powers About Nuclear Program," Associated Press, January 5, 2012.

Figure 2.1
Uranium Fuel Cycle

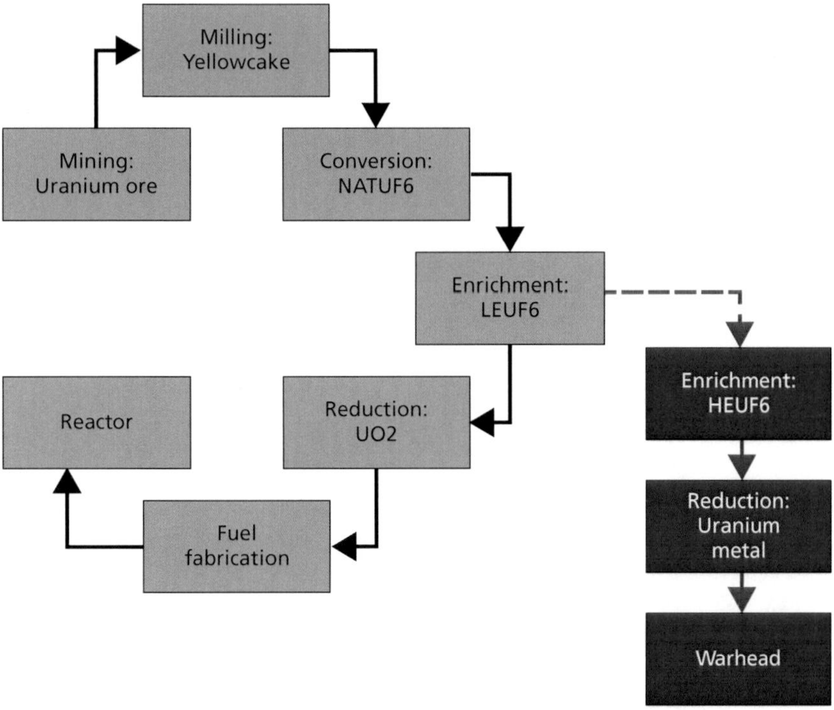

NOTE: NATUF6 = natural uranium hexafluoride; LEUF6 = low enriched uranium hexafluoride; UO2 = uranium dioxide; HEUF6 = highly enriched uranium hexafluoride.
RAND *MG1180-2.1*

cost-effective. There also are doubts about Iran's ability to mine enough uranium to fuel even a single commercial nuclear reactor.

After the uranium ore from the mines is milled to form uranium yellowcake, the yellowcake is then converted to NATUF6 gas at Iran's UCF at the INTC. The NATUF6 is then brought to the FEP, where it is enriched by centrifuge to 3.5% LEUF6, a task that requires thousands of centrifuges.[43] In theory, Iran's stockpile of 3.5% LEUF6 could

---

[43] Naturally occurring uranium consists almost entirely of the isotope U-238. U-235, which occurs naturally in very small amounts, is the isotope required for a self-sustaining fission chain reaction. The U-235 concentration in natural uranium is roughly 0.7%. The purpose

be used to fuel an LWR such as the Bushehr reactor. However, at present, Bushehr is the only operational reactor in the country, and its fuel is provided by Russia. Additionally, Iran would have difficulty producing enough LEU to fuel Bushehr, and does not have the ability to make the fuel assemblies the reactor requires.

In 2010, Iran began to further enrich some of its stockpile of 3.5% LEUF6 to 20% using cascades in the PFEP. The TNRR, which is used to produce medical isotopes, requires 20% LEU fuel. Iran is unable to acquire 20% LEU for this reactor from foreign suppliers; however, it can purchase medical isotopes from abroad. Iran refused a deal in 2009 that would have supplied fuel for the TNRR in return for most of its stocks of 3.5% LEU. It is also unclear whether Iran will be capable of producing the fuel assemblies required for the TNRR.[44]

Iran is currently constructing a fuel manufacturing plant (FMP), also at Isfahan, for the purpose of producing fuel rods and assemblies from its LEU. This would require first converting gaseous LEUF6 into uranium oxide metal, then using the metal to make fuel assemblies. Nuclear reactors typically require fuel assemblies built according to unique designs, something Iran would have to master in order to fuel either the TNRR or the Bushehr reactor. Iran's decision to produce large stockpiles of LEU before demonstrating an ability to turn that product into fuel assemblies raises serious questions about Tehran's nuclear intentions.

Although uranium enrichment is the core of Iran's nuclear fuel cycle effort, the Iranians also have been working toward acquiring the means to produce plutonium. Plutonium is produced by irradiating natural uranium fuel rods in a reactor. The plutonium is then separated from the spent rods through a chemical process known as plutonium

---

of uranium enrichment is to separate U-235 from other isotopes and thereby increase its concentration. Separation of U-235 can be achieved in different ways. Iran's program uses centrifuges that separate uranium isotopes by taking advantage of their tiny differences in mass. Because a single pass through one centrifuge can only accomplish a near-trivial amount of separation, enrichment to useful concentrations of U-235 requires thousands of centrifuges.

[44] In January 2012, Iran announced that it had successfully produced a fuel rod, and had irradiated it in the TNRR. The claim has not been independently verified. "Iran Says It Has Produced Its First Nuclear Fuel Rod," Associated Press, January 1, 2012.

reprocessing. The separated plutonium can be used to fuel commercial reactors. It also can be used to fuel nuclear weapons. Iran is currently constructing an HWR at Arak, the IR-40, which would run on natural uranium and could produce weapons-grade plutonium. Iran is still a year or more away from completing the IR-40, and there are doubts about its ability to complete the reactor at all.[45] Iran claims it is now capable of producing the natural uranium fuel assemblies needed to fuel the IR-40, using designs adapted with Russian assistance. Iran also has begun operating a heavy water production plant at Arak that is capable of producing the heavy water required for reactor operation. Iran has no known reprocessing facilities.

Major Program Elements and Facilities

Uranium Mining and Milling

Iran has uranium mining facilities in two locations: Gchine, near Bandar Abbas in the southern part of the country; and Saghand, in central Iran. Iran's deposits of natural uranium are relatively small, with total reserves estimated to be roughly 20,000 metric tons.[46] The Gchine site is currently the only mining and milling operation in Iran at which yellowcake is actively being produced. The milling operation is co-located with the mine. Gchine began producing yellowcake in 2006, and underwent a significant expansion in 2009.[47] Iranian mining and milling operations are not subject to IAEA safeguards. As a result, there is little data on these operations. It has been reported that the annual output of the Gchine facility is roughly 25 tons of yellowcake, or 21 tons of uranium.[48] This would be enough for Iran to

---

[45] Iran has stated that the Arak reactor will begin operations in late 2013. The most recent IISS strategic dossier expresses doubt that Iran will be able to complete the reactor on this schedule, and the May 2012 IAEA report noted no apparent progress at the site. IAEA, GOV/2012/23, May 25, 2012; and IISS, 2011, p. 80.

[46] Measured in tons of uranium oxide metal. IAEA, "Islamic Republic of Iran," *IAEA Country Nuclear Power Profiles*, December 2002, para. 1.1.2.

[47] Jonathan Tirone, "Iran Raises Uranium Output as Photos Show Need for Wider Checks," Bloomberg News, November 3, 2009.

[48] IAEA, GOV/2004/83.

produce roughly 2.1 tons of 3.5% LEUF6 per year. At existing rates of production, it would require more than a decade for Gchine to produce enough LEU for one reloading of the Bushehr reactor. This rate of yellowcake production is also insufficient to operate the Isfahan UCF at capacity. Although Iran's indigenous uranium production is insufficient to fuel commercial reactors, it is enough for a nuclear weapons program.

Iran has been conducting work at the Saghand mining site for decades, yet has not been able to extract and mill ore from the site. It has repeatedly announced and then delayed target dates for the beginning of mining and milling operations. According to the AEOI, the uranium content of the site's ore is 553 parts per million, far lower than what is typically considered economical to mine. A milling facility for the mine is being constructed at Ardakan, roughly 120 km away.

There are indications that Iran is having trouble obtaining adequate supplies of yellowcake.[49] Iran has tried to obtain yellowcake from foreign suppliers but has been unable to do so. Iran had imported over 500 tons of yellowcake from South Africa in the early 1980s.[50] This stock is now nearly gone, having almost entirely been converted to uranium hexafluoride (UF6) at Isfahan. Iran, however, already has more than enough NATUF6 to produce nuclear weapons. Its shortage of yellowcake would only be problematic if its intention is to operate commercial nuclear reactors.

Isfahan: Uranium Conversion Facility (UCF)

At the UCF, the uranium yellowcake produced at Iran's mining operations is converted into uranium hexafluoride gas that can be fed into centrifuge cascades for enrichment. The conversion of yellowcake to UF6 is a necessary step in the fuel cycle. The Iranians have mastered the uranium conversion process and are capable of producing industrial-scale quantities of UF6 for enrichment.

---

49 See David Albright and Jacqueline Shire, "Iran's Uranium Stockpile Dwindling," ISIS, December 30, 2009.

50 David Albright, Jacqueline Shire, and Paul Brannan, "Is Iran Running Out of Yellowcake?" ISIS, February 11, 2009.

The UCF at Isfahan originated as a Chinese-supplied turnkey facility. China agreed to build the facility in 1990, but in 1997 pulled out of the project in response to U.S. pressure, leaving the UCF unfinished. Iran decided to complete the facility on its own, relying on Chinese-supplied blueprints. Tehran declared the facility to the IAEA in 2000. The facility became operational in 2004. The UCF is capable of producing 200 tons of NATUF6 annually; however, Iran lacks sufficient yellowcake to operate the facility at its peak capacity (see the previous section on mining and milling). Iran stopped producing UF6 in August 2009, after having produced a total of 271 tons of NATUF6.[51]

When the facility first went online, Iran reportedly experienced problems with molybdenum contamination of its UF6 product. This problem has apparently since been resolved, and Iran has had no difficulty enriching UF6 to 20% U-235, which would have been complicated by a significant presence of molybdenum.

Natanz: Fuel Enrichment Plant (FEP)

The FEP is Iran's industrial-scale uranium enrichment facility at Natanz. It contains nearly all of Iran's centrifuges that are being fed NATUF6, and is where nearly all of Iran's 3.5% LEUF6 has been produced. The FEP contains two cascade halls: Production Halls A and B. Hall A is, according to the Iranians, intended to hold roughly 25,000 centrifuges. Iran has not provided details on their intentions for Hall B to the IAEA. As of May 2012, no centrifuges had been installed in Hall B. All nuclear material and centrifuges at the FEP are under IAEA surveillance and safeguards, and are subject to regular IAEA inspections.[52]

All centrifuges used in the FEP are of the IR-1 type. Centrifuges are connected in cascades that usually consist of 164 machines, although some cascades (as of May 2012, 31 of them) contain 174 machines. Cascades, in turn, are arranged into units of 18 units. In Hall A, the

---

[51] IAEA, GOV/2011/54, September 2, 2011. According to the report, Iran announced its intention to the IAEA of restarting NATUF6 production beginning October 23, 2011.

[52] All of the figures provided in this section are from the IAEA Report to the Director General released on May 25, 2012. IAEA, GOV/2012/23.

only section of the facility that has operational cascades, there are now three units installed (of the planned eight), which contain a total of 54 installed cascades, 52 of which are currently being fed with NATUF6 feedstock. In total, there are about 9,300 installed centrifuges in the hall, of which roughly 8,800 are being fed with NATUF6.

As of May 11, 2012, the FEP had produced 6,197 kg of 3.5% LEUF6. This amount is sufficient to produce between three and six weapons.[53] The LEUF6 is stored on site under IAEA seal, although some of this product has been used for further enrichment to 20% LEUF6 at the PFEP (see below).[54] Over the six-month period from November 2011 to May 2012, Iran produced 3.5% LEUF6 at a rate of roughly 200 kg/month. Iran's rate of LEUF6 production has increased steadily over time. For the six months ending November 2011, Iran produced 3.5% LEUF6 at a rate of roughly 145 kg/month, and during

[53] There is significant debate regarding how much LEU would be required to make a weapon. There is general agreement that 25 kg (the IAEA's "significant quantity") of HEU is required for a bomb. There is disagreement, however, regarding how much 3.5% LEUF6 feedstock is required to produce that much HEU. The exact amount would depend on the efficiency of the process used to enrich to weapons grade, and the wastage that would be produced. One would need 983 kg of 3.5% LEUF6 to produce 25 kg of 93% HEU metal if there were no wastage. Albright estimates that a bomb could be produced with as little as 1,030 kg of 3.5% LEUF6, and Kemp and Glaser provide a similar figure, although they assume a tails assay of 0.4%. An FAS report authored by Ivanka Barzashka assumes a tails assay of 0.7%, and calculates that 1,300 kg would be required, assuming ideal cascades. The IISS estimates the first bomb would require 2,900 kg LEUF6, and each subsequent bomb 1,300 kg. The amount for the first bomb is much higher to account for the inevitable inefficiencies that would result from a real-world breakout attempt. In general, in choosing its breakout options, Iran would face a trade-off between efficiency (how much uranium would be wasted) and speed (how long it would take to produce a bomb's worth of HEU). The text here takes the IISS and ISIS estimates as the upper and lower bounds, with the ISIS estimate as a worst-case scenario. David Albright, Jacqueline Shire, and Paul Brannan,"Can Military Strikes Destroy Iran's Gas Centrifuge Program? Probably Not," ISIS, August 7, 2008; Ivanka Barzashka, "Using Enrichment Capacity to Estimate Iran's Breakout Potential," FAS Issue Brief, January 21, 2011; R. Scott Kemp and Alexander Glaser, "Statement on Iran's Ability to Make a Nuclear Weapon and the Significance of the 19 February 2009 IAEA Report on Iran's Uranium Enrichment Program," March 2, 2009; and IISS, 2011, p. 120.

[54] In October 2011, Iran transferred a single cylinder containing 3.5% LEUF6 from Natanz to the FFEP at Fordow in preparation of beginning production of 20% LEU at that location. IAEA, GOV/2011/69, para. 23.

the previous six months at a rate of roughly 140 kg/month.[55] At these rates, Iran produces enough 3.5% LEUF6 for an additional bomb every 5–7 months (if further enriched, and assuming each additional weapon requires 1,030–1,300 kg 3.5% LEUF6). Iran's progress in expanding its uranium enrichment program is represented in Figures 2.2 and 2.3.

Natanz: Pilot Fuel Enrichment Plant (PFEP)

Construction began on the PFEP in 2001, and it became operational in October 2003. Unlike the FEP, which is buried underground, the PFEP is above ground. Originally used for centrifuge research and development (R&D), as of May 2012 it is used both for R&D and the enrichment of 3.5% LEUF6 to 20%. The facility is designed to contain six 164-machine cascades (about 1,000 centrifuges). At present, there

Figure 2.2
Centrifuges at FEP Being Fed NATUF6

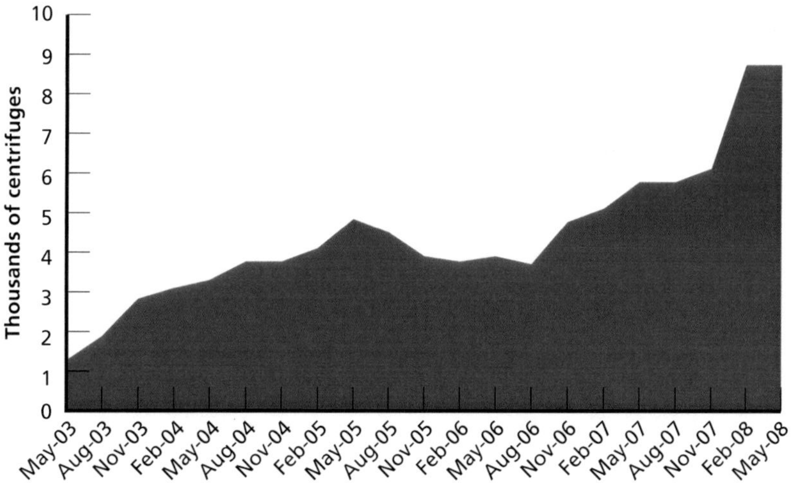

SOURCE: IAEA.
RAND *MG1180-2.2*

[55] As of May 11, 2012, Iran had produced 6,197 kg of 3.5% LEUF6. As of November 2, 2011, the total was 4,922 kg. As of May 14, 2011, it was 4,105 kg. IAEA,GOV/2012/23, para. 14; IAEA, GOV/2011/65, para. 15; IAEA, GOV/2011/29, para. 10.

Figure 2.3
Cumulative Production of 3.5% LEUF6 at FEP

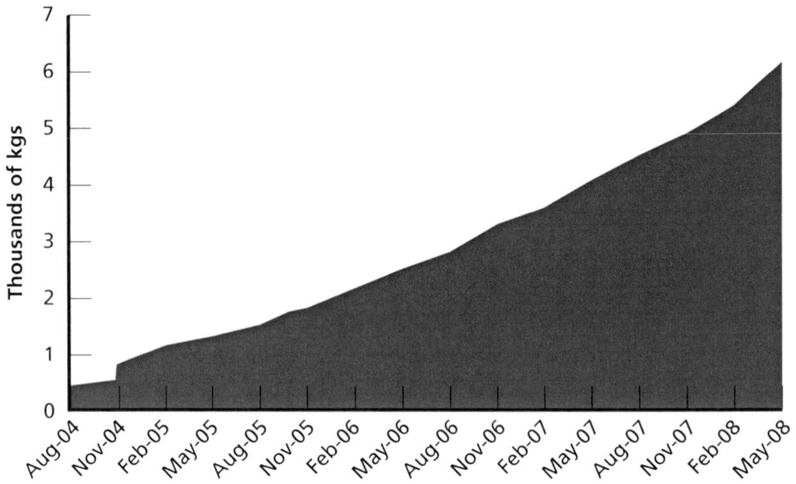

SOURCE: IAEA.
RAND *MG1180-2.3*

are two cascades used for 20% enrichment, and the area for the other four cascades is used for R&D on newer centrifuge models.[56]

In 2010, Iran began enriching to 20% in the PFEP using two centrifuge cascades.[57] One cascade enriches 3.5% LEUF6 to roughly 20%. The other cascade is fed the tails assay from the first, which is around 2% U-235, and enriches it to 10%. The 10% product is then fed back into the first cascade at an intermediate point in order to enrich it to 20%. This procedure greatly improves overall efficiency. This is important from a cost perspective in producing fuel for the TNRR, Iran's stated objective in enriching to 20%. However, it is also a useful way for Iran to improve its breakout capability should it ever choose to

---

[56] Information on the PFEP used here is from IAEA, GOV/2012/23, May 25, 2012, and IISS, 2011.

[57] Enrichment to 20% began in February 2010 using one cascade. A second cascade for enrichment of the tails assay from the first became operational in July 2010.

attempt a "batch recycling" process to quickly enrich 3.5% LEUF6 to 90% (this process is discussed in more detail in the section on breakout scenarios below). As of May 2012, Iran had produced 110.1 kg of 20% LEUF6 at the PFEP.[58]

Fordow Fuel Enrichment Plant (FFEP)

The Fordow Fuel Enrichment Plant is a heavily fortified underground facility located near the holy city of Qom. Iran reported the existence of the FFEP to the IAEA on September 21, 2009, after it learned the facility had already been discovered by Western intelligence agencies. Iran and the IAEA agreed on a safeguards approach for the facility in August 2011. The FFEP is intended to hold roughly 3,000 centrifuges in 16 cascades. Iran has stated that it intends to use 12 cascades for uranium enrichment. The other four cascades will be used for centrifuge R&D, including R&D on advanced centrifuge models.[59] Iran's reasons for constructing the site are unknown, and it has refused to provide such information to the IAEA. The site's existence raises substantial concerns that there may be more clandestine enrichment facilities. In fact, in November 2009, shortly after the existence of Fordow was revealed, Iran announced its intention to construct another ten enrichment facilities, and that it had already chosen sites for five of them. Iran has provided no information about where these sites will be located.[60]

In June 2011, Iran announced its intention to expand its production of 20% LEU to the FFEP. That August, Iran began to install IR-1 centrifuges at the site for this purpose. In December 2011, Iran began to enrich uranium to the 20% level using two interconnected cascades at the FFEP similar to the two cascades used for this purpose at the PFEP. In January 2012, Iran began to produce 20% LEU using a second set of interconnected cascades at the site, raising the total number of cascades at Natanz and Fordow dedicated to the production

---

[58] As of May 15, 2012, 43 kg of the 20% LEUF6 Iran has produced has been used to make fuel plates for the TNRR, thereby lowering Iran's stocks of 20% LEUF6. IAEA, GOV/2012/23, para. 38.

[59] IAEA, GOV/2010/62, November 23, 2010.

[60] "Iran, Defiant, Approves Plan for 10 Enrichment Sites," Associated Press, November 29, 2009.

of 20% LEU to six.[61] As of May 13, 2012, Iran had produced 35.5 kg of 20% LEUF6 at the FFEP.[62]

Plutonium Fuel Cycle Facilities

Iran's plutonium program is less advanced than its uranium enrichment program. As of May 2012, Iran is not able to produce plutonium for a nuclear weapon, and there are doubts as to whether Iran will be able to acquire such a capability in the foreseeable future. The production of weapons-grade plutonium requires the irradiation of uranium in a nuclear reactor. Iran currently has four small research reactors (including the TNRR), an industrial-scale LWR at Bushehr, and an HWR under construction at Arak. The research reactors are too small to produce significant quantities of plutonium (although Iran has produced experimental quantities of plutonium in the past using the TNRR). The Bushehr reactor could, in theory, produce plutonium for nuclear weapons; however, this would be difficult for Iran to do (see below). The Arak IR-40 reactor would be ideally suited to produce plutonium; however, that reactor is not scheduled to be completed anytime soon, and it is very possible that it will not be completed in the foreseeable future.[63]

The IR-40 HWR at Arak is a 40 MWt natural-uranium fueled, heavy water cooled, and heavy water moderated reactor capable of producing roughly 11 kg of weapons-grade plutonium, enough for at least one bomb per year (assuming a minimum of 6 kg of plutonium are required for a bomb). The IR-40's design is one of the more suspicious aspects of the Iranian nuclear program: there is little justification for such a reactor as part of a purely civilian program. On the other hand, the design is ideally suited for the production of plutonium for nuclear weapons. Few reactors of similar design are in operation in other countries. The ones that are—chiefly located in India, Pakistan, North Korea, Israel, and France—are almost all used to make fuel for nuclear

---

[61] IAEA, GOV/2012/9, February 24, 2012, para. 25; Olli Heinonen, "The 20 Percent Solution," *Foreign Policy*, January 11, 2012.

[62] IAEA, GOV/2012/23, para. 27. As of May 2012, 43 kg of Iran's stocks of 20% LEUF6 had been converted to fuel plates.

[63] IISS, 2011, pp. 78–83.

weapons. Iran began to pursue the acquisition of a heavy water reactor before the A.Q. Khan network made centrifuges available in the 1990s. As a result, the Arak reactor and related facilities likely represented an attempt to develop a nuclear weapon capability via the plutonium route as an alternative path should uranium enrichment prove unfeasible. Possession of a plutonium reprocessing capability also would offer Iran a more effective way to produce large quantities of fissile material over the long term, and would be an important part of an advanced nuclear weapons program.

The IR-40 was designed and built indigenously after repeated attempts in the 1990s to purchase a reactor from a foreign supplier. Iran likely received foreign help in the design of the reactor. At a minimum, it appears that the Russian design institute NIKIET gave Iran advice on how to fuel the reactor, which involved adapting the reactor's design to accommodate a type of Russian LWR design (RBMK) fuel assembly.[64] Ground was broken for construction in 2004.

Iran expects the reactor to go online in 2013, however there are a number reasons to doubt that Iran can meet this goal. For example, Iran will have a great deal of difficulty producing the pressure vessel for the reactor, which will require forging large pieces of metal without welding. A Russian company that was originally contracted to supply these parts pulled out of the deal in 2008. Even if Iran were to acquire these components, a start-up date of 2013 would still be overly ambitious.

There also are questions about whether Iran will be able to produce sufficient heavy water for the reactor. Iran's Heavy Water Production Plant (HWPP) at Arak began operating in 2004. Because the facility requires no nuclear materials, Iran has refused to allow IAEA inspections at the site, and information about it is limited. It is believed, how-

---

[64] Arak uses a heavy water cooled and moderated design, with which NIKIET has no past experience. NIKIET's standard HWR design is the RBMK, which is heavy water cooled and graphite moderated. Also, the RBMK is fueled with 3.5% LEU, while the Arak reactor uses natural uranium. The Arak reactor was modified so that it could be fueled with RBMK-type fuel assemblies using natural uranium fuel rods rather than LEU. The necessary redesigns of both the reactor and the fuel assembly would have required substantial assistance from the Russians. ISIS, "Update on the Arak Reactor in Iran," August 25, 2009.

ever, that the capacity of the plant falls short of being able to supply the IR-40. With an estimated production rate of 8 metric tons per year, it would take the plant roughly 12 years to produce enough heavy water for the reactor.[65] Iran has claimed that it intends to greatly expand the plant's capacity, but it is unknown whether there has been significant progress.

Iran will also face challenges fueling the IR-40. Iran began constructing a commercial-scale FMP at the INTC in 2003. Iran announced in 2009 that it had mastered the necessary steps to produce fuel assemblies for the IR-40. As of May 2012, Iran had begun producing UO2 pellets for fuel assemblies for the IR-40, and had produced two dummy fuel assemblies. It remains unclear, however, whether Iran will be capable of producing fuel assemblies that can be successfully used by the IR-40.[66] Should Iran begin operation of the IR-40, it would still need to reprocess the spent fuel from the reactor in order to separate the plutonium. Iran is not believed to possess a reprocessing facility, and it would be technically challenging for Iran to build such a facility. It also would be difficult to acquire such a capability without detection.

The LWR at Bushehr

The single Russian-built LWR at the Bushehr power plant was completed in 2010 and began commercial operation in September 2011.[67] The Bushehr reactor is a 1,000 MWe LWR based on the Russian Vodo-Vodyanoi Energetichesky Reaktor (VVER-1000) design. In 2005, Russia and Iran signed an agreement under which Russia will provide fuel for the reactor for ten years. Iran agreed to return all spent fuel

---

[65] This estimate is based on the assumption that the IR-40 reactor would require roughly 90 tons of heavy water at start-up, and another 1 ton of replacement heavy water annually. Assuming that Iran's heavy water plant has been operated at capacity continuously since 2004—a large assumption—then it would take until roughly 2016 to stockpile enough heavy water to begin operating the reactor. IISS, 2011.

[66] IAEA, GOV/2011/23, para. 36, 37.

[67] Peter Crail, "Iran's First Power Reactor Goes Critical," *Arms Control Today*, Vol. 41, No. 5, June 2011; "Iranian Nuclear Power Station Begins Generating Electricity," Reuters, September 4, 2011.

to Russia. Russia began delivering the initial fuel load for Bushehr in late 2007, even though the reactor was not loaded until October 2010 because of repeated delays (largely orchestrated by the Russians). In early 2011, technical problems led to a partial unloading of the fuel, and the reactor did not go critical until May.

Although Bushehr will produce hundreds of kilograms of plutonium in normal operation, it will be in a form that is not suitable for weapons production. Additionally, Iran and Russia have agreed that spent reactor fuel will be returned to Russia. In general, it would be extremely difficult for the Iranians to use the Bushehr reactor to produce weapons-grade plutonium. Freshly loaded fuel would have to be removed after weeks in the reactor at full power, or months at low power. This would be nearly impossible to do without detection. Additionally, the spent fuel could not be reprocessed immediately after removal. It would first have to cool for months.[68] Iran also would be confronted with the difficulty of constructing a reprocessing facility, something that would be difficult (but far from impossible) to do in secret. In sum, while it is technically possible for the Iranians to use Bushehr to produce fuel for a bomb, the difficulties of doing so relative to its already-available uranium options are so great that such a scenario is unlikely.

Ballistic Missile Program

If Iran were to develop nuclear weapons, it would rely on its ballistic missiles to deliver them. Because Iran's missile research lacks transparency, few details about its capabilities are publicly available, and there is disagreement about Iran's missile program in the open-source litera-

---

[68] Declassified information on the construction of nuclear weapons from LWR spent fuel has been available for decades. The central problem with using an LWR to produce plutonium is that the plutonium in the spent fuel, under normal reactor operations, contains high concentrations of the isotope Pu-240. This "reactor-grade" plutonium is less suitable for making a bomb than "weapons-grade" plutonium, which generally contains Pu-239 concentrations in excess of 80%. However, by changing the operations of the reactor, it is possible to produce weapons-grade plutonium. See J. Carson Mark, "Explosive Properties of Reactor-Grade Plutonium," *Science & Global Security*, Vol. 4, No. 1, 1993.

ture.[69] Iran has a long-standing ballistic missile program, and a relatively advanced capability, given the country's overall technical limitations. It has received substantial foreign assistance in these efforts, but has in recent years likely acquired most—if not all—of the necessary capabilities to develop and manufacture ballistic missiles indigenously. It is likely, however, that Iran still depends on outside assistance to some degree.[70]

Iran's efforts have centered on the development of medium-range ballistic missiles that are capable of hitting targets anywhere in the region. Such a capability would be required for Iran to hit targets in Israel. The core of Iran's program has been the Shahab series of short- and medium-range ballistic missiles (SRBMs and MRBMs). Iran may have as many as 200–400 Shahab-1 and Shahab-2 missiles. The Shahab-1, based on the Soviet-designed SCUD-B, has a range of roughly 300 km. The Shahab-2, based on the SCUD-C, has a range of about 500 km. Although these missiles likely have poor accuracy, they are based on proven, battle-tested designs and likely have a reasonably high degree of reliability.[71] Their ranges would allow them to reach tar-

[69] Because capability estimates can be based on Iranian claims, weapon designs rather than actual test-flight data, or very limited numbers of tests, these estimates can often be little more than guesswork. They also, understandably, are often based on worst-case scenarios. The 1998 Rumsfeld Report (Commission to Assess the Ballistic Missile Threat to the United States, "Executive Summary of the Report of the Commission to Assess the Ballistic Missile Threat to the United States," July 15, 1998) should serve as a caveat when interpreting these estimates. Also, the real-world performance of these missile systems will depend on a number of exogenous factors that cannot be accounted for here (e.g., warhead design).

[70] International Institute for Strategic Studies, *Iran's Ballistic Missile Capabilities: A Net Assessment*, London: IISS, 2010, pp. 140–141. According to the IISS report, Iran likely still depends on foreign suppliers for rocket engines and guidance systems. Historically, North Korea and China have been the most important sources of assistance for Iran's missile program. Assistance from North Korea likely continues.

[71] Ranges for the Shahab-1 and -2 are taken from Department of Defense, "Unclassified Report on Military Power in Iran," April 2010. Iran obtained hundreds of SCUD-Bs and components for SCUD-Bs from several countries, mostly from North Korea. The Soviet-designed SCUD-B can carry a 1,000 kg payload and has a maximum range of 300 km. It is unknown whether Iran can indigenously manufacture all of the necessary components of the Shahab-1. Estimates of the number of missiles vary widely. Most estimates are in the 200–300 range. The SCUD-C is an improved version of the SCUD-B. Iran likely continues

gets in several of the GCC states, including Kuwait, Qatar, Oman, and the United Arab Emirates (UAE). A number of U.S. bases, including bases in Iraq and Bahrain, are within these ranges as well.

The Shahab-3, an MRBM based on the North Korean Nodong missile, is believed to be capable of carrying a 1,000 kg payload at a range of more than 1,000 km.[72] Iran has developed modified versions of this design, including the Ghadr-1, which may have a substantially longer range, although its payload capacity may be less than the Shahab-3. The Ghadr-1, and possibly the original Shahab-3 model as well, are capable of putting all of Israel at risk.[73]

Iran has also tested solid-fueled MRBMs. A solid-fueled missile would offer a number of advantages of the liquid-fueled Shahab-3 design, such as a shorter launch sequence, which would make a preemptive counterforce strike more difficult. Since 2009, Iran has conducted test flights of the Sejil-2, which is believed to have a range over 2,000 km. The payload capacity for the Sejil, however, is believed to be considerably less than 1,000 kg. This would present Iran with a sig-

---

to depend on foreign components to manufacture the Shahab-2, which is the Iranian version of the SCUD-C. Some estimates give the Shahab-2 a range as great as 1,000 km. Iran is believed to have deployed between 50 and 150 of these missiles. Anthony H. Cordesman and Martin Kleiber, *Iran's Military Forces and Warfighting Capabilities: The Threat in the Northern Gulf*, Washington, D.C.: Center for Strategic and International Studies, 2007, pp. 134–156.

[72] The Department of Defense estimates a range of over 1,200 km for the Shahab-3. Department of Defense, 2010. The missile is based on North Korea's Nodong, which is itself a scaled-up version of the SCUD design. Iran's development of the Shahab-3 likely involved substantial assistance from North Korea, and possibly other countries.

[73] Iran has revealed several variants of the Shahab-3. The Ghadr-1 variant was first displayed in 2007, and reportedly has a range of 1,800 km (IISS estimates a range of 1,600 km, with a 750 kg payload). There have been reports that Iran has been working to develop an IRBM. Iran has claimed such efforts were canceled, and that it instead will focus on its space program rather than longer-range missiles. Jane's Strategic Weapon Systems, "Shahab-3/4 (Ghadr-1)," July 20, 2010; Department of Defense, 2010; IISS, 2010. Cordesman and Seitz offers a range of CEP from 190 m to 4,000 m or more depending on the sort of guidance system that is used. Anthony H. Cordesman and Adam C. Seitz, *Iranian Weapons of Mass Destruction: The Birth of a Regional Nuclear Arms Race?* Santa Barbara, Calif.: Greenwood, 2009, pp. 114–115.

nificant challenge in developing a warhead that is light and compact enough to be mated to the Sejil.[74]

Although concerns are often voiced about potential Iranian development of longer-range missiles, or even an intercontinental ballistic missile (ICBM) that could reach the United States, there is substantial disagreement among experts on this point. Similarly, there is insufficient evidence in the open-source literature to conclude that Iran has an active ICBM program, or is nearing the ability to deploy ICBMs.[75] Iran would probably seek to develop an intermediate-range ballistic missile (IRBM) capability before pursuing missiles that could reach the United States. Such a program would likely require timescales and testing that would provide substantial forewarning to the United States and its allies. The Department of Defense has estimated that Iran could develop an ICBM by 2015, although this estimate assumes the availability of significant foreign assistance.[76] It is worth noting that to date, only five countries—the United States, Russia, China, Great Britain, and France—have deployed ICBMs.

Technical Problems and Setbacks

Even as Iran approached—and by the end of 2010 had likely crossed—the threshold of a single bomb's worth of 3.5% LEUF6 (1180–2900 kg), problems with the enrichment program were becoming increasingly apparent. In 2008, there was an apparent decline in the efficiency of Iran's centrifuges. Then in 2009 there began a noticeable slowdown

---

[74] See Uzi Rubin, "Showcase of Missile Proliferation: Iran's Missile and Space Program," *Arms Control Today*, Vol. 42, No. 1, January/February 2012; Steven A. Hildreth, *Iran's Ballistic Missile Programs: An Overview*, Washington, D.C.: Congressional Research Service, RS22758, February 4, 2009.

[75] See Uzi Rubin, "Showcase of Missile Proliferation: Iran's Missile and Space Program," *Arms Control Today*, Vol. 42, No. 1, January/February 2012; Steven A. Hildreth, *Iran's Ballistic Missile Programs: An Overview*, Washington, D.C.: Congressional Research Service, RS22758, February 4, 2009.

[76] Specifically, the DoD report states that, "[w]ith sufficient foreign assistance, Iran could probably develop and test an intercontinental ballistic missile (ICBM) capable of reaching the United States by 2015." Department of Defense, 2010. Iran's potential to develop an ICBM is heatedly debated among experts.

in enrichment activity at the Natanz facility. Although Iran continued to install more centrifuges throughout most of 2009, the number of machines being fed with NATUF6 declined from a reported peak of 4,920 in May to 3,772 by January 2010.[77] By November 2009, the majority of centrifuges installed in the FEP were not being fed with NATUF6.[78] In late 2009 and early 2010, the Stuxnet computer virus forced the Iranians to remove roughly 1,000 centrifuges from the FEP.[79] By late 2010, the centrifuge program was showing signs of recovery; however, the September 2011 IAEA report revealed that the effective separative power in the FEP had slightly declined from the previous reporting period.[80]

There are several likely causes of Iran's technical problems with its enrichment program. One is that Iran's enrichment program was likely hindered by the haste with which centrifuges were installed in the FEP in 2007, before sufficient testing could be performed. In 2007, the Iranians installed roughly 3,000 centrifuges in the FEP, with nearly all being fed UF6. This is remarkable considering that between December 2007 and August 2010, the net increase in the number of UF6-fed centrifuges in the facility was only about 800. This rush to expand the program may have led to many of the technical problems that were later experienced.[81]

An additional problem is that the centrifuge model currently used in the FEP—the IR-1, which is based on a discontinued model designed by the European conglomerate URENCO—is known to have substantial flaws.[82] The model is estimated to have a fail rate of

---

[77] Gas centrifuges are fed uranium in a gaseous form, uranium hexafluoride (UF6). The gas is produced through a complex chemical process at a uranium conversion facility.

[78] David Albright and Christina Walrond, *Iran's Gas Centrifuge Program: Taking Stock*, Washington, D.C.: Institute for Science and International Security, 2010.

[79] David Albright, Paul Brannan, and Christina Walrond, "Stuxnet Malware and Natanz: Update of ISIS December 22, 2010 Report," ISIS, February 15, 2011.

[80] Effective separative power refers to the average separative work per machine in the facility per unit of time. See Barzashka, 2011.

[81] IISS, 2011, pp. 65–66.

[82] IISS, 2011, pp. 65–66.

10%. Iran is currently seeking to develop much more efficient and reliable centrifuge models, including IR-2m, IR-4, and "third-generation" designs. Some of these have already been tested using UF6 feedstock. If these efforts are successful, this could greatly advance Iran's enrichment capabilities.

Iran made progress with the efficiency of the IR-1 before encountering setbacks in 2011. Effective separative power at the FEP grew from 0.4 separative work units (SWU) per centrifuge per year in 2006, to 0.9 SWU by the end of 2009, but this declined to less than 0.8 SWU based on the September 2011 IAEA report for the latest reporting period. Iran also appears to be making progress with next-generation centrifuge designs to replace the first-generation IR-1 machines it currently employs in the FEP. Most important of these designs are the IR-2m and the IR-4, which are based upon the German G-2 centrifuge. Iran obtained this design from the A.Q. Khan network in the mid-1990s, but has been unable to obtain the maraging steel necessary for their rotors in sufficient quantity. It appears that Iran is now producing a modified design that employs a carbon-fiber rotor instead, which could allow for even greater efficiency. It would also allow Iran to avoid the problem of having to find foreign suppliers for maraging steel (the IR-2m still depends on a maraging steel bellows for the rotors; the IR-4 does not). As of August 2011, Iran had installed 127 IR-2m machines and 27 IR-4 machines in the PFEP, although there is uncertainty about whether Iran can overcome the necessary material and technical problems required to deploy these centrifuges in large numbers.[83]

A third problem is that it is uncertain whether Iran has the required materials and resources to manufacture more than about 15,000 centrifuges (it has already deployed about 11,000). Iran had originally announced that it planned to deploy 48,000 centrifuges at Natanz. There is substantial doubt about its ability to reach this target, or to deploy a sufficient number of machines to produce the quantity of LEU required to fuel a commercial reactor. As pointed out above, Iran

---

[83] David Albright and Christina Walrond, "Iran's Advanced Centrifuges," ISIS, October 18, 2011.

can already produce enough LEU for nuclear weapons, which require much less.[84]

It is likely that the sanctions that have been progressively enacted against Iran have succeeded in erecting serious barriers to the country's ability to procure needed equipment, raw materials, and assistance from abroad.[85] Iran operates a sophisticated international smuggling operation that has proven capable of obtaining equipment and supplies in spite of international efforts to restrict them. However, sanctions have greatly complicated this task, and have raised costs.[86] They also have made it difficult for Iran to rely on regular suppliers. The more Iran must seek out new suppliers for parts and materials, the less it will be able to trust their quality. Over the past year, the United States and its allies have voiced growing confidence in the success of efforts to delay Iran's program through both sanctions and sabotage, and have claimed that these measures have resulted in years of additional delay.[87]

One major cause of technical problems has been the U.S.-Israeli effort to use cyberwarfare capabilities to sabotage Iran's centrifuge program, most notably with the Stuxnet computer worm.[88] Stuxnet is a precisely targeted virus that affects the functioning of the Siemens programmable logic controller (PLC) that controls the operation of the IR-1 centrifuge. Specifically, the worm radically manipulates the centrifuge's rate of spin, causing catastrophic and irreversible damage, while hiding its tracks by sending false data to operators. It is believed that the worm began to infect computers used by four Iranian organi-

---

[84] Albright and Walrond, 2010.

[85] Kenneth Katzman, *Iran Sanctions*, 2011.

[86] Evan Perez, "Iran Faces Nuclear Smuggling Charges," *Wall Street Journal*, February 2, 2011; Mark Hosenball and John Shiffman, "U.S., European Officials Probe Iran Nuclear Smuggling," Reuters, March 28, 2012.

[87] Jill Dougherty, "Clinton: Sanctions Against Iran Helping Delay Its Nuclear Program," CNN, January 10, 2011; Mark Landler, "U.S. Says Sanctions Hurt Iran Nuclear Program," *New York Times*, January 10, 2011.

[88] Albright, Brannan, and Walrond, 2011. As this monograph was going to press, information began to emerge that Stuxnet was part of a wider U.S.-Israeli effort to conduct cyberwarfare attacks against Iran called Olympic Games. See David E. Sanger, "Obama Ordered Sped-Up Wave of Cyberattacks Against Iran," *New York Times*, June 1, 2012.

zations in summer 2009, and from these organizations spread to the PLCs that controlled centrifuges at Natanz. Around late 2009 and early 2010, Stuxnet destroyed about 1,000 of the 9,000 centrifuges installed in the FEP. This forced the Iranians to shut down a number of centrifuge cascades for months.

Although it may have been the most impressive sabotage attack on Iran's nuclear program, Stuxnet has not been the only one.[89] There have been a number of covert attacks on Iranian nuclear and missile facilities and equipment, as well as assassinations of Iranian nuclear scientists. Although the provenance of these attacks is not publicly known, it is possible that they are part of a coordinated effort to set back Iran's nuclear program.[90] Beyond the direct damage caused by these measures, the attacks have necessarily given Iran reason to be concerned about the capabilities of its adversaries, and will likely force the Iranians to expend resources to try to protect themselves from future attacks. Stuxnet and other attacks may also lead the Iranians to second-guess their ability to conduct activities in secret, as the worm was very specifically targeted to Iran's centrifuges, and detailed knowledge about the program.[91]

Evidence of a Weapons Program

Iran has consistently claimed that its nuclear program is purely civilian in nature, and that it does not intend to acquire nuclear weapons. To support this claim, the Iranians point to statements by Ayatollah Khomeini indicating that nuclear weapons are contrary to the teachings of

---

89 Mike Shuster, "Inside the United States' Secret Sabotage of Iran," NPR, May 9, 2011; William J. Broad, John Markoff, and David E. Sanger, "Israeli Test on Worm Called Crucial in Iran Nuclear Delay," *New York Times*, January 15, 2011.

90 As of January 2012, there had been four assassination attacks against Iranian nuclear scientists. At the time of this writing, the most recent assassination took place on January 11. Iran has blamed Israel and the United States for these attacks. The United States has strongly denied responsibility. Iran also has suggested it might carry out retaliatory attacks. Rick Gladstone, "Iran Signals Revenge over Killing of Scientist," *New York Times*, January 12, 2012.

91 Roula Khalaf, James Blitz, Daniel Dombey, Tobias Buck, and Najmeh Bozorgmehr, "The Sabotaging of Iran," *Financial Times*, February 11, 2011.

Islam, and to a *fatwa* issued by Supreme Leader Khamenei forbidding nuclear weapons.[92]

The formally declared elements of the Iranian nuclear program are "dual use" (i.e., they have both legitimate applications in nuclear energy and also can be used to make nuclear weapons). The fuel cycle is a case in point: the enrichment of uranium can be used to make fuel for nuclear reactors or to produce fuel for a bomb. Thus far, Iran has only enriched uranium to levels suitable for nuclear reactor fuel (approximately 3.5% and 20%), whereas weapons-grade uranium is typically more than 90% enrichment. However, enrichment to lower levels nonetheless brings Iran closer to making bomb-grade fuel should it eventually choose to do so.

There are reasons to believe that Iran is, at a minimum, seeking to give itself the future option of making weapons quickly and with relatively little difficulty (i.e., acquire a virtual capability). Iran's enrichment program in its current state is not well suited for making fuel for reactors. At present, Iran has one commercial nuclear reactor, at Bushehr. Although it has repeatedly announced plans to build more, and has actively sought foreign suppliers, under current conditions there is little reason to believe that the country can acquire additional commercial-scale reactors anytime in the foreseeable future. Yet the Bushehr reactor has a guaranteed supply of fuel from the Russians, obviating any need for Iran to produce its own. The Iranians have voiced anxieties over future fuel supplies given their uncertain political relationship with the international community, but the Russians have proved willing to keep the Bushehr reactor running throughout the nuclear crisis. Most importantly, even if the Iranian goal were to indigenously fuel Bushehr, they are a long way off from being able to do so. To run the Bushehr reactor for one year, the Iranians would need to produce roughly 37 metric tons of 3.5% LEUF6 per year, which is many times greater than their current production rate (more than 20 times greater, in fact). Iran would need roughly 50,000 IR-1 centrifuges running at their current peak efficiency to fuel Bushehr, something the

---

[92] IAEA, INFCIRC/657, September 15, 2005, pp. 121–122.

Iranians do not appear close to doing.[93] Iran also has not demonstrated the ability to turn its 3.5% LEUF6 into fuel assemblies suitable for the Bushehr reactor—no simple engineering feat, particularly if Russian assistance is not forthcoming. Tellingly, Iran's enrichment program is much better suited for producing weapons. At 2011 production rates, Iran could produce enough 3.5% LEUF6 for an additional nuclear weapon every 8–9 months.

In addition to these suspicions, key pieces of evidence have emerged indicating that Iran has conducted—and may continue to conduct—a number of activities that are uniquely related to weapon development. The 2007 U.S. National Intelligence Estimate on the Iranian nuclear program concluded with "high confidence" that "Iranian military entities were working under government direction to develop weapons" until 2003, after which, the report concluded, "Tehran halted its weapons program."[94] Also, the IAEA's safeguards reports on Iran, starting in 2008, began to document evidence—mostly supplied by Western intelligence agencies—of past weapons-related activities.[95] Beginning in 2010, the IAEA has suggested that some of these activities may have been resumed. In November 2011, the IAEA released a report that provided an unprecedented level of detail about this evidence, lending credibility to earlier claims and suspicions, and corroborating them with new details. Although the report does not demonstrate that Iran continued to operate a nuclear weapon program after 2003, it does

[93] David Albright, Jacqueline Shire, Paul Brannan, and Andrea Scheel, "Nuclear Iran: Not Inevitable," ISIS, January 21, 2009. Even more than enrichment capacity, a greater barrier to producing fuel for a commercial reactor could be Iran's limited ability to make sufficient NATUF6 feedstock. It would require over 250 metric tons of NATUF6 to produce enough fuel to run Bushehr for one year. It is highly questionable whether Iran could actually mine enough uranium to produce this amount on a yearly basis, and sanctions have effectively barred Iran from purchasing yellowcake from abroad. But Iran has more than enough uranium to produce a decently sized nuclear weapons arsenal.

[94] The judgment that Iran's weaponization efforts ceased in 2003 was provided in the NIE with "moderate confidence." Office of the Director of National Intelligence, 2007.

[95] The IAEA has referred to this evidence as "issues which give rise to concerns about possible military dimensions." IAEA, GOV/2008/15, May 26, 2008.

suggest that Iran has undertaken a number of weapon-related tests and activities with no civilian justification since that time.[96]

Since the early 2000s, several key pieces of evidence have arisen that cast a suspicious light on Iran's nuclear program. One is a 15-page document shown to the IAEA by the Iranians in 2005. This document describes processes for producing uranium metal from UF6 and machining the metal into hemispheres appropriate for a warhead. Iran did not allow the IAEA to make copies of the document. Tehran has argued that the document was provided, unsolicited, by the A.Q. Khan network when Iran purchased P-1 centrifuges from the network in 1987, and they claim that the information was never used to pursue a nuclear weapons capability. The document is additionally concerning because it is known to also have been included in a larger package of information that was given to Libya by the A.Q. Khan network that included detailed designs for a nuclear weapon. It is likely that the Khan network made similar design information available to Iran. The November 2011 IAEA report cites additional evidence (all previously known) that Iran had access to weapon design more advanced and sophisticated than that provided to Libya.[97]

Another key piece of evidence has been the contents of a laptop that was acquired by the United States from an Iranian defector in 2004.[98] The laptop contained voluminous technical information on the conversion of UF4 (uranium tetrafluoride or "green salt," an intermediate stage in the conversion of UF6 into uranium metal for a bomb), the design of a reentry vehicle consistent with a nuclear warhead, designs for an underground tunnel that could be used for a nuclear test, and the development and testing of high explosives consistent with those required for an implosion device. According to the documents, these projects were overseen by Mohsen Fakhrizadeh, a high-ranking officer in the Iranian Revolutionary Guards Corps (IRGC) who headed

---

[96] IAEA, GOV/2011/65, November 8, 2011.

[97] The IAEA report refers to this 15-page document as "the uranium metal document." IAEA, GOV/2011/65, Annex, para. 5, 33.

[98] Jeffrey T. Richelson, *Spying on the Bomb*, New York: W.W. Norton & Co., 2007, pp. 545–554. Also, IISS, 2011, pp. 86–88.

Iran's Physics Research Center (PHRC), an organization linked by other sources to nuclear weapons development. The documents portray steady progress on these programs up to 2003 (they make no reference to program activity after this date). The Iranians have denied the existence of these programs, and have suggested that the laptop documents are forgeries.[99]

The laptop data features prominently in the IAEA's November 2011 report, which offers details about the activities it describes and cites corroborating evidence.[100] According to the report, prior to 2004, Iran conducted extensive research and experiments on high explosives that can be used in an implosion weapon. Several elements of this work, including a multipoint initiation system, exploding bridgewires, and monitoring equipment for tests, have few or no uses aside from nuclear weapon development. The report also suggests that Iran conducted at least one experiment to initiate a high explosive charge in the form of a hemispherical shell consistent with a warhead. Most damningly, the IAEA report connects the programs described in the laptop files—green salt, high explosives, and a reentry vehicle—to one another, and describes them as part of a single, coordinated program under the direction of Iran's military that operated until 2003. The report also states that work on a "scaled down" version of the multipoint initiation system may have continued after 2003, but does not provide specific evidence. It also suggests that the work may have been limited to computer simulations and was not part of a coordinated weapon program.[101]

A final key piece of evidence is a document, reported in 2009 by the *Times* of London and later corroborated by the IAEA, which describes a program to develop a uranium deuteride neutron initiator. This is an unusual form of neutron initiator, but consistent with techniques used by Pakistan that would have likely been available to

---

[99] IAEA, GOV/2011/65, Annex, para. 8.

[100] The report refers to the laptop data as "the alleged studies documentation." IAEA, GOV/2011/65, Annex, para. 21, 31–65.

[101] IAEA, GOV/2011/65, para. 45.

Iran via the Khan network.[102] The evidence about Iran's work on a neutron initiator is particularly important because it suggests that some of this work took place after 2003. The IAEA report suggests that Iran may have conducted a research effort from 2006–2010 to validate the design of the initiator.[103]

Consistent with earlier findings of the U.S. Intelligence Community, the November 2011 IAEA report suggests that Iran's nuclear program came to a sudden halt in 2003. It also suggests that Iran may not have completed the development of a viable warhead that could be delivered by missile by that point.

Some analyses have suggested that this evidence is less than conclusive about either Iran's progress toward weaponization or its political commitment to making weapons. Studies conducted by Sandia National Laboratory have suggested that many of the designs uncovered from the laptop—including those related to mating a warhead to a missile—would not work, indicating that as of 2003, Iran had not yet achieved the ability to weaponize. Other Western analysts have noted that it is possible that the work depicted in the laptop data represents feasibility studies rather than a determined effort to produce weapons.[104]

---

[102] See Jeffrey Lewis, "Uranium Deuteride Initiators Redux," *Arms Control Wonk*, May 25, 2011, http://lewis.armscontrolwonk.com/archive/4032/uranium-deuteride-initiatiors-redux.

[103] IAEA, GOV/2011/65, Annex, para. 56.

[104] Former IAEA chief of safeguards Olli Heinonen, who made numerous visits to Iranian nuclear facilities, told *Ha'aretz* in 2010 that Iran's efforts were "likely part of a feasibility study into examining aspects of the assembling of a nuclear warhead, but not, at this stage, the actual manufacturing of a nuclear device." Yossi Melman, "Behind the Scene of UN Nuclear Inspection of Iran," *Ha'aretz*, October 22, 2010. The article also references videos obtained by the IAEA that apparently depict work on a reentry vehicle suitable for a nuclear warhead. Other sources have questioned whether Iran would be capable of building a warhead small enough to fit the reentry vehicle design from the laptop. See Paul Kerr, "Questions Surround Iran's Nuclear Program," *Arms Control Today*, Vol. 36, No. 2, March 2006. David Albright also questions whether Iran could build a warhead this small. He also argues that the publicly known information from the laptop is not sufficient to determine whether Iran has an active nuclear weapons program, and that the design work could have been initiated by missile scientists rather than the government. The full text of Albright's November 2005 comments can be found at http://lewis.armscontrolwonk.com/archive/858/sanger-hypes-the-laptop.

In any case, this evidence raises substantial concerns about Iran's nuclear activities prior to 2004 and supports the 2007 NIE's finding that Iran had a weapon program in place until that time. It also raises substantial concerns about Iran's behavior and intentions after 2003, and undercuts Iran's claims that its nuclear program is entirely peaceful in nature. The available evidence suggests that by 2003, Iran may not have had perfected its ability to produce a weapon, but had made significant progress with virtually every element of weaponization. It is unclear what, if any, progress Iran has been able to make in its weaponization efforts since its formal program was halted in 2003.

Iran has thus far failed to satisfactorily address the above evidence to the IAEA, and has in fact refused to answer any weapons-related questions from the IAEA since August 2008, other than to claim that allegations of weapons-related work are "baseless" and that evidence of weapons work is "forged" and "fabricated."[105]

Breakout

This section lays out Iran's available paths to a nuclear bomb, provides estimates of how long it would take Iran to produce a nuclear bomb, and discusses how difficult it would be for Iran to achieve such a goal. These estimates are applicable to Iran's technical and political situation at the beginning of 2012. As Iran continues to improve the technical sophistication of its program, these estimates will inevitably shorten. While it cannot be known how quickly such changes may come, or how much breakout times will be shortened by specific dates, it is possible to identify a number of key milestones Iran could achieve that would significantly improve its breakout capabilities.[106] This section will consider the most important of these milestones, as well as their policy implications.

---

[105] IAEA, GOV/2011/65, para. 8.

[106] The term "breakout capability" as used here refers to the speed and effectiveness with which Iran could produce at least one nuclear weapon should it choose to devote all available resources to doing so. The question of when or whether Iran will develop a nuclear weapon is both technical and political. Breakout estimates here refer only to the technical component of this question.

Even though Iran may already have developed the necessary technical components to produce a bomb, as of January 2012, Iran would likely need over a year to do so. This correlates well with the conclusions of the U.S. Intelligence Community, which has estimated that it would require Iran at least a year to produce a single nuclear weapon even if all available resources were swiftly dedicated to the task.[107] Other credible sources, however, arrive at estimates as short as 6 months, or as long as 19 months.[108] These estimates vary according to the assumptions they make about a number of uncertain variables. They also vary according to whether the intent is to identify likely or merely plausible—but unlikely—outcomes. Both worst-case and likely estimates will be provided in this section where appropriate.[109]

The reader is cautioned not to allow technical breakout estimates to become a distraction from the more important question of Iran's

---

[107] Greg Miller and Joby Warrick, "U.S. Report Finds Debate in Iran on Building Nuclear Bomb," *Washington Post*, February 19, 2011.

[108] The Institute for Science and International Security (ISIS), a non-profit organization in Washington led by David Albright that is a respected authority on nuclear weapon proliferation, offers a breakout estimate of six months. The International Institute for Strategic Studies (IISS), a London-based think tank that is a similarly respected authority, estimates it would take Iran 19 months to make a weapon. These estimates differ largely because the shorter estimate excludes the time needed to reconfigure centrifuge cascades (it assumes a secret facility already prepared for HEU enrichment), and assumes a level of centrifuge efficiency more than twice the level Iran has yet to demonstrate with working centrifuges (it uses idealized efficiency estimates based on what an IR-1 centrifuge can achieve in theory). In other words, the estimates do not so much disagree as they measure different things. Specifically, the shorter estimate makes a number of low-probability worst-case assumptions that the IISS estimate does not. Albright and Walrond, 2010; IISS, 2011, pp. 70–74.

[109] However, the utility of worst-case estimates here should not be overstated. A significant problem with worst-case scenarios in the Iranian nuclear context is that Iran's most attractive path to a bomb is likely via the use of a secret facility. The facilities at both Natanz and Fordow were, in fact, not declared to the IAEA until their existence had already been detected. Yet, if the existence of secret facilities is assumed in worst-case estimates, then the resulting breakout estimates can collapse to zero. It is possible, for example, that Iran has possessed a parallel, undetected nuclear program for years, and is right now in the very final stages of building a weapon. This being the case, the utility of adopting worst-case scenarios on the scale of months that employ more sanguine, but not necessarily plausible, assumptions is questionable. In this case, it is important to note that the U.S. Intelligence Community estimate is intended to offer a likely outcome rather than a worst case.

political will. All breakout estimates assume that Iran has decided to produce a weapon. Yet this is likely not so. Additionally, as will be discussed in greater detail later in this report, if Iran were dedicated to acquiring nuclear weapons, the United States and its allies would possess few—if any—cost-effective options for preventing them from succeeding, at least over the long term. Iran already has the technical wherewithal to build a bomb. Although air strikes and economic sanctions may set the Iranians back in their efforts, this would likely be only temporary, as the Iranians would continue to possess the underlying technical resources to reconstitute its program and acquire a weapon. The only thing preventing such an outcome is Iran's own decisionmaking calculus.

This report also agrees with the most recent National Intelligence Estimates (2007 and 2011) in finding that Iran has likely not yet made a definitive decision to acquire nuclear weapons.[110] There is no evidence to suggest that Iran has turned its existing capabilities to affect a nuclear breakout. Instead, Iran's behavior suggests it seeks to shorten the time required to build a bomb, improve the ease of doing so and the reliability and effectiveness of the resulting weapon and delivery systems, and increase the number of weapons such a breakout "dash" could produce. Iran is also likely working to improve its ability to pursue a breakout without detection, while reducing the ability of the United States and its allies to use military or other measures to stop a breakout once it is discovered. The pace of Iran's technical progress thus far suggests that the fruition of such efforts will require years of further progress. In theory, however, the Iranians could eventually reduce the time required for nuclear breakout to a matter of weeks.[111]

---

[110] In his testimony on the 2011 NIE on Iran, DNI Clapper stated that the Intelligence Community estimated with "high confidence" that Iran had "not decided to restart the [nuclear weapon] program" after 2003. DNI James Clapper, Testimony Before the Senate Committee on Armed Services, March 10, 2011. Secretary of Defense Leon Panetta confirmed in January 2012 that the United States continued to hold this judgment. "Panetta: Iran Is Seeking Capability to Build Nuclear Weapon but Hasn't Decided to Develop One," Associated Press, January 8, 2012.

[111] The basis of these estimates is explained later in this section. In general, the most important determinants of how short Iran's breakout time can become are whether it possesses a

What Iran Would Need to Make a Bomb

Any attempt at nuclear breakout would require two distinct steps: the production of weapons-grade fissile material, and the construction of an actual nuclear warhead. Two types of fissile material can be used to produce a nuclear weapon: uranium and plutonium. In either case, it is necessary to produce a significant quantity of a particular isotope of the element at a very high level of purity. In the case of uranium, the isotope U-235 must be enriched to a purity of roughly 90%, something that Iran already has the technical capacity to do with its centrifuge facilities. The alternative is to purify the plutonium isotope Pu-239. Pu-239 is produced as a by-product of nuclear fission in reactors, and can be purified through a process known as plutonium reprocessing.

Iran currently does not have the ability to produce weapons-grade plutonium, and will not likely acquire such a capability in the near future. The HWR at Arak, which could in theory produce enough plutonium for at least one bomb per year, is unfinished. It is unknown when this reactor will come online or, given their shortage of materials, whether the Iranians can ever finish it. In theory, the Russian-built reactor at Bushehr could produce plutonium. This too, however, is also likely beyond Iran's capability. The Bushehr LWR is poorly suited for producing Pu-239. The reactor would have to be freshly fueled and its operation parameters changed in order to produce Pu-239 that could be reprocessed and used in a weapon. The spent fuel from this process would have to cool for months before Iran could reprocess it. At present, Iran does not possess the ability to reprocess the necessary quantity of plutonium for a bomb. For the foreseeable future, the uranium route to the bomb gives Iran its only attractive breakout scenarios. As a result, this study considers the enrichment of uranium to weapons-grade HEU to be an essential step for Iran to acquire a nuclear weapon.

Once the appropriate fissile material is obtained in sufficient quantity, it must be crafted into a functioning warhead. It is assumed here that the Iranians would choose to produce a nuclear warhead with

---

secret facility for enrichment to weapons grade, whether it can deploy more advanced centrifuge models in large numbers, and whether it can stockpile sufficient 20% LEUF6 to use as initial feedstock to produce HEU.

an implosion design, which requires less HEU and is easier to mate to a missile.[112] Iran would need to overcome several technical challenges to construct a functioning implosion warhead that could be effectively mated to one of Iran's ballistic missile designs. The HEUF6 produced in its centrifuges would have to be converted to uranium metal first, then machined into hemispheres for the warhead pit. Iran would need the high-explosive lenses necessary to implode the uranium core, which would have to be shaped into the right configuration so that the pit implodes uniformly. Iran also would need to have an appropriate neutron emitter to act as a trigger. While these are all challenging steps, there is evidence that Iran has already made progress with them, and may have already mastered many or all of them. Still, assembly of a warhead for the first time would be challenging and time consuming, even if the individual steps had been worked out in advance.[113] Although the time required to make a weapon once sufficient fissile material has been produced is important, it is excluded from the breakout estimates provided in this section. This is because once sufficient HEUF6 has been produced, it can be removed to a secret location. Therefore, once

---

[112] A nuclear weapon works by creating a chain-reacting supercritical mass of fissile material. This can be accomplished in two ways: the gun-type design, which fires one subcritical mass of HEU into another to create a supercritical mass from the combination of the two; or an implosion-type design, which compresses a subcritical mass of HEU or plutonium using high-energy conventional explosives, and thereby creating a supercritical mass. "Little Boy," the atomic bomb dropped on Hiroshima, was a gun-type weapon, while "Fat Man," the bomb dropped on Nagasaki, was an implosion-type device that used plutonium. Despite its greater simplicity (the United States found it so simple that it used the design for Little Boy without having previously field tested it), the gun-type design is far from optimal, and it is unlikely that Iran would use it. It requires more HEU than an implosion design (as much as 2–3 times more), is less efficient, and is relatively unsafe. Additionally, in the case of Iran, there is evidence that the Iranians have already obtained proven designs for an implosion warhead. See Li Bin, "Nuclear Missile Delivery Capabilities in Emerging Nuclear States," *Science & Global Security*, Vol. 6, No. 3, 1997; IISS, 2011, p. 121. Nonetheless, if Iran's priority were to be to fashion a crude weapon without consideration of wastage or efficiency, it could choose to go this route.

[113] Even if all of the necessary components to a weapon had been prepared and tested, and all of the technical steps had been mastered in advance—including the reduction of uranium metal and machining of hemispheres, which in theory could be mastered by experimenting with non-fissile substitutes—the time to prepare the uranium core and assemble the weapon would still not be zero. The IISS estimates this could take six months.

Iran can produce enough HEU for a bomb, the chances for successful interdiction by the United States and its allies diminishes greatly. Nonetheless, it should be kept in mind that it would still require time for Iran to build a weapon, and this time could be substantial.

Possible Breakout Paths

An Iranian breakout could begin with different initial feedstocks. The higher the enrichment level of the initial feedstock, the shorter the breakout time. One breakout path Iran could take to a bomb would be to enrich its existing stock of either 3.5% LEUF6 or NATUF6 to weapons grade. Both stocks are sufficient to produce at least one bomb.[114] However, because both are under IAEA safeguards, it would be difficult for Iran to do this without relatively quick detection.[115] Because either would require months, given Iran's capabilities as of January 2012, the United States would receive sufficient warning of a breakout to organize a response months before Iran could produce enough HEU for a bomb.[116]

---

[114] This assumes 1,030–2,900 kg to make the first bomb and 1,030–1,300 kg LEUF6 to make each successive bomb (using the Pakistani four-stage enrichment process). As of May 2012, Iran had already stockpiled more than 6,000 kg of 3.5% LEUF6. The IISS estimates that roughly 11 metric tons of NATUF6 would be required to make a single bomb using a facility with 5,832 IR-1 centrifuges with cascades arranged according to the Pakistani method. Iran's stockpile as of September 2011 was roughly 350 metric tons. IISS, 2011, pp. 70–75.

[115] IISS, 2011, p. 71; Peter Crail, "Iran Raising Uranium-Enrichment Level," *Arms Control Today*, Vol. 40, No. 2, March 2010. Iran's entire stock of 3.5% LEUF6 is contained in one capsule, which is stored at the FEP. The IAEA conducts up to 24 inspections at Natanz per year, up to 12 of which can be unannounced (minimum of two hours' notice). Materials such as LEUF6 are under seal, and surveillance cameras are installed. See Ivanka Barzashka and Ivan Oelrich, "Increased Safeguards at Natanz: What Does It All Mean?" FAS Strategic Security Blog, August 28, 2009, http://www.fas.org/blog/ssp/2009/08/increased-safeguards-at-natanz-what-does-it-all-mean.php.

[116] In clarifying remarks by Defense Secretary Leon Panetta in December 2011, Pentagon Press Secretary George Little stated that because IAEA inspectors have "good access" to Iran's enrichment facilities, the United States would learn of any Iranian attempt at a nuclear breakout and "retain sufficient time under any such scenario to take appropriate action." Thom Shanker, "Aides Qualify Panetta's Comments on Iran," *New York Times*, December 20, 2011.

Another option would be for Iran to initiate breakout using natural uranium ore or yellowcake. In principle, uranium could be taken from Iran's mines, which are not under safeguards, or yellowcake could be illicitly imported from abroad. Such a move would avoid immediately triggering detection. However, Iran would still need to convert the uranium to UF6, which would involve using the UCF at Isfahan (or at a secret UCF, the construction and concealment of which would raise its own complications). This, too, would likely be quickly detected.

In the near future, Iran could potentially be able to use uranium enriched to 20% to initiate a breakout dash. In 2010, Iran began enriching 3.5% LEUF6 to 20% using cascades in the PFEP at Natanz. Enrichment from 3.5% to 20% brings Iran much of the way toward the 90% enrichment required for fueling a nuclear bomb. As of November 2011, Iran had produced 76.8 kg of 20% LEUF6, not nearly enough uranium for a weapon. Using Iran's 2011 rate of production of roughly 4 kg per month of 20% LEUF6, it would take Iran at least three years to produce enough to fuel a single weapon.[117] However, in January 2012 Iran began to increase its production of 20% LEUF6 when it initiated an additional enrichment line at its Fordow facility. Iran also has announced that it plans to further increase its rate of production by adding additional centrifuges and replacing IR-1 centrifuges with more advanced models. This could greatly shorten the time needed to stockpile enough 20% LEUF6 to fuel a bomb (if further enriched to 90%). As of January 2012, Iran has not demonstrated the ability to dedicate newer-model centrifuges to this task.

While Iran's stock of 20% LEUF6 would be under IAEA safeguards, if Iran were to initiate a breakout using these stocks the required time to produce sufficient HEU for a bomb would be much less than if it started with 3.5% feedstock, giving the United States less time to

[117] This assumes it would require at least 150 kg of 20% LEUF6 for a bomb. It should be noted that this is an extremely conservative estimate, as 150 kg of 20% LEUF6 is mathematically equivalent to only 21.8 kg of 93% U-235 metal (i.e., with perfect efficiency and no wastage at all, an impossibility to be sure, 150 kg of 20% LEUF6 would produce less than the 25 kg of 90% U-235 metal used by the IAEA to represent a significant quantity of fissile material). Between September 19, 2010, and August 20, 2011, Iran produced 45.7 kg of 20% LEUF6 at the PFEP using two 164-centrifuge cascades. IAEA, GOV/2011/54, p. 4.

intervene. Given Iran's current efforts and the advantages that would accrue from stockpiling greater quantities of 20% LEUF6, Iran has an incentive to wait until it has at least a single bomb's worth of 20% LEUF6 in its stockpile before attempting a breakout. The current production of 20% LEUF6 could, therefore, be the beginning of a "slow-motion" breakout. Additionally, because, as of November 2011, Iran had installed only 412 IR-1 centrifuges at the FFEP for the purpose of enriching uranium to 20%, it has an incentive either to greatly increase the number of cascades at Fordow before trying a breakout or to use the cascades installed at the FEP for this purpose.[118]

If Iran were to decide to use the FEP for a breakout dash, however, it would either have to reconfigure the cascades—which would require the time-consuming and highly visible work of repiping the machines—or attempt to use the untested, more inefficient process of "batch recycling." The likeliest path would be for Iran to use Pakistan's method, which involved a four-stage process of enrichment to 90% HEU. The A.Q. Khan network is known to have sold the plans for this method to other states on the black market, and likely gave it to Iran as well.[119] This process would require the reconfiguration of centrifuges at Natanz, repiping, and the installation of new equipment. This would be technically challenging to do, and nearly impossible to carry out without alerting inspectors. The IISS estimates that such a reconfiguration at the FEP would take a minimum of three months.[120]

The alternative would be to use a process called "batch recycling" or "batch enrichment," which would not require reconfiguring centrifuges. In the batch-recycling process, 3.5% LEUF6 would be fed into cascades at the FEP using their existing configuration to produce 16% LEUF6 as an intermediate. The process would then be repeated to pro-

---

[118] IAEA, GOV/2011/65, para. 22–24.

[119] Iran is believed to have received the plans for this method from A.Q. Khan. See IISS, 2011, pp. 73–74.

[120] IISS, 2011, pp. 70–74. This section largely follows the logic of the IISS report, which is consistent with estimates made by other organizations, including the U.S. Intelligence Community. For more information on the relative challenges of batch recycling, see Alexander Glaser, "Characteristics of the Gas Centrifuge for Uranium Enrichment and Their Relevance for Nuclear Weapon Proliferation," *Science & Global Security*, Vol. 16, No. 1, 2008.

duce weapons-grade HEU. This would require far less time than the Pakistani four-stage process. Assuming no wastage or technical problems, it could take as little as four months, as opposed to a minimum of eight months, and would be less obvious to inspectors.[121] It would, however, be both risky and inefficient. Batch recycling is an untested process, and Iran would be taking a significant risk in attempting it. The four-stage process, on the other hand, is a proven method of HEU enrichment. Also, because batch recycling is highly wasteful (it involves a high tails content, and the tails are not further enriched, at least not to make the first bomb), it requires about twice as much initial feedstock. Given Iran's stockpile of LEU as of November 2011, Iran would risk not being able to produce enough HEU for a weapon by using this method.

It is possible, though unlikely, that Iran has one or more secret facilities where it could enrich its LEU stocks to weapons grade. This could involve either a single large secret facility or multiple smaller facilities. In the latter case, HEU could be enriched in stages, with intermediate batches being moved from one location to another. The advantage of this would be to make it more difficult for air strikes to destroy all the equipment and UF_6 stocks, and to end the breakout dash. The construction and operation of small facilities also could involve a reduced footprint and fewer signs of activity for Western intelligence agencies to detect. The disadvantages would include the difficulty of secretly constructing multiple sites, the inefficiencies involved in moving intermediate batches from one facility to another, and the additional time that would be involved in the enrichment process. Iran also would face the challenge of using its limited pool of scientists and technicians to operate and maintain diverse enrichment facilities, all without detection.

---

[121] IISS, 2011, pp. 72–73. Because these figures assume no wastage, they should be read as the absolute and ideal minimum time required for enrichment. The IISS report also assumes that the effective separative power for the centrifuges would be 0.9 SWU per machine per year. Given that over the most recent reporting cycle (ending August 2011) the effective separative power at the FEP was less than 0.8 SWU/machine/year, this too should be read as a worst case. Three of the eight months required using the Pakistani method are the months required (again, a bare minimum estimate) to repipe the cascades.

A secret enrichment program would likely be the most attractive breakout option to the Iranians, because it may offer the best opportunity to avoid detection, as well as an improved ability to successfully survive an attack. Iran would, however, face a number of trade-offs in pursuing this option, and there would be strong incentives to wait until its program were more advanced before attempting a breakout. In particular, there would be a trade-off between the size of the secret facilities and the speed with which HEU could be produced. A small facility has a better chance of avoiding detection (it could, for example, even be hidden within an urban area), but it would take longer for it to produce a significant quantity of HEU. As a result, Iran has a strong incentive to wait. If it first masters the operation of more advanced and efficient centrifuge models, and stockpiles more LEU (and potentially more 20% LEU), it can greatly improve this trade-off by allowing for shorter enrichment times using smaller (and potentially more reliable) facilities.

Iran also could construct an entirely secret and parallel nuclear program, from uranium ore to HEU. If successful, this could entirely avoid detection. However, the technical and resource barriers to achieving this are likely prohibitive. It is unlikely Iran would be able to produce sufficient yellowcake indigenously for a parallel program. Similarly, under tight multilateral sanctions and intense scrutiny, Iran would find it challenging to locate a foreign supplier that is both willing and able to provide a sufficient supply of yellowcake secretly and without detection. Iran also would have to build and operate a number of secret facilities to accomplish this, including a UCF, which would be technically challenging. All of this would have to be done using Iran's existing pool of scientists and engineers. Most importantly, it would involve a sizable investment of resources, while accepting a significant risk of detection.

Implications for U.S. Policy

Breakout estimates are relevant to U.S. policy choices only insofar as the United States or its allies would be given sufficient warning to mount a military response, and would have a known target against which the use of force could effectively stop a breakout dash. These conditions would likely not hold if Iran were to use a secret facility to produce HEU for a bomb. If the United States did not already know where such a facility was located, it is unlikely it could do so before Iran had completed the work. Even in this case, however, unless Iran is operating an entire (and secret) parallel program, it would have to divert UF6 from its existing stocks, something that would be detected within several weeks at most. Air strikes would be useless without a target; however, the United States might decide to use other forms of punishment to retaliate. In any case, the lack of obvious policy choices the United States would have in such a scenario suggests that the possibility of secret enrichment facilities ought to be a central concern.

The United States would have superior options should Iran choose to conduct a breakout dash using its existing, declared facilities. Iran would have to either expel IAEA inspectors—which the United States and Israel could choose to treat as a red line by itself—or it would have to begin production of HEU while IAEA seals and monitoring equipment remained in place, and while its facilities were subject to frequent and unannounced inspections. Because periods between on-site inspections are between one and three weeks, Iran would have to be able to enrich its existing stocks of UF6 to 90% and then remove the product to a hidden facility for bomb assembly within this time in order to deny the United States and its allies the ability to destroy the facility before the work could be finished.[122] Additionally, Iran would have to have a high level of confidence that it could achieve its goals within such a short time frame, or accept a high risk of failure.

Given Iran's capabilities and resources as of the beginning of 2012, even under worst-case assumptions, Iran would not be able to produce enough HEU for even a single weapon without providing the United States months of forewarning. A reasonable worst-case estimate in this scenario would be roughly four months. This would assume that Iran could, using all of the centrifuges at Natanz successfully being fed UF6 as of May 2012, successfully use the untested batch-recycling method to produce 90% HEUF6 from its existing stocks of 3.5% LEUF6.

---

[122] The IAEA guarantees that it would detect the diversion of the amount of uranium needed for a bomb within one month. Barzashka and Oelrich, 2009.

Even leaving the issue of detection and possible interdiction aside, Iran would have to be willing to accept a very high risk of technical failure to even attempt such a breakout dash. If Iran were to use the Pakistani four-step method instead—still using worst-case assumptions such as peak efficiency and no wastage or technical problems—it would take almost a year to produce enough HEUF6 for a bomb. Given that Iran will almost certainly encounter wastage and decreased efficiency when enriching uranium to higher purity than it has in the past, it is unlikely that Iran would be able to make enough HEU for a bomb in under a year.

Possible Future Developments and Implications

These estimates would change considerably, however, if Iran were to make significant technical progress with its program. If Iran could stockpile enough 20% LEUF6 for a weapon, it could, using the same worst-case assumptions above—including the use of the batch-recycling method—reduce the four-month breakout time to about six weeks. Using the much more plausible four-step method, the figure would be roughly three months. A more worrying scenario would be if Iran were to successfully deploy next-generation centrifuges with much greater efficiencies than the IR-1. Improved centrifuge designs such as the IR-4 could, in theory, increase efficiency severalfold, and potentially cut enrichment times to a fraction of what they would be otherwise. According to the IISS, with 5,832 "third-generation" centrifuges with an efficiency of 10 SWU, Iran could enrich uranium to weapon grade in less than two weeks. So far, however, Iran has not demonstrated that it can successfully build or operate such a centrifuge model even on an experimental level.

As of January 2012, it seems unlikely that Iran could produce enough HEU for a bomb in under a year. It could potentially take Iran significantly longer. It would also take Iran months more to reduce the HEUF6 to metal and machine it into hemispheres. It is further uncertain whether Iran can build a warhead it can mate to a missile for delivery. Even if Iran could do all of this, it would, at best, have a single, untested weapon. Unless Iran possesses a secret facility fully equipped with centrifuges primed for use, it would be forced to carry out the enrichment at Natanz, which is under IAEA inspections and safeguards. Even under the most remotely plausible worst-case scenarios, the United States and its allies would be given months of forewarning, and could—if they chose—use military force to prevent Iran from achieving its goals. While the use of air strikes against Iranian facilities would win little international support at present, the situation would likely be very different if Iran were to initiate a breakout, and the threat of military force by the United States or its allies under such circumstances would likely be very credible to Tehran. As a result, Iran has little incentive to undertake such a risky endeavor.

However, these circumstances would change if Iran could successfully build a large-scale secret enrichment facility, deploy significantly more advanced centrifuge models in large numbers, or stockpile enough 20% LEUF6 for a bomb. If Iran possessed an SQ-worth of 20% LEU feedstock, its breakout times would be greatly shortened, but it would still be very unlikely it could achieve a breakout without giving the United States warning. The United States and its allies may, however, judge that such shortened time lines would leave them without sufficient time to guarantee an effective response, in which case they could establish the acquisition of such stocks as a red line itself. Similarly, the United States may declare the deployment of more advanced centrifuges by the thousands as a red line as well.

The more serious problem, and the most likely to arise, is the possibility that Iran could construct a secret facility for the enrichment of HEU. Although it would be difficult for Iran to do this without detection, and it would also be difficult for it to mount such a large-scale expansion of its centrifuge program, it is important to note that both the Natanz and Fordow facilities were undeclared, and Iran may have intended to keep them secret even after they began operation. Ultimately, the threat posed by the possibility of a secret facility greatly outweighs the threat presented by Iran's declared facilities, at least until Iran can make significantly more technical progress with its program. The prevention and detection of such secret facilities should therefore be a priority for the United States.

CHAPTER THREE

Explaining Iran's Nuclear Policy Choices

Iran's nuclear decisions are shaped by the external threat environment, the internal domestic political process, and the state's technical capabilities. The discussion in this text so far has focused largely on the last of these: the technical and material factors that determine which nuclear outcomes are *possible*. Ultimately, though, Iran's nuclear future will be determined by all of these factors. Over the long term, in fact, technical restraints will likely be the least significant of these. This is particularly the case now that Iran has demonstrated it is capable of carrying out all of the essential elements of the nuclear fuel cycle. If the regime is determined to develop nuclear weapons and is willing to devote the necessary resources and run the required risks to accomplish that task, there is little that the United States and its allies will be able to do to prevent Iran's success.

Although Iran's external threat environment has likely had a strong influence on nuclear policies, its role is not deterministic. Many states with the technical wherewithal to effectively pursue a nuclear weapons program, and with hostile security environments similar to Iran's, have decided to forgo nuclear weapons. To fully understand Iran's nuclear choices, it is necessary to pry open the black box of Iran's domestic politics.

The nuclear decisionmaking process is characterized by two related factors: the beliefs and preferences of Iranian elites, and the relative influence these elites have over the policy process. Iranian elites can loosely, but usefully, be categorized into several factions according to their preferences on the nuclear issue. The domestic balance of political power among these factions—which groups dominate the decision process or how unified or divided influential elites are—determines which preferences are expressed in policy.

The external security environment, technical capabilities and resources, and domestic politics all interact with one another to shape Iran's nuclear policy. The relationships among these variables are complex and often difficult to predict, particularly with a state like Iran whose decisionmaking processes are opaque and convoluted. Changes in one of these areas can have important effects on the others. Changes in the security environment, not least from U.S. policy choices, can affect the domestic political balance in Tehran and the policy preferences of elites. Reduced technical capacity—from, say, sabotage—can raise the costs of the nuclear effort and shift the preferences of decisionmakers in Iran. Economic sanctions could either discourage elites from weaponizing or encourage them. Similarly, sanctions could strengthen the position of moderates in Iran or that of conservatives. Figure 3.1

Figure 3.1
Iran's Nuclear Policymaking Process

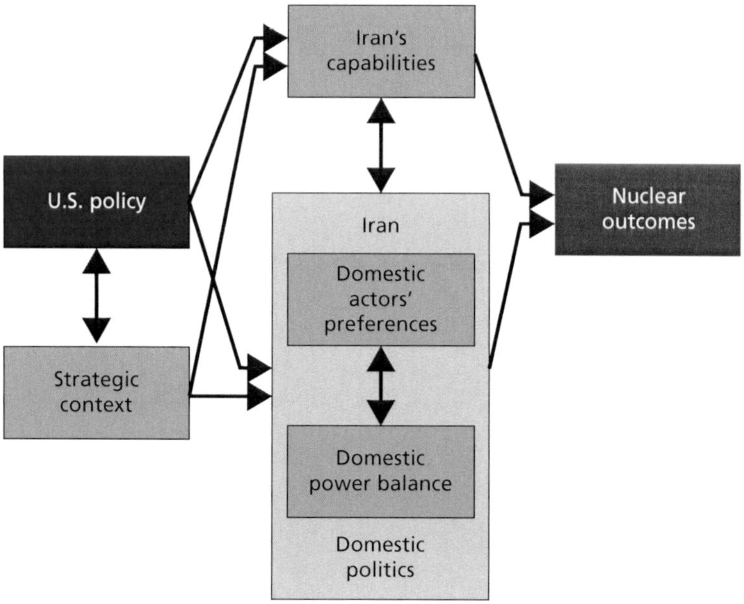

RAND *MG1180-3.1*

illustrates these interactions and the relationship of Iran's nuclear decisionmaking to domestic, international, and technical factors.

The following sections lay out the determinants of Iran's nuclear decisionmaking process. In particular, they describe the regional security context as seen from Tehran, the relevant set of beliefs and perceptions of state interest that are widely shared among Iranian decisionmakers, and the relevant informal and formal structures of the domestic political process. The last section considers the factional divides in Iranian politics, and the way in which factional politics affect nuclear policy. Throughout, the objective is to identify points in the decisionmaking process at which U.S. policies can possibly exert leverage.

Iran's Strategic Calculus

External Security Threats

Although Iran's security context has played—and will likely continue to play—an important role in the state's nuclear decisions, it is but one of a number of factors that have shaped Iranian behavior. Iran's security environment has, in fact, undergone significant change over the course of its nuclear program, and these changes have had no clear and consistent relationship to the regime's nuclear decisions. One implication of this is that security assurances alone are unlikely to be successful in resolving the nuclear standoff.

Iran had begun to entertain the possibility of developing nuclear weapons as early as the 1970s, when the country was still ruled by the shah, and the country's strategic environment was quite different than it is today. At that time, the United States was Iran's most important ally, and Israel, in many ways, played the role of a strategic partner. Tehran was more greatly concerned about Pakistan's nuclear weapons program during this period than it was Israel's already substantial nuclear capabilities.[1]

---

[1] See Etel Solingen, *Nuclear Logics: Contrasting Paths in East Asia and the Middle East*, Princeton, N.J.: Princeton University Press, 2007, p. 165.

Even after the Iranian Revolution, the new regime's greatest threat came not from the United States or Israel, but from Saddam Hussein's Iraq. Iraq's nuclear program, and its use of chemical weapons against Iran during the Iran-Iraq War (and the international community's failure to react to it), both likely had an important effect on Iran's nuclear decisions. In 1987, Hashemi Rafsanjani, then-president of Iran, suggestively stated the following:

> With regard to chemical, bacteriological, and radiological weapons training, it was made very clear during the war that these weapons are very decisive. It was also made very clear that the moral teachings of the world are not very effective when war reaches a serious stage; the world does not respect its own resolutions, and closes its eyes to the violations and all the aggressions which are committed on the battlefield. . . . We should fully equip ourselves in the defensive and offensive use of chemical, bacteriological, and radiological weapons.[2]

After Khomeini's death, Rafsanjani and others spearheaded a revival of Iran's nuclear program.

The U.S. invasion of Afghanistan after 9/11, and especially the 2003 invasion of Iraq, radically redefined Iran's security environment in ways that brought both benefits and challenges, and that had ambiguous implications for the country's nuclear effort. In one fell swoop, the United States removed two of Iran's principal security threats, including its chief adversary. Importantly, the invasion also removed any concern of facing a nuclear-armed Iraq.

The invasion of Iraq also increased the threat that Iran faced from the United States. Always a chief adversary of the Islamic Republic, since 2003, the United States has played the role of Tehran's greatest security threat. Iran was faced with a large U.S. troop presence on its borders, and the prospect of a greater American role in the region for the foreseeable future. This coincided with the Bush administration's use of rhetoric that indicated stronger U.S. support for regime change

---

[2] Quoted in Ray Takeyh, *Guardians of the Revolution: Iran and the World in the Age of the Ayatollahs*, New York: Oxford University Press, 2009, p. 245.

in Tehran, such as the identification of Iran as part of the "axis of evil." However, over time, the occupation of Iraq also helped to draw U.S. attention away from Iran at a time when revelations about the nuclear program had initiated a crisis and weakened America's ability to pursue tougher policies on the nuclear question.

Similarly, the power vacuum left by the removal of Saddam Hussein also has ambiguous implications for Iran's security. On the one hand, it opened up an opportunity for greater Iranian influence in Iraq and a Shia-dominated government in Baghdad. On the other hand, it created instability in a neighboring state, ensured the continued presence of U.S. troops, and raised the possibility of a future regime in Baghdad allied with the United States that offered a political model that could challenge the Islamic Republic's legitimacy.

While Iraq's nuclear and chemical weapons programs may offer an explanation for Iran's renewed interest in a nuclear program in the late 1980s and 1990s, changes in the country's security environment since 2003 have implications for the nuclear program that are less clear. Given the United States' consistent hostility toward the regime and its support for regime change, nuclear weapons, and perhaps even a virtual capability, could be seen as providing Iran with a useful deterrent against the United States. However, Iran also must consider the effect of its ongoing *development* of such a capability. Although possession of nuclear weapons can serve as an effective deterrent, a still-nascent nuclear *program* could invite preventive military force and put the regime at greater risk than it would face otherwise. Iran's nuclear program has already brought diplomatic isolation and punishing economic sanctions.

The threat from the United States also does not fully explain many of Iran's specific decisions with its program. There is evidence that Iran suspended weapons research in 2003, shortly after the United States invaded Iraq. Additionally, Tehran made key concessions to the West during this period, including the suspension of its enrichment activities and the acquiescence to stronger safeguards protocols. It is tempting to explain these concessions as a reaction to an increase in the United States' regional influence and the threat it posed to Iran. However, as pointed out above, the U.S. invasion did not have straightforward security implications for Iran. Also, Iran adopted a more conciliatory position at a time when reformists held power and the country's enrichment capabilities were limited. Furthermore, even in the 2003–2005 period, Iran was steadfast in its refusal to permanently give up the fuel cycle. Iran's subsequent behavior—its decisions to restart enrichment, defy the IAEA and the UNSC, and, possibly, restart nuclear weapons research after 2007—are not easily explained by changes in the external threat environment.

Iran's stance toward Israel also is not well explained by purely strategic considerations. Any current threat to Iran from Israel is largely a product of Iran's provocations since the revolution, and its frequent use of threats and extreme anti-Semitic and anti-Israeli rhetoric. Tehran adopted an adversarial posture toward Israel after 1979, and did so for reasons that had little to do with the regional military balance or a security threat from Israel. Instead, Iran's hostility was based on regime ideology. Iran also saw strong opposition to Israel as a way to spread its revolutionary appeal across the region.[3]

It is also unlikely that the threat from Israel's nuclear arsenal has played a significant role in Iran's nuclear decisionmaking. Israel's nuclear weapons have been rhetorically useful for Tehran, which has pointed to the "double standard" the West has adopted in taking issue with Iran's ostensibly peaceful nuclear pursuits while remaining reticent about Israel's arsenal.[4] However, such rhetoric likely does not represent a genuine concern about Israel's nuclear arsenal. Iran's relations with Israel did not become hostile until the revolution, long after Israel developed nuclear weapons. Iran even offered to collaborate with Israel on the development of the Jericho II missile, which is capable of delivering nuclear weapons. In fact, one Iran expert concluded from an extensive survey of official statements that Israel has played a very

---

[3] Marc Lynch, *Upheaval: U.S. Policy Toward Iran in a Changing Middle East*, Washington, D.C.: Center for a New American Security, June 2011; Takeyh, 2009.

[4] Dana H. Allin and Steven Simon, *The Sixth Crisis: Iran, Israel, America, and the Rumors of War*, New York: Oxford University Press, 2010, pp. 107–111.

small role in nuclear deliberations, and that the leadership is not "inordinately concerned about Israel's nuclear monopoly."[5]

Although security may be an important factor in Iran's nuclear decisionmaking, it is likely neither sufficient nor even necessary to explain the regime's current behavior. It is likely that the principal motivation for Iran's renewal of its nuclear efforts in the 1980s was the threat from Saddam Hussein's Iraq.[6] However, even after that threat was definitively eliminated, Iran's efforts continued. Iran's foremost security threat since 2003 has been the United States. Although nuclear weapons would greatly enhance the regime's security and ensure its survival against a U.S. attack, it is not clear that Iran sees nuclear weapons as a necessary measure to deter the United States. In fact, Iran's pursuit of nuclear weapons could put the regime at greater risk than it would otherwise be by potentially inviting preventive attack, rallying Iran's adversaries around a common position, pushing its Arab neighbors further into alignment with the United States, and leaving the country isolated.

As a result, the United States should view with skepticism the idea that security assurances alone can resolve the Iranian nuclear crisis. Assurances may be a useful tool in dealing with Iran, but they are most likely to be productive by creating favorable domestic political incentives in Tehran, and by helping to win international support for U.S. nonproliferation policies. Because Iran's motivations for its nuclear program are likely not entirely—or even primarily—based on external security threats, assurances alone cannot convince Tehran to reverse course. Similarly, because it is unlikely that Israel's nuclear arsenal is a significant influence on Iran's nuclear decisions, the United States should avoid efforts to create a nuclear weapon–free zone (NWFZ) in the Middle East as a means to win Iranian compliance.

---

[5] Quoted in Ray Takeyh, "It's Not Israel That's Driving Tehran to Nukes," *International Herald Tribune*, August 27, 2005.

[6] Karl Vick, "Blame Iran: Another Way of Seeing Iran's Nuclear Program," *Time*, April 19, 2012.

Iranian Expansionism

Iran's decisionmaking is influenced not only by the presence of external threats, but also opportunities to expand its regional influence, and to further establish itself as a dominant regional power. These hegemonic ambitions are informed by deeply rooted Iranian nationalism, the country's revolutionary ideology, and elite conceptions of Iran's rightful place in the world.

As a Persian, Shia Muslim state in a region dominated by Sunni Arabs, Iran has no natural allies, and has long been in competition with its neighbors for regional power and influence. This has particularly been the case with Saudi Arabia, which shares ambitions for regional dominance. Especially since 2003, Iran also has been faced with in the United States' regional influence, and the possibility of a permanent U.S. military presence. These factors have led to a sense of strategic encirclement in Iran. In part, Iran's efforts to expand its regional influence are a reaction to its fear of encirclement.

Iran seeks to extend its influence in three principal areas: to establish itself as the preeminent power in the Persian Gulf; to spread its revolutionary ideology and political influence across the region, particularly in the neighboring states of the GCC and Iraq; and to challenge Israel's power—if not its very existence—through regional proxies such as Hezbollah and Hamas. The pursuit of these goals has necessarily brought Iran into direct conflict with the United States, as their achievement would involve a sharp reduction in the role of the United States in the region.[7]

Iran strongly opposes the U.S. presence in the Persian Gulf, and has repeatedly expressed a preference for an exit of U.S. forces from the Gulf and the creation of a regional security order among the Persian Gulf States, with Iran at its fulcrum. These ambitions have created tensions with both the other Gulf States and the United States, which has long dominated the Gulf, headquarters the U.S. Fifth Fleet there, and manages the security of the Persian Gulf as an "American lake."[8]

---

[7] As Hassan Rowhani, Iran's former nuclear negotiator, once put it, "wherever Iran goes, it faces the United States." Quoted in Chubin, 2006, p. 117.

[8] Allin and Simon, 2010, p. 96.

Iran's relationship with the Gulf States has been tense since the Iran-Iraq War, during which the Gulf States supported Baghdad. One way in which Iran has sought to extend its influence among these states has been to appeal to their large minority Shia populations (in the case of Bahrain, Shia are in the majority). Although Iran's ability to sow political subversion, and its appeal to Arab Shias, is limited, the Gulf monarchies have viewed Iran as a threat to their domestic political legitimacy and stability. These tensions have increased as a result of recent Shia protests and uprisings in Bahrain.

Iran also has sought to subvert the U.S. position in Iraq, and to support Iraqi Shias in an effort to push Iraqi politics into alignment with Tehran. However, these ambitions have been tempered by concerns that Iraq could descend into greater domestic turmoil, creating instability on Iran's border. Iran has therefore tried to strike a careful balance between promoting Shia groups sympathetic to Tehran and challenging U.S. influence in the country, while avoiding any moves that it believes could trigger a spiral of political destabilization.[9]

Since the Iranian Revolution, Iran has adopted an unwaveringly hostile stance toward Israel. Iran is the only Middle Eastern state that openly denies Israel's right to exist. Aside from its venomous rhetoric, Iran has provided substantial support to anti-Israeli terrorist organizations such as Hezbollah, Hamas, and Islamic Jihad. The Shia group Hezbollah has been Iran's most important proxy in the region. Iran relies on its relationship with Syria to exert its influence in the Levant. The Arab Spring political movements, however, have brought the future of Iran's influence in the region into question. Tehran's ability to support proxies and expand its political influence will largely depend on how the current political changes taking place in Syria and Egypt play out.

Iran's hostility toward Israel stems from both genuine animosity based on its ideology, and a desire to use the Israel-Palestine conflict instrumentally to build popular support among Sunni Arabs and to

---

[9] Chubin, 2006, pp. 117–122. These competing policy goals have sometimes led to surprising policy choices, such as support for Sunni insurgents simply because they oppose the U.S. presence. Iran has faced a similar set of competing incentives in Afghanistan.

undermine Arab governments. By establishing itself as the vanguard of the anti-Israeli and anti-American sentiment in the region, Iran can win regional support while putting pressure on Arab governments that are unwilling to take a similarly rejectionist stance, or renounce their security relationships with the United States.

Iran may see its nuclear program as a way to further these regional strategic goals. Much of this may be symbolic: Iran likely views the nuclear program as a symbol of anti-American and anti-Israeli defiance, and a way to gain support within the region. The United States, Israel, and the Gulf States, however, are additionally concerned that Iran may seek to use nuclear weapons as a "shield" that would allow it to become more assertive regionally. The worry is that Iran might conclude, rightly or wrongly, that its possession of a nuclear deterrent will allow it to engage in threats, military excursions, and—most likely—increased support for its terrorist proxies with impunity. This could lead to an expansion of Iranian influence. More likely, though, it would simply lead to regional instability and, potentially, war.

Negative Security Consequences of Weaponization for Iran

If Iran were to acquire nuclear weapons, the strategic results would not be all positive. In fact, Iran faces a complex and uncertain strategic calculus over the question of weaponization. The way that this calculus is approached, moreover, very likely varies across domestic political actors in Iran, with many elites more willing to accept the risks and costs of weaponization than others.

The development of nuclear weapons could invite a preventive attack, and would likely trigger efforts on the part of other states to balance against Iran's nuclear capabilities through arms buildups and possibly through the pursuit of nuclear weapons of their own. Iran would not be able to count on a benign response from Israel, and could find itself in a confrontation with a state that possesses far greater conventional and nuclear military capabilities. Weaponization could lead to a greater and permanent U.S. military presence or, in the worst case, military conflict with the United States. It could also increase Iran's diplomatic and economic isolation, particularly with the West. Although some in Iran might believe that, eventually, they could go down the path of India and achieve a level of international acceptance as a nuclear power, they would not be able to count on such an outcome.

For Iran, the security implications of weaponization are uncertain. Not all Iranian elites will recognize these potential trade-offs, however. The way in which Iran's decisionmakers interpret the costs and benefits of nuclear policy choices will have at least as much to do with their particular views and assumptions as any objective calculation of rational regime interests.

International and Domestic Political Factors

International Prestige

In addition to the security benefits that Iran could gain from nuclear weapons, Iranian decisionmakers may perceive nuclear weapons as having a potential symbolic value. Specifically, the possession of a nuclear arsenal, however small or limited, could have a psychological effect across the region that benefits Iran more than any actual effect on the material balance of power. This could be important in several contexts. It could create a rallying effect among Shia populations across the Middle East. It could affect perceptions among Sunni Arabs of the relative balance of power between Israel and Iran and encourage Arabs to view Tehran as the most legitimate challenger to Israel. It also could have a similar effect on perceptions of Iran as a champion of anti-Americanism and anti-imperialism. If these effects were to materialize, Iran could reap benefits beyond the actual military capabilities that would accrue from a small number of weapons.

Domestic Legitimacy

Iran's nuclear decisionmaking is also influenced by the domestic political legitimacy that the regime can gain from the country's nuclear progress. Conservative leaders in particular have taken pains to link the nuclear program to Iranian nationalism, holding the program's fuel-cycle achievements up as signs of Iranian technological sophistication and prowess. The nuclear program also symbolizes the country's self-sufficiency and independence from foreign—and especially Western—influence, a core political value among Iranians and a central legitimizing principle of the Islamic Republic.

This effort has served the regime well. Public support for the nuclear program is strong, and there is consensus about the desirability of fuel-cycle development across the political spectrum.[10] This consensus, however, is complicated by two factors: the nuclear program is publicly discussed only in terms of its civilian potential, and there is little agreement about the costs that Iran should be willing to incur in order to pursue it.

The Iranian leadership presents the nuclear issue to the public strictly in the context of Iran's right to possess the full nuclear fuel cycle as part of a civilian nuclear energy program. The U.S.-led opposition to Iran's efforts is portrayed as an attempt to deny Iran legitimate technologies for nuclear energy self-sufficiency that it has a legitimate right to, as enshrined in the NPT. The development of nuclear weapons is eschewed in the strongest terms, and the regime has repeatedly argued that nuclear weapons contradict the religious precepts of Islam and are contrary to the will of God.

As a result of this framing, the nuclear policy serves as a useful political football in the domestic arena. Moreover, by framing it as an issue of rights devoid of any considerations of risk or cost, ruling conservatives have been able to use the issue as a cudgel against political moderates who question whether the nuclear program is worth incurring the wrath of the international community.[11] It has also led to a dynamic in which all parties have a political incentive to take a hard

---

[10] A 2011 RAND survey in Iran found that 87% of Iranians support a civilian nuclear energy program and 32% strongly favor developing nuclear weapons. Sarah Beth Elson and Alireza Nader, *What Do Iranians Think: A Survey of Attitudes on the United States, the Nuclear Program, and the Economy*, Santa Monica, Calif.: RAND Corporation, TR-910-OSD, 2011.

[11] David E. Thaler, Alireza Nader, Shahram Chubin, Jerrold Green, Charlotte Lynch, and Frederic Wehrey, *Mullahs, Guards, and* Bonyads*: An Exploration of Iranian Leadership Dynamics*, Santa Monica, Calif.: RAND Corporation, MG-878-OSD, 2010, pp. 92–96.

line on nuclear negotiations, regardless of what is in the national best interest.

Ideology

The preferences and beliefs of Iranian elites on the nuclear question are shaped by the regime's ideology. This ideology assigns Iran a particular place and role in the world, and casts Iran's strategic choices in the context of a revolutionary narrative. Ideological assumptions and beliefs influence perceptions of external threats, calculations of potential costs and benefits of different policy choices, and expectations about the consequences of actions and the likely reactions of critical actors, including the United States.

This ideology does not, however, make Iran an "irrational" actor. As with all states, Iran's foreign policy is influenced both by domestic belief systems and the constraints imposed by the country's strategic environment. The interaction between the two is complex. Although Iran may have pursued imprudent policy courses out of ideological zeal in its early revolutionary period, in general, it has adopted an increasingly pragmatic foreign policy, particularly when regime survival is at stake. Also, there are ideological differences across Iran's main political factions, particularly over the trade-offs between spreading the revolution and adopting the pragmatic policy course of a "normal" state. These differences have implications for the willingness of different factions to make compromises over the country's nuclear program, and the desirability of acquiring nuclear weapons, particularly at the expense of Iran's relationships with the outside world.

Iranian political ideology and strategic culture are strongly rooted in the 1979 Iranian Revolution. The revolution cast itself as a transnational phenomenon that placed Tehran at the vanguard of a movement aimed at overturning an illegitimate and oppressive world order that was built on maintaining Western (and particularly U.S.) hegemony at the expense of non-Western nations. In particular, the revolution sought to overturn U.S. influence in the Islamic world, to remove U.S.-supported Arab authoritarian regimes, and to spread Islamic rule ordered on Iran's system of *velayat-e faqih* (rule of the jurisprudent). The extension of Iran's political and religious principles was therefore imagined as a liberation of oppressed peoples and a rejection of Western imperialism.[12]

Although the revolution is typically conceived in universal terms, it bears elements of Iran's particular identity.[13] Iranian nationalism and Shia Islam strongly shape Iran's view of itself and the world. In many ways, the revolution's themes of anti-colonialism and independence match Iranian national sentiments of victimization and entitlement. Iranian nationalism paints Iran as the inheritor of an ancient civilization uniquely destined for regional domination. This view long predates the 1979 revolution, and its wide acceptance contributed to the appeal of Khomeini's message. According to this narrative, Iranian hegemony has been unjustly thwarted by both Iran's neighbors and Western outsiders. As a Persian and Shia state surrounded by Sunni Arabs, Iran has long cast itself as a vulnerable and excluded outsider. The country's historic experience with Western imperialist designs has reinforced Iran's view of itself as excluded and vulnerable.

The early experiences of the Islamic Republic forced Iranian leadership to temper its ideological designs by adopting a more pragmatic approach to foreign policy. Particularly as a result of the Iran-Iraq War, Tehran was forced to reconcile its ideology with the realities of international politics. For the regime to survive, it would have to adapt to these realities and moderate its behavior in the region. Iran's growing pragmatism can be seen in many of its foreign policies over the past decades. It has maintained an alliance with Syria despite substantial ideological differences between the two states. It has exercised restraint in its relations with the newly independent Islamic peoples of Central Asia in order to maintain a stable relationship with Russia. In

---

[12] See Chubin, 2006; and Jerrold D. Green, Frederic Wehrey, and Charles Wolf, Jr., *Understanding Iran*, Santa Monica, Calif.: RAND Corporation, MG-771-SRF, 2009.

[13] Takeyh, 2009. Takeyh describes the ways in which Khomeini's universalist, Islamist vision found a receptive audience in Iran in part due to the ways in which it fit with existing nationalist themes. Khomeini nonetheless described the revolution in anti-nationalist terms. He argued (as quoted on p. 18) that "[w]e don't recognize Iran as ours, as all Muslim countries are a part of us," and that the revolution he led was a "revolution without borders."

many ways, it has moderated its approach to the Gulf States and has even cooperated with the United States in certain ways after the 9/11 attacks.[14]

However, there is disagreement among the leadership on how Iran ought to approach trade-offs between the pursuit of revolutionary goals and pragmatism. Iran's conservatives in particular tend to see the world in terms of a zero-sum competition between Iran on the one hand and the West (and especially the United States) and its proxies on the other.[15] At the extreme, this view makes any compromise with the United States undesirable, and even threatening. Any accommodation is by definition a devil's handshake that could potentially be exploited in the future to Iran's disadvantage. At the same time, greater openness with the United States puts the revolution itself at risk by providing the Americans with a route to subvert Islamic values.

As a result, conservatives have tended to see IAEA and UN actions as part of a U.S.-led effort to keep Iran down and deny Iran a nuclear capability that could enhance the state's self-sufficiency and regional influence. The nuclear issue in this sense is simply part of a wider competition between oppressed and oppressor. Viewed this way, the issue becomes one that is less about the specific elements of the program or the details of negotiations, and more about resisting compromise with an adversary that is fundamentally hostile. The United States, in this view, is motivated by the desire to deny Iranian independence and crush the revolution rather than legitimate security interests.

Pragmatists and reformists, on the other hand, have shown a greater willingness to compromise with the West in part because their ideological beliefs differ from traditional conservatives. While they, too, see the nuclear issue largely in terms of broader themes of self-sufficiency and independence, they do not see compromise as a funda-

---

[14] Takeyh, 2009, pp. 205–219.

[15] These factional disputes are described in Thaler et al., 2010. Factional differences in Iran stem in large part from the diversity of views among the original pro-Khomeini coalition that led the revolution. Although these groups were united in their support for an Islamic state, their interpretations differed on what exactly such a political order entailed. Also see Mehdi Moslem, *Factional Politics in Post-Khomeini Iran*, Syracuse, N.Y.: Syracuse University Press, 2002.

mental rejection of these principles but rather as a necessary means of achieving them.

Domestic Politics and Factions

The nuclear issue is highly politicized in Iranian domestic politics, and has become a political football in factional disputes. Actual policy preferences can be secondary to the instrumental use of the issue for political advantage. Nor is the nuclear issue an independent one. It is linked to broader political debates about Iran's general orientation toward the world economy and the international political order, and economic and political liberalization. This issue linkage is both direct and symbolic. In direct terms, Iran's nuclear choices will affect the country's trade and access to the international financial system. These are critical issues in a country in which the domestic economy remains at the top of the political agenda. Symbolically, the nuclear program is a surrogate for self-sufficiency and independence from the Western-centered international order.

Iranian elites are broadly in agreement in their support of the nuclear program and the desirability of an enrichment capability. They differ, however, over how the program's benefits ought to be weighed relative to other policy priorities, especially the country's economic and political orientation toward the West, in particular, and the international community in general. While some decisionmakers are willing to incur substantial costs in the form of economic sanctions and diplomatic isolation in order to keep the nuclear program, others are more willing to make compromises in order to improve ties with potential foreign trading partners and to reduce external security threats. These varying policy preferences correlate with several broad and informal political factions.

Many Iran experts group Iranian political elites into four broad and loosely defined political factions: *principlists*, *traditional conservatives*, *pragmatic conservatives*, and *reformists*.[16] These factions differ

[16] The typology used here is taken from earlier RAND works on Iranian domestic politics, including Lynn E. Davis, Jeffrey Martini, Alireza Nader, Dalia Dassa Kaye, James T. Quin-

according to their respective worldviews, policy preferences and priorities, and views about Iran's general orientation in the international system. None of the four factions challenges the legitimacy of the regime, or the principal of *velayat-e faqih* that puts the Supreme Leader at the apex of Iran's political system. They are informal groupings of elites that are better described as broad networks of political alliances rather than tight or formal political groupings. They transcend the formal institutions of the state and compete for control over them.[17] Each faction contains its own sub-factions that compete for political influence. All of these groupings are fluid and overlapping entities, and political alliances may form that cross factional lines.

The two most ideologically conservative factions—the principlists and the traditional conservatives—are broadly aligned across policy preferences, and differ more in terms of domestic power struggles than desired policy outcomes. These two factions adhere most closely to the ideological underpinnings of the Iranian Revolution. They reject the international status quo, and see Iran as the vanguard of an international Islamic revolutionary movement that is locked in a zero-sum competition with both regional and global adversaries. In particular, they see the United States as both a threat to the regime's existence, as well as the primary obstacle to the expansion of Iran's revolution throughout the region. Both factions place a high value on self-sufficiency and autonomy, and view accommodation with the United States and greater international and domestic openness as potential threats to the revolution and the regime. They see the United States and the West as corrupting influences, and hold cultural purity as a lofty value. Any

livan, and Paul Steinberg, *Iran's Nuclear Future: Critical U.S. Policy Choices*, Santa Monica, Calif.: RAND Corporation, MG-1087-AF, 2011; Thaler et al., 2010; Green et al., 2009; and Alireza Nader, David E. Thaler, and S.R. Bohandy, *The Next Supreme Leader: Succession in the Islamic Republic of Iran*, Santa Monica, Calif.: RAND Corporation, MG-1052-OSD, 2011. Also see Moslem, 2002; Mehran Kamrava, "The 2009 Elections and Iran's Changing Political Landscape," *Orbis*, Vol. 54, No. 3, Summer 2010; and Chubin, 2006. Kamrava details how the principlists emerged as a distinct and powerful faction after the 2005 election of Ahmadinejad.

[17] Splits within the principlist faction have become increasingly relevant since the 2009 presidential election. Kamrava, 2010.

opening to the Western-dominated international system would therefore put Iran's social and political order at risk.[18]

Although recent years have seen principlists in ascendance, traditional conservatives in Iran remain the largest faction. They dominate a number of key state institutions, including the Majlis, the Guardian Council, and the Assembly of Experts, and they command broad support within the IRGC. Their support is drawn from the ideologically conservative old guard of the clerical establishment, and the lower-middle classes.

Supreme Leader Khamenei is identified most closely with the traditional conservatives, and his rise to power after the death of Khomeini cemented their preeminence in Iranian politics.[19] While Khamenei has backed Ahmadinejad, and gave critical support to President Ahmadinejad after the disputed 2009 election, recent political events in Iran suggest that this support is ending.[20] This could have important consequences for Iran's factional alignment, and the relative influence of traditional conservatives.

The principlist faction, built around a core of IRGC and Basiji veterans who rose to influential positions, emerged as the politically dominant group after the 2003 local elections, the 2004 Majlis elections, and the 2005 election of Mahmoud Ahmadinejad to the presidency. They are most strongly associated with the IRGC and the Basij, and represent the rise of a new guard of IRGC cohorts to political influence. Much of the leadership of this group served in the IRGC during the Iran-Iraq War. These elites were politically sidelined for much of the post-war period, when the pragmatic conservatives controlled the

---

18 Traditional conservatives and principlists are the most conservative factions of the Islamist Right in Iranian politics. Nader et al., 2011, pp. 11–15.

19 Ray Takeyh, *Hidden Iran: Paradox and Power in the Islamic Republic*, New York: Holt, 2006, pp. 33–44.

20 Saeed Kamali Dehghan, "Ahmadinejad Fights to Preserve His Dwindling Power," *Guardian*, May 9, 2011; "Ahmadinejad v Ayatollah: Who Will Win Iran Dust-Up?" BBC News, July 8, 2011; Alireza Nader, "Ahmadinejad vs. the Revolutionary Guards," *PBS Frontline*, July 11, 2011; Farideh Farhi, "Iran's Deepening Internal Battle," *PBS Frontline*, June 7, 2011.

presidency. They emerged strengthened, however, from the political battles between conservatives and reformists during the Khatami era.[21]

The principlists have drawn popular support from the country's lower classes and the religiously devout. They have portrayed themselves as the guarantors of the revolution and Khomeini's legacy, and share traditional conservatives' preferences for a closed and inward-looking political orientation, self-sufficiency, and cultural purity. Principlists tend to be hardliners who support a deep Islamization of society and strong state control over the economy to pursue ideological goals such as social justice for the lower classes. Some principlists, including Ahmadinejad, have followed an anti-clerical bent, and challenge the supremacy of the clerics in the political order.[22] Although Ahmadinejad led the principlists' rise to power, and as President acted to strengthen their political influence, many within this faction are fierce political opponents of the President, and it is far from homogeneous.

Particularly in the wake of the 2009 presidential elections, increasing divisions have appeared both between traditional conservatives and principlists as well as within the principlist camp. President Ahmadinejad has played a polarizing role, as he has sought to consolidate political gains by expanding the power and political independence of the presidency, and to restrict the decisionmaking process to a small circle of loyalists. Powerful conservative elites such as Ali Larijani have vocally challenged Ahmadinejad and have sought to build their own political networks in order to contest Ahmadinejad's power. Recently, Supreme Leader Khamenei has become more assertive in challenging Ahma-

---

[21] Frederic Wehrey, Jerrold D. Green, Brian Nichiporuk, Alireza Nader, Lydia Hansell, Rasool Nafisi, and S.R. Bohandy, *The Rise of the Pasdaran: Assessing the Domestic Roles of Iran's Islamic Revolutionary Guards Corps*, Santa Monica, Calif.: RAND Corporation, MG-821-OSD, 2009. The IRGC itself does not act as a homogeneous political bloc, and in many ways exhibits the same factional divisions that characterize the broader political system. In general, though, the IRGC leadership has been conservative and reactionary, and led both the fight against reformists during the 1997–2005 period and the crackdown on the Green Movement after the 2009 election.

[22] See Ali M. Ansari, *Iran Under Ahmadinejad: The Politics of Confrontation*, New York: Routledge, 2007. Ahmadinejad is among an influential group in the principlist faction that adheres to a millenarian Mhadist view. This group believes in a direct link with the Twelfth Imam that does not require the mediation of a clerical authority.

dinejad, and has successfully removed several important presidential appointees from power. As of fall 2011, it is unclear what implications these moves have for Ahmadinejad's future role in the political system, or how it will affect the influence and makeup of the principlist faction. It does suggest, however, that Ahmadinejad's hold on power is likely to weaken substantially.[23]

The pragmatic conservative faction is also ideologically conservative, but its members have been more willing to temper ideological zeal and pursue pragmatic policies to advance the regime's interests. Pragmatic conservatives share the commitment of traditionalists to the revolution, and tend to support the traditionalists' repressive cultural and social policies and their opposition to political liberalization. However, they differ with traditional conservatives and principlists over economic liberalization. The pragmatists believe that greater economic openness, both in terms of opening Iran's markets to the international economic order and liberalizing the domestic economy, will benefit Iran and promote economic growth and, in turn, enhance Iran's regional power. They see revolutionary goals and openness as complementary, whereas conservatives see them as naturally antagonistic. The pragmatists also support efforts to reduce tensions with the United States, and to achieve a political settlement that promotes regional stability. This is viewed instrumentally, as a way to create the necessary strategic and political environment for Iran to rapidly grow its economy. The most visible and influential member of this faction has been Hashemi Rafsanjani, who held the presidency from 1989 to 1997. The faction's popular support is drawn most strongly from the country's merchant class (*bazaari*) and the urban middle and professional classes.

The reformists represent the ideological left in Iranian politics. Reformists' interpretations of the revolution tend to differ markedly from members of the more conservative factions. The reformist faction supports economic openness and liberalization, and also favors politi-

---

[23] Karim Sadjadpour, "The Rise and Fall of Iran's Ahmadinejad," *Washington Post*, July 13, 2011; Muhammad Sahimi, "Khamenei Versus Khamenei: Will Ahmadinejad Be Impeached?" *PBS Frontline*, July 10, 2011. For a different view, see Roshanak Taghavi, "Iran's Power Struggle Is Set to Escalate," *Guardian*, July 15, 2011.

cal openness and domestic reform. This group's policy preferences are the most moderate of the major political factions. They favor a relaxation of cultural and social policy, rapprochement with the West, and steps toward greater democratization. This faction was briefly ascendant between 1997 and 2005, when President Khatami was in power. In contrast to Ahmadinejad's policies, Khatami favored a "dialogue of civilizations," and pursued a "grand bargain" with the United States to resolve a number of outstanding disputes. However, even when they controlled the presidency, the reformists consistently lacked the broader political authority in the country to successfully pursue such initiatives, and ultimately proved unable to achieve them.

After the 2005 election of Ahmadinejad, the reformist faction became increasingly marginalized in Iranian politics and ceased to control any major formal political institutions. After the contested 2009 elections, the reformists became most closely associated with the Green Movement, and key reformist elites such as Mir Hossein Moussavi and Mehdi Karroubi assumed leadership roles of the movement. The 2009 elections also had the effect of pushing pragmatic conservatives and reformists into greater political alignment, and Rafsanjani himself came to publicly support the Green Movement. Ultimately, though, the result of these protests, at least in the near term, has been the greater consolidation of political power in the hands of conservatives, and the further marginalization of reformists and pragmatic conservatives.

All four political factions support the nuclear program and Iran's development of the full nuclear fuel cycle. They differ in how they value the nuclear program relative to the costs of continued defiance of the West, increasingly strict international sanctions, and isolation from the international economic system. Both traditional conservatives and principlists are not only willing to push forward with the nuclear program at the expense of relations with the West, but can reap domestic political benefits from it. These factions both derive domestic political legitimacy from a state of mutual hostility with the United States and its allies. The nuclear program is used instrumentally as a way to demonstrate resolve in the face of Western pressure, and strength in the face of Western coercion. Both the principlists and the traditional conservatives have used the nuclear issue as a way to signal their revolutionary credentials to a domestic audience, and to challenge the political legitimacy of the reformists, whom they have painted as weak, lacking in resolve, and easily cowed by the United States.[24] In this sense, the recalcitrant position in nuclear negotiations favored by Ahmadinejad and Supreme Leader Khamenei has reflected the domestic struggle for political authority as much as actual policy preferences.

While the pragmatic conservatives and reformists also support Iran's nuclear efforts, they are not so prepared to incur the costs of a continued dispute with the West, and do not see domestic political value in a hostile relationship with the United States. These two factions both support rapprochement with the West—the pragmatists have sought to achieve this through gradual steps, the reformists through a grand bargain—and believe that regime survival can best be achieved by promoting regional stability and integration with the international economic order. Unlike conservatives, they see continued conflict with the United States as a potential threat to the regime.

Both pragmatists and reformists wish to pursue a negotiated settlement of the nuclear question, and are willing to make compromises in order to do so.[25] However, there are likely hard limits to how far even these groups are willing to go in negotiations. Importantly, no political faction in Iran has signaled a willingness to completely give up uranium enrichment at any price. Even if reformists were to gain control over policy, the United States and its allies would still likely have to make significant concessions in order to achieve a deal. This probably would have to include, at a minimum, allowing Iran to maintain a token enrichment capability, if not a full-scale industrial capacity to produce nuclear reactor fuel.

Bargaining preferences aside, it is unlikely that pragmatic conservatives or reformists will be in a position to set Iran's nuclear policy at any point in the foreseeable future. In fact, the most pertinent char-

---

24 Chubin, 2006; Shahram Chubin, "The Domestic Politics of the Nuclear Question in Iran," in Joachim Krause and Charles King Mallory IV, eds., *The Strategic Implications of the Iranian Nuclear Program*, Berlin: Aspen Institute, 2010, pp. 84–93.

25 Chubin, 2010.

acteristic of current Iranian domestic political dynamics for negotiations may be that the leadership is currently extremely divided, there is substantial political polarization among the competing factions, and the outcome of current power struggles is highly uncertain.[26] These divisions serve both to focus the attention of the leadership inward and to increase the difficulty of winning the necessary political support for any potential negotiated settlement. Each group has an incentive to deny the others the political capital that could accrue from striking a favorable deal with the United States. Opponents of any proposed settlements also can appeal to the Supreme Leader, whose own positions on both the nuclear issue and relations with the United States are very conservative.

The effect this has on the nuclear issue was perhaps most visible in 2009, when Iran first agreed to, and then reneged on, the fuel-swap deal with the P5+1. This deal was favored by principlists surrounding President Ahmadinejad, and the negotiators who first agreed to the deal were among that group. However, other political factions quickly took issue with the deal, not necessarily because they opposed it on the merits, but because they did not wish to hand Ahmadinejad and his supporters a political victory that could be used to increase his power. It is telling that Moussavi, who as a leader of the reformist faction has favored a more accommodating bargaining stance with the West in general, was one of the most vocal critics of the fuel swap, and was allied with traditional conservatives in putting an end to the deal.

The continued rise of the IRGC as a potent political and economic force in Iran will also likely complicate efforts to negotiate a settlement with Iran. Although the IRGC leadership is subject to many of the same political divisions and factional disputes as the polity as a whole, it is currently dominated by conservatives. The IRGC also has

---

[26] As this report was going to press, there were a number of indications that the political fortunes of President Ahmadinejad and his supporters had substantially declined, and the Supreme Leader had begun to exert more unified control over Iran's decision-making process. The implications of this development for negotiations over the nuclear program are unclear. See Rudy deLeon, Brian Katulis, and Peter Juul, *Strengthening America's Options on Iran: 10 Key Questions to Inform Debate*, Washington, D.C.: Center for American Progress, 2012, pp. 43–52.

a vested interest in Iran acquiring nuclear weapons, because it is likely that the IRGC would have stewardship over the arsenal.

The current domestic political dynamics in Iran, therefore, make it unlikely that the United States and its partners can successfully negotiate a resolution to the nuclear issue, or coerce Iran into a more favorable bargaining position. Because conservatives can use tensions with the United States to their domestic political benefit, coercion could even strengthen their control over the policy process. Conservatives currently control the major centers of power, dominate the leadership of the IRGC, and have the sympathy of the Supreme Leader, who will have the ultimate say on whether or not Iran pursues nuclear weapons. Divisions between and within the conservative factions only reduce the chance of a negotiated solution by creating gridlock and providing incentives for the different groups to oppose any deal supported by rivals. The best path available to the United States and its partners is to encourage positive political change in Iran over time, and to avoid any measures that could reinforce the power and legitimacy of conservatives or help to unite them.

CHAPTER FOUR

Constraints on U.S. Policy

Previous chapters have discussed the potential capabilities, limitations, and strategic and political motivations of Iran's nuclear program. All of these factors will be important in shaping the future course of Iran's program, and the decision of whether or not to weaponize. This chapter puts the nuclear issue into a broader context by considering external factors that U.S. policymakers must consider when addressing the nuclear issue. The United States, as the world's dominant power, has a large and diverse set of interests that must always be considered when choosing its foreign policy. This chapter seeks to highlight the most important considerations for the United States when choosing an Iran policy. In particular, U.S. policymakers must take into account the important roles that Israel and the states of the GCC, especially Saudi Arabia, play. These states, and particularly Israel, are among the United States' most important allies in the region. They are also among the most directly impacted by Iran's nuclear decisions, and their interests, preferences, and policy choices will have an important effect on outcomes.

Beyond the region, the United States will have to coordinate its policies on the Iranian nuclear issue with its global partners. Most challenging will be winning broader support from Russia and China for U.S. policy objectives. U.S. policy choices could have important consequences for the broader international nonproliferation regime. The Iranian case is setting important precedents for how the United States and its allies, the P-5, the IAEA, and the UN Security Council will approach future proliferation cases. The case also highlights the weaknesses and contradictions that are inherent to the existing regime and the NPT, which—depending on how these are reconciled—could affect the choices of future nuclear proliferants.

Israel

In order to maintain regional stability and its relationship with its ally, the United States will need to reassure Tel Aviv of its commitment to Israel's defense, and its resolve in addressing the Iranian nuclear program. Most importantly, the United States will have to convince Israel to support U.S. policy initiatives and not adopt an independent and potentially destabilizing policy course of its own. An effective policy toward Iran will depend on the United States and its allies, especially Israel, presenting Tehran with a unified front.

The United States will have to convince Israel not to launch air strikes unilaterally against Iran's nuclear facilities or to openly declare its nuclear capabilities. The United States can best achieve these goals by reassuring Israel of its commitment to Israel's defense, emphasizing the costs of any action not coordinated with the United States, and convincing Israel that the United States is committed to an effective policy course toward Iran.

Israel has identified Iran's nuclear program as an "existential threat," and has stated its willingness to use unilateral military force, if necessary, to prevent Iran from developing nuclear weapons. It has expressed impatience with open-ended negotiations, and supports a more coercive approach toward Iran than the one that the United States and the other members of the P5+1 have followed. Israel has consistently favored keeping the threat of a military strike on the table, and has conducted military exercises that resemble preparations for such a strike.[1]

---

[1] Jeffrey Goldberg, "Point of No Return," *Atlantic Monthly*, Vol. 306, No. 2, September 2010; Michael R. Gordon and Eric Schmitt, "U.S. Says Exercise by Israel Seemed Directed at Iran," *New York Times*, June 20, 2008; Goldberg, 2010.

It is difficult to tell, however, where rhetoric ends and sincere commitments to military force begin. Israel has an interest in using the threat of a military attack as a way to apply pressure on the United States to pursue a resolution of the Iran nuclear crisis that favors Israel, and as a way to coerce Iran.[2] Israel also has an interest in keeping the Iran issue at the top of the United States' list of priorities, and the threat of unilateral military action furthers that. In November 2011, Israeli Defense Minister Ehud Barak stated that in nine months from that time, Iran could enter a "zone of immunity," in which actions to prevent Iran from acquiring nuclear weapons could become impossible.[3] While it is unclear what specific thresholds Iran could cross with its program in that time, the issuance of a public deadline serves to put pressure on the Obama administration to act in the months before the 2012 presidential election. Yet in January 2012, Defense Minister Barak stated that an Israeli attack on Iran's nuclear sites was still "very far off."[4] Aside from Iran's acquisition of a weapon, it is unclear what Israel's red lines are, or under what circumstances the Israelis would be willing to carry out air strikes.

Although Israel's leaders have suggested that the Islamic Republic is irrational—and, presumably, could be willing to launch a nuclear attack on Israel despite the fact that this would bring certain and swift destruction to Iran—Tel Aviv's strategic calculus is more nuanced than such statements suggest. Israel fears the regionally destabilizing effects of a nuclear-armed Iran. Israelis are concerned that Iran will seek to use nuclear weapons as a shield that enables them to behave more aggressively in the region without fear of retaliation. A nuclear-armed Iran could provide cover for attacks by Hezbollah or other terrorist groups against Israel. Such attacks could be orchestrated by Tehran, or by

---

2 According to Marc Lynch, senior Obama administration officials have described having to deal with three "ticking clocks": Iran's technical progress with its nuclear program, growing domestic political pressure in the United States, and the possibility of an Israeli attack on Iran. Lynch, 2011.

3 John Vinocur, "Clock Ticking for West to Act on Iranian Nuclear Program," *New York Times*, December 29, 2011.

4 Isabel Kershner and Rick Gladstone, "Decision to Attack Iran Is 'Far Off,' Israel Says," *New York Times*, January 18, 2012.

anti-Israeli groups themselves, which could be emboldened by Iran's arsenal.[5]

Israel also worries that an Iranian nuclear capability could reduce America's ability to project power in the region, and this would begin a longer-term shift in the balance of power.[6] Similarly, there is concern that whatever security cooperation Israel now receives from Arab states would gradually evaporate in such a climate.[7] Finally, an Iranian nuclear arsenal could trigger additional nuclear proliferation across the region. Such changes in the strategic environment could, in the eyes of many Israelis, present an "existential threat" over the long term by encouraging emigration, forestalling any resolution to the Israeli-Palestinian conflict, or forcing Israel to permanently become a garrison state.[8]

Israel's view of Iran's nuclear program is informed by its history of facing existential threats from its neighbors in the region. Repeatedly, Israelis have been reminded of the degree to which their existence as an independent state depends on the country's superior military capabilities and preparedness. Many Israelis believe that their success in the face of these threats has depended not only on its military might but the resolve to use it, and even the willingness to use it preemptively against materializing threats.[9] This has particularly been so with nuclear weapons. Beginning with the 1981 Israeli attack on Iraq's

---

[5] Nonetheless, many Israelis take Iran's rhetoric at face value, and see the Islamic Republic as fundamentally driven by ideology, prone to irrational behavior, and capable of launching a first strike on Israel even if it means state suicide. For a discussion of Israel's perceptions of the Iran nuclear issue, see Davis et al., 2011, pp. 95–112.

[6] Davis et al., 2011, pp. 105–108.

[7] Lynch, 2011; Allin and Simon, 2010, pp. 75–106. At present, a number of Arab states are willing to cooperate with Israel behind the scenes, something that would likely become more difficult to do in the wake of an Israeli attack on Iran. The degree to which this would be true would depend on the specific circumstances and consequences of the attack. These concerns are exacerbated by the region's strategic uncertainties brought on by the Arab Spring.

[8] Allin and Simon, 2010, pp. 64–65.

[9] A poster at the Israeli Air Force Headquarters in Tel Aviv depicts three Israeli F-15s flying above Auschwitz to illustrate the central role of the legacy of the Holocaust in Israel's perception of its threat environment. Allin and Simon, 2010.

Osirak nuclear facility, Israel has demonstrated its commitment to the Begin Doctrine, which holds that Israel will not allow a potential adversary to develop weapons of mass destruction that could be used against it.[10] The doctrine was reaffirmed in 2007 when Israel bombed a nuclear facility in Syria.

Since the revolution, Iran has established itself as one of the most hostile states in the region toward Israel.[11] Iranian leaders have adopted inflammatory anti-Israeli and anti-Semitic rhetoric, and have frequently expressed their desire to see an independent Israeli state vanish from the region. Moreover, Iran has provided substantial military and financial support to Israel's most dedicated and capable adversaries, especially Hezbollah and Hamas. Using Syria as a conduit, Iran has succeeded in establishing Hezbollah as a potent proxy in Lebanon. The terrorist organization has proved itself to be an enduring political and paramilitary force in Lebanon and an enduring security challenge to Israel. Using Iranian weaponry and funds, Hezbollah has conducted attacks against Israel, including rocket attacks against Israeli civilians. Despite Israeli military action against Hezbollah strongholds in Lebanon in 2006, the organization retains its ability to inflict casualties on Israel, while the group's dedication to opposing Israel has only increased.[12]

---

[10] Prime Minister Menachem Begin issued a directive in 1977 that Israel would not allow states in a "state of war" with Israel to acquire the means of producing nuclear weapons. After the 1981 attack on Osirak, Begin stated that Israel would use "all the means at our disposal" to prevent a rival from acquiring such a capability. In 1981, Defense Minister Ariel Sharon stated that an adversary acquiring the means to produce nuclear weapons was "not a question of a balance of terror but a question of survival," and that Israel would use preventive military force to eliminate such a threat "at its inception." Shai Feldman, *Nuclear Weapons and Arms Control in the Middle East*, Cambridge, Mass.: Center for Science and International Affairs, Harvard University, 1997, p. 109.

[11] Takeyh, 2009; Kenneth Katzman, *Iran: U.S. Concerns and Policy Responses*, Washington, D.C.: Congressional Research Service, RL32048, March 4, 2011. Supreme Leader Khamenei has frequently referred to Israel as a "cancerous tumor," and in 2010 called Israel a "disease." President Ahmadinejad has denied the Holocaust took place, and in 2005—echoing Ayatollah Khomeini—stated his desire to see Israel "wiped off the map." Rafsanjani suggested that Israel could be destroyed with a single atomic bomb.

[12] Patrick Devenny, "Hezbollah's Strategic Threat to Israel," *Middle East Quarterly*, Vol. 13, No. 1, Winter 2006; Thanassis Cambanis, "Stronger Hezbollah Emboldened for Fights

Iran also has successfully established ties of support with Palestinian organizations, especially Hamas, which politically controls Gaza and has used the territory to launch attacks against Israel. Israel's invasion of Gaza in 2009 uncovered evidence of Iranian support for Hamas in the form of finances, arms, and materiel. Iran's support for terror attacks on Israel, its efforts to undermine the Israeli-Palestinian peace process, and its rhetorical commitment to the destruction of Israel has, in Israel's eyes, justifiably made Iran a chief security threat. A nuclear-armed Iran would be an unacceptable threat to many Israeli decisionmakers.

Tensions between Israel and Iran worsened after the election of Mahmoud Ahmadinejad and the political ascendancy of conservatives in Iran. Ahmadinejad has adopted unusually inflammatory anti-Israeli rhetoric, even by Iran's normally hostile standards. The rise of political conservatives and their willingness to adopt a more confrontational posture toward the United States and the West on the nuclear issue has increased Israeli anxieties about Iran's nuclear program, which many in Israel doubt is aimed at developing nuclear weapons.

Israel's military capabilities are likely sufficient to conduct operationally successful air strikes against Iran's principal nuclear facilities at Fordow, Natanz, Isfahan, and Arak. However, it is questionable whether such an attack could sufficiently delay the Iranian nuclear program to justify the cost.[13] Many Israelis have expressed an appreciation of these potential costs, which include regional diplomatic fallout, the possibility of Iranian retaliation, and negative effects on Israel's relationship with the United States.[14] Air strikes could trigger retaliatory attacks by Iran's regional proxies, and could even lead to a wider

---

Ahead," *New York Times*, October 6, 2010.

[13] The possible benefits and costs of a military strike against Iran are discussed in greater detail in the following chapter. For a detailed look at the operational challenges Israel would face in conducting such an attack, see Whitney Raas and Austin Long, "Osiraq Redux? Assessing Israeli Capabilities to Destroy Iranian Nuclear Facilities," *International Security*, Vol. 31, No. 4, Spring 2007. For an update on Raas and Long's assessment with respect to the Fordow facility, see Austin Long, "Can They?" *Tablet*, November 18, 2011.

[14] Goldberg, 2010. Officially, Israel has repeatedly stated a preference for the issue to be resolved peacefully if possible, while continuing to keep all options "on the table."

conflict. An Israeli attack also could set back the Arab-Israeli peace process, push Arab states in the region into Iran's orbit, and lead to negative domestic political consequences in nearby states affected by the Arab Spring, such as Egypt, whose domestic politics are already unstable and highly uncertain, and are susceptible to the influence of extremists. These costs and risks are likely viewed in Tel Aviv as being sufficiently high to warrant restraint, particularly while the United States continues to pursue negotiations and sanctions.

A central concern for Israel is its relationship with the United States, and it will be reluctant to use force against Iran without Washington's approval.[15] Nonetheless, there is likely a point at which the Israelis would be willing to act unilaterally against Iran in spite of U.S. opposition. To reach this point, Israel would likely have to be convinced that Iran's crossing of the nuclear threshold was imminent, and that the United States was unprepared to act to stop it. Regardless of where Israel's red line lies, the United States will have significant influence over Israel's decisions.[16]

Another important concern for the United States will be Israel's nuclear posture. Israel has had a nuclear monopoly in the Middle East for more than four decades. Although estimates about Israel's nuclear arsenal range widely, there is no question that it is a mature nuclear power that possesses substantially greater capabilities than Iran would be able to acquire in the foreseeable future. It likely possesses more

---

[15] Davis et al., 2011.

[16] While the United States, as Israel's most important ally, has a substantial ability to influence Israeli decisions, it is not clear exactly how much the United States can influence Israel's decisions regarding a possible attack against Iran. See Jim Zanotti, Kenneth Katzman, Jeremiah Gertler, and Steven A. Hildreth, *Israel: Possible Military Strike Against Iran's Nuclear Facilities*, Washington, D.C.: Congressional Research Service, R42443, March 28, 2012. Also, short of Iran developing a nuclear weapon, Israel's official red lines are unclear. It is also possible that the United States may have already provided Israel with assurances that it will use air strikes against Iranian nuclear facilities should Iran cross certain lines such as the expulsion of inspectors or the initiation of a breakout dash.

than 100 weapons, and has developed the full nuclear triad (i.e., the ability to deliver nuclear warheads from land, sea, and air).[17]

Israel has carefully maintained an ambiguous nuclear policy. It is not a member of the NPT, and has never declared itself a nuclear weapons state. This policy reflects a long-standing tension in Israeli security thinking between the belief that a nuclear deterrent is necessary to ensure Israel's survival, and the fear that an Israeli nuclear arsenal could trigger nuclear proliferation in the region and ultimately leave Israel less secure. As a small state whose population is densely concentrated into a handful of urban areas, Israel sees itself as uniquely vulnerable to a nuclear attack. Many Israelis believe this would put Israel at a disadvantage in a nuclear competition with Arab states, and that it could undermine stable deterrence. Rafsanjani's public remark that one nuclear weapon could destroy Israel—while Iran itself could survive a similar attack on its territory—strongly feeds into this concern.[18] As a result, many Israelis consider the nuclear monopoly to be essential to Israel's survival. The Begin Doctrine reflects this view.

Iran's development of a nuclear weapons capability could lead many Israelis to rethink the country's nuclear doctrine of ambiguity. One concern could be that an undeclared and ambiguous arsenal would be an inadequate deterrent. To effectively deter a nuclear-armed Iran, some Israeli decisionmakers might perceive a need for declared capabilities, clearly articulated red lines, and possibly a nuclear test. There would likely be substantial public support for such a change in Israel's position were Iran to openly declared itself a nuclear-armed state or test a weapon of its own.[19]

On the other hand, Iran itself could maintain ambiguity about its nuclear capabilities, and develop a virtual capability without declar-

---

[17] See IISS, *Nuclear Programs in the Middle East: In the Shadow of Iran*, London: International Institute for Strategic Studies, 2008, pp. 119–134; and Joseph Cirincione, Jon B. Wolfsthal, and Miriam Rajkumar, *Deadly Arsenals: Nuclear, Biological, and Chemical Threats*, 2nd ed., Washington, D.C.: Carnegie Endowment for International Peace, 2005.

[18] Rafsanjani made the statement during his Friday prayer sermon on Quds Day 2001. *Voice of the Islamic Republic of Tehran*, "Quds Day Speech by Chairman of Expediency Council Akbar Hashemi Rafsanjani," December 14, 2001 (BBC Monitoring).

[19] Davis et al., 2011, pp. 108–111.

ing itself a nuclear power, or withdrawing from the NPT. In this case, Israel would be faced with difficult decisions. A declaration on Israel's part could direct regional criticism toward Israel and away from Iran, and could fuel calls for a Middle-Eastern NWFZ. Yet a situation in which both Iran and Israel maintained ambiguity about their nuclear capabilities would likely be unstable over the long term.[20]

Although some influential Israelis have expressed wariness with the Obama administration's Iran policy, and concern that Washington is insufficiently prepared to use coercive measures to resolve the crisis, both Israel and the United States have recognized the importance of maintaining a unified policy stance, and to not provide Iran with an opportunity to divide Israel from its closest ally.[21] Over the past two years, the United States has used sanctions and the threat of military action as a way to reassure Israel and win patience for further negotiations.[22] The success of U.S. policy will likely continue to depend on these efforts to create the necessary space for negotiations and a longer-term resolution of the nuclear issue.

Gulf Cooperation Council

The monarchies of the GCC are a key concern in U.S. regional policy and will be central to any Iran strategy. These states have long-standing

---

[20] A somewhat similar situation held in South Asia before India and Pakistan conducted nuclear tests in the late 1990s. See S. Paul Kapur, *Dangerous Deterrent: Nuclear Weapons Proliferation and Conflict in South Asia*, Stanford, Calif.: Stanford University Press, 2007.

[21] Alon Ben-Meir, "Israel's Response to a Nuclear Iran," *International Journal on World Peace*, Vol. 27, No. 1, March 2010; Goldberg, 2010; and Chuck Freilich, *Speaking About the Unspeakable: U.S.-Israeli Dialogue on Iran's Nuclear Program*, Washington, D.C.: The Washington Institute for Near East Policy, 2007. There are conflicting reports about Israeli attitudes toward the Obama administration's Iran policies, and how these attitudes differ from those toward the Bush administration's approach. Clearly the Netanyahu government seeks to push the United States toward a more coercive approach toward Iran, and is concerned about U.S. resolve. It is important, however, to avoid the temptation of reading too much into these differences, as such concerns would likely arise under any circumstances simply because Israel and the United States have different stakes in the issue.

[22] Lynch, 2011.

cooperative ties with the United States, and an adversarial—but complex—relationship with the Islamic Republic of Iran.[23] The states of the GCC, and Saudi Arabia in particular, will be important partners for the United States in both containing Iran's regional influence and managing regional stability through engagement with Tehran. Also, as some of the world's major oil suppliers, they can play a critical role in U.S. diplomacy by offsetting the potential effects of sanctions against Iran on global oil supplies.

Several factors have led the GCC states to be particularly anxious about the possibility of a nuclear-armed Iran.[24] First, they are geographically proximate to Iran and rely heavily on the free passage of shipping through the Strait of Hormuz to export oil. If a nuclear-armed Iran were to trigger a regional conflict, the Gulf States would be directly affected. Iran could seek to obstruct the sea lanes through the strait and has demonstrated a willingness to do so in the past. In November 2011, Iran threatened that it could seek to close the strait in retaliation against an oil embargo. Iran could also strike Gulf oil infrastructure either through proxy or missile attacks.[25]

Second, several states of the GCC have a history of conflict with Iran. After the 1979 revolution, Ayatollah Khomeini questioned the legitimacy of the Gulf monarchies and called for their overthrow. Iran and the UAE continue to dispute territorial claims over Gulf islands. Iran has been implicated in supporting domestic subversion in a number of Gulf States. During the Iran-Iraq War, relations reached a low point when the Gulf monarchies leant their support to Saddam Hussein's

---

[23] The GCC itself was formed largely in response to the Iranian threat in the wake of the Iranian Revolution and the beginning of the Iran-Iraq War. Treatment here of the GCC as a unified entity, however, should not obscure the fact that the Gulf States have differing interests and policy preferences on a host of issues, including relations with Iran.

[24] Davis et al., 2011, pp. 51–54, 79–93.

[25] Ayatollah Khamenei has threatened to strike Gulf oil infrastructure in retaliation for an attack on Iran's nuclear programs. Michael Smith, "Iran Threatens Gulf Blitz If U.S. Hits Nuclear Plants," *Sunday Times*, June 10, 2007.

Iraq.[26] More recently, the Gulf States have been wary of Iran's influence in Iraq and the country's nuclear program.[27]

In particular, Saudi Arabia has long seen Iran as a regional rival and a competitor for leadership within the Islamic world. Iran and Saudi Arabia also have competing interests regarding the global oil market: Iran has an incentive to maximize short-term prices, while the Saudis are concerned with stability and long-term market trends.[28] In late 2011, tensions between Saudi Arabia and Iran increased after the United States alleged that Iran had been involved in an assassination plot against the Saudi ambassador to Washington. Riyadh has not directly accused the Iranian government of involvement, but has expressed concern about a possible connection.[29] In January 2012, tensions escalated further after the Saudis announced they were prepared to increase oil exports to offset the effects of an oil embargo against

[26] The GCC did not formally throw its weight behind Iraq, and there were divisions among the GCC members over relations with Iran and Iraq during the war.

[27] There have been significant changes in Iran's approach to the Gulf since the revolution. After reaching a low point during the Iran-Iraq War, Iranian relations with the GCC states improved under Rafsanjani and Khatami. Rafsanjani pursued a policy of diplomatic outreach toward the Gulf States in order to reduce tensions with powerful and influential neighbors, and to try to take advantage of splits between the monarchies and Iraq. Part of Iran's policy was to propose a regional security arrangement that excluded the United States. Even though Iran's role in the Gulf War helped smooth tensions with its Gulf neighbors, Rafsanjani's willingness to support subversion and terrorism, and inflammatory rhetoric from conservatives that undermined Rafsanjani's diplomatic efforts, ultimately stalled the outreach initiative. Khatami was more successful, and in 1999 he became the first sitting Iranian president to visit Riyadh. Takeyh, 2009, pp. 130–139, 198–199.

[28] Frederic Wehrey, Theodore W. Karasik, Alireza Nader, Jeremy J. Ghelz, Lydia Hansell, and Robert A. Guffrey, *Saudi-Iranian Relations Since the Fall of Saddam: Rivalry, Cooperation, and Implications for U.S. Policy*, Santa Monica, Calif.: RAND Corporation, MG-840-SRF, 2009, pp. 12–21, 72–75.

[29] The Saudi government successfully sponsored a resolution in the UN General Assembly in November 2011 that condemned the assassination plot, but did not specify Iranian involvement. In an attempt to repair the rift over the allegations of a plot, Iran's intelligence minister visited Riyadh and met with the Saudi crown prince in December 2011. The Iranians also agreed to OPEC production targets preferred by the Saudis. Clifford Krauss, "OPEC Agrees to Raise Its Production Target," *New York Times*, December 15, 2011.

Iran. Saudi Arabia (along with other GCC states) also provided direct assurances to China and other major purchasers of Iran's oil.[30]

Third, the Gulf States are concerned about Iran's ability to interfere with their domestic politics. One major concern is Iran's influence over domestic Shia populations. Shias represent a substantial minority in the Gulf States overall, and are in the majority in Bahrain. The disenfranchisement of this group, particularly in Bahrain, in which a poor Shia majority is ruled by a wealthy Sunni elite, has led to protests and uprisings. The rights of the Shia majority were a central issue in the 2011 Bahraini anti-government protests. In March 2011, military forces from the GCC's multinational Peninsula Shield Force were deployed to secure the Bahraini border and key installations while Bahraini security forces cracked down on protesters. Bahrain and Saudi Arabia have both claimed that Iran has played a key role in inciting sectarian clashes, and have characterized protests as part of the larger GCC-Iran competition.

These claims, however, are likely overblown. A November 2011 report by an independent commission in Bahrain determined that there was insufficient evidence to support the government's claims of Iranian influence in the country's protests.[31] Such claims can serve domestic political purposes as much as they reflect the actual beliefs among the leadership. In fact, Bahraini Shias, like other Shia groups across the Gulf States, have largely sought to distance themselves from Iran, and there are political and cultural differences between Gulf Arab and Iranian Shias that cast doubt on the degree of influence Iran could wield to sow subversion.[32]

Concern among the GCC States about Shia dissent has risen since the United States invaded Iraq in 2003. The removal of Saddam Hussein from power and the political empowerment of Iraqi Shia have

---

[30] Mark Landler and Clifford Krauss, "Gulf Nations Aid U.S. Effort to Choke Off Iran Oil Sales," *New York Times*, January 13, 2012.

[31] Nada Bakri, "Torture Used on Protesters in Bahrain, Report Says," *New York Times*, November 23, 2011.

[32] Allin and Simon, 2010, pp. 88–93; Genieve Abdo and Jasim Husain Ali, "Misunderstanding Bahrain's Shia Protestors," Al Jazeera, April 3, 2011.

raised concerns about domestic Shia populations in the Gulf. This coincides with the perception among the Gulf States of a shift in the region balance of power in Iran's favor. Saudi Arabia in particular worries that the United States' withdrawal from Iraq can create a power vacuum that Iran might fill. GCC-Iran relations in the future will depend in large part on the direction Iraqi politics takes. The GCC and Iran have competing interests in Iraq, but also have a shared interest in maintaining stability.

The GCC states also are concerned about Iran's ability to influence the Sunni Arab majority.[33] Iran has increasingly used its hostility toward Israel, its support for Hezbollah, and its unyielding stance on the Israeli-Palestinian conflict as a way to win support from the Arab "street." While Iran's influence is limited here as well, its efforts have succeeded in putting domestic political pressure on the Gulf monarchies by challenging their legitimacy and the Saudis' pretensions to represent pan-Arab interests. This will likely impose increasing limits on the ability of the GCC states to adopt cooperative policies toward Israel.

Finally, several of the Gulf States host major deployments of U.S. military forces, including the headquarters of the U.S. Fifth Fleet in Bahrain. The presence of these forces on their territories, and their close geographic proximity to Iran and Iran's possession of missiles capable of targeting their territories, makes the GCC states vulnerable to retaliatory strikes should there be a conflict between Iran and the United States or Israel. The U.S. military presence and its influence in the Persian Gulf also has been a principal source of tension with the Iranians, who have long opposed a U.S. security role in the region and have repeatedly promoted a regional security plan that excludes the Americans.

The Gulf States have followed a two-pronged strategy toward Iran. On the one hand, they have sought to shore-up their alliances with the United States, and have solicited security guarantees and the transfer of sophisticated American military systems such as missile defenses and advanced fighter aircraft. On the other, they have, to varying degrees,

---

[33] Wehrey et al., *Saudi-Iranian Relations Since the Fall of Saddam*, 2009, pp. 21–29.

taken measures to accommodate Iran and reduce sources of hostility with their powerful neighbor. This has particularly taken the form of improved diplomatic relations, trade, rhetorical restraint, and efforts to convince Iran that they will not host any forces that would be used for an attack on the nuclear program.[34] Although the states of the GCC enjoy close ties with one another and seek to coordinate their foreign policies, there are differences among them in their approaches to Iran. States such as Bahrain and Saudi Arabia have been more confrontational with Iran than have Oman and Qatar, for example, despite the fact that all of these states are close U.S. allies.

Of significant concern to the United States is the possibility that the GCC states will question the U.S.'s commitment to their security, and more greatly seek to hedge their bets in the face of an Iranian nuclear threat. Hedging strategies could take the form of further accommodation toward Iran, the forging of closer ties with Russia and China in an effort to diversify their security relationships, a reluctance to grant the United States basing and overflight privileges on their territories, or even the development of their own nuclear weapons programs. Recent behaviors by these states have reinforced U.S. concerns. Some GCC states such as Qatar and Oman have demonstrated a willingness to accommodate Iran, and there have been differences among the emirates of the UAE over that country's Iran policy.[35] Finally, there is concern that a perceived weakening of the U.S. defense commitment could create incentives for nuclear weapons development by GCC

---

[34] Marina Ottaway, "Iran, the United States, and the Gulf: The Elusive Regional Policy," *Carnegie Paper No. 105*, Washington, D.C.: Carnegie Endowment for International Peace, November 2009; Davis et al., 2011, pp. 52–53; Anna Mulrine, "Blockbuster U.S. Arms Sale to Saudi Arabia," *Christian Science Monitor*, September 21, 2010.

[35] Abu Dhabi has been more supportive of sanctions and coercion than Dubai, which hosts substantial Iranian investments and a large Iranian diaspora, and whose second largest trading partner is Iran. However, Dubai's financial crisis has given Abu Dhabi a stronger hand in shaping UAE policy toward Iran. See Casey L. Addis, Christopher M. Blanchard, Kenneth Katzman, Carol Migdalovitz, Jim Nicol, Jeremy M. Sharp, and Jim Zanotti, *Iran: Regional Perspectives and U.S. Policy*, Washington, D.C.: Congressional Research Service, R40849, January 13, 2010, pp. 12–14.

members, and the Saudis have suggested they might seek to develop nuclear weapons should Iran acquire nuclear weapons.[36]

The complex relationship between the Gulf monarchies and Israel is a complicating factor for U.S. regional policies in general, and for the United States' Iran policy in particular. The GCC and Israel are aligned in their interest to forestall an Iranian nuclear bomb and to contain the growth of Iranian regional power. At the same time, the historical tensions between Israel and its Arab neighbors and popular opinion about the Israeli-Palestinian dispute make a formal alliance against Iran impossible, and provide an opening for Iran to sow discord between Israel and the Arab states. The Gulf States would be forced to strongly condemn an Israeli attack on Iran's nuclear program even if Gulf leaders were to privately welcome the destruction of Iran's facilities. Similarly, support by a nuclear-armed Iran for attacks on Israel through Hezbollah or other terrorist proxies could increase domestic instability in Saudi Arabia and other states of the GCC, just as Israel's war in Lebanon had done in 2006.[37]

Divisions among the GCC states, concerns about domestic stability, and the complex relationships these states have with Israel, Iran, and Iraq all impose limits on the degree to which the GCC can serve as a part of a unified bulwark in the region against Iranian expansion. The Gulf States will likely resist any U.S. effort to develop a balancing coalition against Iran, particularly one that includes Israel. They will also likely oppose any coercive measures against Iran that could trigger instability or retaliatory attacks on their territories or against Gulf shipping. They will instead likely prefer to continue to try to manage regional security through bilateral security relationships with the United States and improved missile and air defense capabilities on the one hand, and hedging strategies aimed at reducing tensions with Iran on the other.

---

36 Davis et al., 2011, p. 61; Moseley, 2011.

37 Lynch, 2011.

Russia

The need for Russian support will continue to be an integral part of the United States' nonproliferation policy toward Iran. U.S. efforts to win Russia's support must take into account the fact that Russia has strategic and economic interests in Iran, and perceptions of the nuclear threat that fundamentally differ from Washington's.[38] Russia's Iran policy is based on a rational accounting of long-standing interests, and is unlikely to change dramatically in response to U.S. pressure or incentives. As a result, there are limits to the degree to which Moscow will support policies such as more coercive multilateral sanctions. In particular, it is unlikely that Russia will favor any measures that jeopardize its regional strategic cooperation with Iran or its investments in the Iranian energy sector, or that risk creating greater instability on Russia's southern frontier.

Russia's interests in the Iran nuclear issue are complex and often contradictory. As one of the five NPT-sanctioned nuclear-armed states, Russia has an interest in preventing Iran from developing nuclear weapons and in upholding the nuclear nonproliferation regime. Russia also has a strong interest in preventing the acquisition of nuclear weapons by a major regional actor in a key border region, and is necessarily concerned that such a development would be destabilizing for the Middle East, Central Asia, and the Caucasus. Perhaps most importantly, Moscow values a cooperative and stable relationship with the United States and Western Europe, and is not willing to jeopardize that relationship in its efforts to promote good relations with Iran.

At the same time, Moscow has cultivated its relationship with Tehran since the early 1990s, and stated that Iran is an important regional partner.[39] Russia enjoys closer relations with Iran than with

---

[38] For a more detailed treatment of the themes raised in this section, see Robert J. Reardon, "Russia, Iran, and the Nuclear Nonproliferation Regime," paper presented at the International Security Studies Section (ISA)/International Security and Arms Control Section (APSA) Joint Annual Conference, Irvine, Calif., October 13, 2011.

[39] Moscow has been careful with the language it has chosen to describe its relations with Tehran. In particular, Moscow has assiduously avoided using the term "strategic partner," preferring instead to emphasize the "friendly" and "important" relationship between the two

most other Middle Eastern states, and Russian public and private firms have invested substantially in developing Iran's energy sector.[40] Russia seeks to use this relationship with Iran to maintain stability on its southern border, and has cooperated with Tehran on regional issues such as ethnic disputes in the Caucasus and in Central Asia, and the convoluted pipeline politics of the Caspian. Although the two states are competitors in many ways in the region—including over access to the Caspian Sea's enormous gas fields—they share an interest in maintaining regional stability and preventing the encroachment of outside powers, especially the United States and Turkey.[41]

Although the Iranian regime's revolutionary Islamist ideology should make Tehran a natural ally of co-religionist extremists in former Soviet territories in Central Asia and the South Caucasus, particularly in places such as Chechnya where Muslim separatists were brutally suppressed by the Russians, in fact, Iran's regional policies have been pragmatic and remarkably restrained. Much of this comes from the shared Iranian-Russian interest in maintaining regional stability and quashing ethnic unrest in the region. Both Russia and Iran are multiethnic states, and both contain large minorities whose population centers lie across borders. Moscow and Iran are both concerned that ethnic disputes in these regions could spill over into their own territories. This has given both sides a reason to moderate their policies in the region.[42]

"neighbors." See John W. Parker, *Persian Dreams: Moscow and Tehran Since the Fall of the Shah*, Washington, D.C.: Potomac Books, 2009, pp. 83–102, 208–211, 305.

[40] Anders Aslund, "Gazprom: Challenged Giant in Need of Reform," in Anders Aslund, Sergei Guriev, and Andrew Kuchins, eds., *Russia After the Global Economic Crisis*, Washington, D.C.: Peterson Institute for International Economics, 2010, pp. 151–168; Celeste Wallander, "Russia's Interest in Trading with the 'Axis of Evil,'" *PONARS Policy Memo 248*, October 2002.

[41] Andrei Shleifer and Daniel Treisman, "Why Moscow Says No," *Foreign Affairs*, Vol. 90, No. 1, 2011.

[42] Brenda Shaffer, *Partners in Need: The Strategic Relationship of Russia and Iran*, Washington, D.C.: Washington Institute for Near East Policy, 2001, pp. 38–48; Martin Malek, "Russia, Iran, and the Conflict in Chechnya," *Caucasian Review of International Affairs*, Vol. 2, No. 1, 2008.

Russia's relationship with Iran has soured in recent years, however, and Moscow has grown increasingly unwilling to provide diplomatic cover for Tehran in its nuclear efforts. Some of this change is explained by U.S. concessions to win Russian support for economic and diplomatic sanctions against Iran, and American pressure on Moscow to end its arms, missile, and nuclear sales. Also important has been Iran's increased intransigence—particularly since the election of Mahmoud Ahmadinejad in 2005—and the country's willingness to challenge the international community with its nuclear program.[43] Iran's reluctance to negotiate a freeze of its enrichment program, and its rejection of a fuel-swap proposal that the Russians had strongly backed, has forced Moscow's hand, and pushed its policies further into alignment with the West.

Over time, Iran has become an increasingly less attractive customer for Russia's military-industrial complex, and Moscow has come to view Iran as more of a liability than an asset. Despite repeated talk of increased civilian nuclear cooperation, ultimately Russia's nuclear assistance to Iran has been limited largely to completing a single LWR at Bushehr, which it had contracted to build in the early 1990s.[44] Even the $1 billion Bushehr contract has proved to be unprofitable, and Russia's commitment to finish it likely rested more heavily in the need to maintain its reputation as an independent nuclear exporter that could not be easily pressured by the West than in any hope for gain from the project itself. By the late 2000s, countries such as China and India had become far more profitable destinations for Russian nuclear and arms technologies than Iran.[45]

---

[43] Pavel Felgenhauer, "The 'Unraveling Relationship' Between Russia and Iran," BBC News, July 24, 2010.

[44] Parker, 2009, pp. 248–249, 289–292; Dmitri Trenin and Alexey Malashenko, *Iran: A View from Moscow*, Washington, D.C.: Carnegie Endowment for International Peace, 2010.

[45] Bulent Aras and Fatih Ozbay, "Dances with Wolves: Russia, Iran, and the Nuclear Issue," *Middle East Policy*, Vol. 13, No. 4, 2006; Anton Khlopkov, "Iran Breakthrough for Russian Nuclear Industry," *Moscow Defense Brief*, Vol. 1, No. 19, 2010. According to Khlopkov, "The project has largely lost its economic importance to Russia, and become more of a political cause. The chances of turning a profit on the whole venture are remote: the costs of this 1bn

As Russian nuclear and arms sales have diminished, Russia's investments in the Iranian oil and gas sector have grown, and have become the central focus of Russia's economic interests in Iran.[46] This relationship may continue to be a barrier to Russian support for more coercive sanctions against Iran if doing so jeopardizes Russian oil investments.

Yet Russia's interests are also complicated by Iran's status as a key competitor in the energy export market. In fact, Russia benefits in some ways from the status quo, as Iran's pariah status and U.S. and European economic sanctions against it give Russia the upper hand in the competition for Caspian pipelines and strengthen Russia's monopoly hold on the European energy market. China's increasing presence in the Iranian market, and the growth in energy exports to China from Iran, also serve Russia's interest insofar that increased demand in China raises global oil and gas prices, while the more Iran's exports are oriented toward the East, the less competition Russia faces in the West.[47] Finally, the longer the Iranian nuclear crisis simmers, the higher world oil and gas prices will be. As one of the world's largest oil and gas exporters, Russia, in this sense, benefits from the stalemate.

Since the low point in U.S.-Russian relations after the Russian invasion of Georgia, the United States has been successful in gaining increased support from Moscow for its nonproliferation policies toward Iran. In particular, the Obama administration's "reset" policy has helped to build greater Russian cooperation on the nuclear question. Russia supported a relatively tough sanctions package in 2010, and agreed to cancel the planned sale of its S-300 air defense system to Iran. Some of this success is explained by the United States' more conciliatory approach on issues such as missile defense. The current administration's ability to persuade Russia that support for the U.S.

---

dollar contract have now spiraled to 3bn euros or more. Therefore the key benefits of Bushehr are political" (p. 8).

[46] Shleifer and Treisman, 2011; Helen Belopolsky, *Russia and the Challengers: Russian Alignment with China, Iran, and Iraq in the Unipolar Era*, New York: Palgrave Macmillan, 2009.

[47] Shleifer and Treisman, 2011. The influence over Europe that Russia's exporter status provides should not be overstated. The trade relationship provides Europe, as a monopsony buyer, with substantial influence over Russia.

position is the best way to prevent the use of military force against Iran—a principal concern for Moscow—has likely been important as well. No less critical, however, has been the overall deterioration of the Russian-Iranian relationship, independent of U.S. policies.

Russia's strategic and financial interests in Iran make it unlikely that the United States can win Moscow's support for "crippling" sanctions, or for sanctions that impose serious restrictions on Iran's oil and gas sector. Nor will Russia support measures that could risk turning what it sees as a rising regional power on its southern frontier into an adversary, with regionally destabilizing results.

Russia's resistance to coercive measures is compounded by the Kremlin's doubts about the effectiveness of sanctions, and their ability to coerce Iran to comply with IAEA and UN demands.[48] From Russia's point of view, "crippling" sanctions could leave Moscow with the worst of both worlds by sacrificing Russian interests while failing to resolve the nuclear crisis. Furthermore, because Russia has long-term strategic interests in Iran, there will be limits to Washington's ability to win Russian support by offering short-term concessions such as offsets for lost investments.

China

The need to win Chinese cooperation has been one of the thorniest challenges for U.S. nonproliferation policy toward Iran. Beijing's status as one of the five permanent members of the UN Security Council has given it a key role in deliberations on Iran, and veto power over sanctions. At the same time, China has large and growing economic ties with Iran, is the largest single investor in Iran's energy sector and the largest importer of Iranian energy, and has consistently fought to water down or delay sanctions measures favored by the United States.

China's position on Iran has not been entirely at odds with that of the United States. The Chinese have supported four UN sanctions

---

[48] See, for example, Vladimir Putin's statements quoted in "Putin: Russia Opposes Force, Sanctions on Iran," Associated Press, June 21, 2011.

resolutions against Iran, and have participated in P5+1 negotiations. Despite previously providing substantial nuclear and ballistic missile assistance to Iran, China agreed in 1997 to restrict its nuclear transfers under pressure from the United States.[49] Instead, China's approach has been similar to Russia's, in that it seeks to balance a set of competing interests on the Iranian nuclear issue.

China's interest in Iran centers on that country's sizable energy resources. The rapid growth of the Chinese economy has made Beijing increasingly dependent on foreign sources of oil. China is currently the second largest consumer of oil after the United States, and recently eclipsed Japan to become the second largest importer.[50] As a result, China has sought to expand its ties with oil- and gas-producing states. Beijing's political relationship with Iran has been an important part of this effort. More than a tenth of China's oil imports come from Iran, making Iran China's third largest source of oil after Saudi Arabia and Angola. Importantly, the overall trade relationship between Iran and China is rapidly growing, going from $4 billion in 2003 to more than $20 billion by 2009.[51]

China is not only a major trading partner with Iran, but also Iran's largest foreign investor. China's national oil companies (NOCs) have established themselves as the largest players in a market that, thanks in large part to U.S. efforts, has become increasingly devoid of other investors. China's late entrance into the international energy

---

[49] Although the Chinese have cut nuclear assistance to Iran, Chinese firms—with or without the knowledge and approval of Beijing—have continued to provide assistance with Iran's ballistic missile program. Shirley A. Kan, *China and Proliferation of Weapons of Mass Destruction and Missiles: Policy Issues*, Washington, D.C.: Congressional Research Service, RL31555, December 13, 2007. The Clinton administration negotiated a pledge from China to end civilian nuclear cooperation with Iran in return for a U.S.-Chinese civilian nuclear cooperation agreement in 1997.

[50] Five sanctions resolutions were passed by the UN Security Council against Iran, but one of these did not impose additional sanctions.

[51] Because some trade between Iran and China is funneled through third parties, actual trade figures are likely larger. UPI, "China Passes E.U. in Trade with Iran," February 9, 2010; Christian LeMiere, "Tighter Bonds—China Strengthens Ties with Iran," *Jane's Intelligence Review*, November 11, 2009; John S. Park, "Iran and China," in Wright, ed., 2010, pp. 182–185.

market has increased the Iranian market's allure, as Chinese firms do not have to compete with better-financed and more technologically sophisticated Western firms.[52] Today, China is by far the leading foreign investor in Iran's energy sector. This relationship has improved China's access to Persian Gulf oil and gas, but has also increasingly complicated Chinese strategic interests by creating a set of growing incentives that are at odds with the U.S.-led effort to prevent Iran from developing nuclear weapons.

Iran has added value for China because it is the only state in the Persian Gulf that is not an ally of the United States. China views the United States' vast influence over the world's energy suppliers and key supply routes as a security challenge, and a reservoir of power that the United States could exploit to its benefit should a crisis erupt between China and the United States. China therefore sees its relationship with Iran—as well as other states outside the United States' orbit—as being of strategic importance. Beijing may fear that if the United States can influence all of the major oil and gas exporters in the Gulf, it could use that influence to restrict China's supply of energy resources during a crisis. Although China views this as unlikely under present circumstances, it is justifiably concerned that the United States might take such a course should a major conflict erupt over Taiwan.[53]

Yet, at the same time, China shares the United States' interest in maintaining stability in the Persian Gulf region.[54] As an energy importer, China does not benefit from a rise in oil prices as Russia does. China also has important and growing relationships with U.S. allies in the Persian Gulf, especially Saudi Arabia, and must balance these interests with those in Iran. As much as a nuclear-armed Iran could give China a hedge against U.S. influence in the Gulf, it would

---

[52] Erica Downs, "Beijing's Tehran Temptation," *Foreign Policy*, July 30, 2009.

[53] John W. Garver, "Is China Playing a Dual Game in Iran?" *Washington Quarterly*, Vol. 34, No. 1, Winter 2011.

[54] Jon B. Alterman, "China's Hard Choices on Iran," *Middle East Notes and Comment*, Center for Strategic and International Studies, October 2009; Garver, 2011. China in fact benefits from U.S. hegemony in the Persian Gulf insofar as it guarantees the free flow of oil for China's economy, and does so without China having to pay for it. The Chinese, however, are at least as aware of the vulnerabilities that arise from this as they are of the benefits.

also put China's energy supplies at risk by creating regional instability. In this sense, the U.S. naval presence in the Persian Gulf actually furthers China's interests.

The tension between China's interests in Iran's energy sector and its relationship with the West have come to the fore in the wake of new sanctions against the Iran Central Bank, and the United States' efforts to build global support for an oil embargo against Iran. China has been vocal in its opposition to these measures, and has pledged to continue its oil trade with Iran. At the same time, Chinese buyers have become noticeably more reluctant to sign new contracts with Iran for oil deliveries, and the volume of oil traded has begun to decline. As of January 2012, it is unclear which path China will take, but a likely course would be for China to reduce its trade with Iran in order to maintain good relations with Europe and the United States, while simultaneously exploiting the sanctions as an opportunity to extract price discounts from the Iranians as they become increasingly dependent on Chinese buyers.[55] It is possible for China to reap a windfall both by enjoying lower prices on oil for domestic consumption, and by reselling or swapping Iranian oil on the international market, buying Iranian crude oil at a discount and selling it closer (or at) global market prices.

China also has interests in Iran beyond the energy sector. It views Iran as a growing regional power in an important geographical region, and one in which the United States has vital interests. Beijing sees a relationship with Iran as a way to improve its influence in that region as well as a potential bargaining chip that can be used in its relationship with the United States. China also views its relationship with Iran in the context of its efforts to squelch Islamic separatist movements in Xinjiang province. Similar to its relations with Russia in the Caucasus, Iran has moved from a position of confrontation to one of silence and restraint on the question of China's treatment of Uighur separatists as ties between Beijing and Tehran have grown.[56]

---

[55] Michael Wines, "Middle East Trip Suggests Change in Policy by China," *New York Times*, January 13, 2012.

[56] Carrie Liu Currier and Manochehr Dorraj, "In Arms We Trust: The Economic and Strategic Factors Motivating China-Iran Relations," *Journal of Chinese Political Science*, Vol. 15, 2010.

As one of the five nuclear weapons states that are signatories to the NPT, China has an interest in preventing the spread of nuclear weapons to more states. However, China has traditionally placed much less importance on the nonproliferation regime than has the United States.[57] China's status as a non-aligned state led it to be suspicious of U.S.-USSR efforts to restrict the spread of nuclear weapons technology, and it did not sign the NPT until 1992. As China has increasingly emerged as a global power, its views on nonproliferation have shifted, and it has accepted a greater degree of responsibility in furthering the regime. Yet its commitment to its enforcement has been weak.

As a state with increasingly global interests, China also seeks to portray itself as a responsible stakeholder in world affairs. This has put a limit on Beijing's willingness to buck the international consensus in order to pursue its particular interests with Iran. Notably, even as China has worked to water down UN sanctions and delay their passage, it has consistently voted in line with the other permanent members of the Security Council. Beijing has been particularly willing to follow Moscow's lead. Russia's similar reluctance to support coercive measures against Iran has allowed China to work against U.S. and European efforts without appearing as an outlier. As Russia moves toward a position more in line with the United States, however, China will increasingly feel pressure to do the same.

Iran's nuclear program is useful to China insofar as it directs U.S. attention toward Iran and away from East Asia. A U.S. containment strategy would force the United States to commit more military resources to the region—forces that otherwise could be committed to Northeast Asia, or to the defense of Taiwan. The nuclear issue is also a useful bulwark against greater U.S. regional hegemony. Iran is the only Persian Gulf State that is not in the U.S. orbit. So long as the nuclear crisis continues, there is little concern for a rapprochement between the United States and Iran, which would result in a significant expansion in the United States' regional influence.

---

[57] Evan S. Medeiros, *Reluctant Restraint: The Evolution of China's Nonproliferation Policies and Practices, 1980–2004*, Stanford, Calif.: Stanford University Press, 2007.

China's interest in Iran as a way to block U.S. hegemony, however, should not be overstated. While these benefits are real, there are also costs to such a policy. China's grand strategy is built on creating the necessary stability to continue its remarkable economic growth. It is unlikely that China will risk jeopardizing stability in the Persian Gulf, or particularly in its relationship with the United States, in order to challenge U.S. power in a region where the United States has long been dominant. Similarly, it is unlikely that China will pursue policies that create a serious risk of U.S. or Israeli military action against Iran, which would have similarly negative implications for Beijing.

In fact, however important Iran may be for Beijing, it greatly pales in comparison to China's relations with the United States, which are central to China's foreign policy. This fact provides the United States with substantial leverage with China on the Iran issue. China's approach will mirror Russia's in this regard: it will likely seek to protect its interests in Iran insofar as it does not disrupt its relationship with the United States. One result of this is that Iran's increasingly oppositional stance toward the IAEA and the UN has forced China toward a more supportive position on sanctions. The Obama administration's willingness to engage with Iran also has positively influenced China's position by making Iran appear as the more unreasonable party.

China is thus torn between a desire to protect and to expand its investments in Iran and the need to toe the line on sanctions in order to maintain international legitimacy and avoid confrontation with the United States. As a result, Chinese firms have adopted a delaying strategy with Iran by increasingly signing contracts for oil and gas development, then foot-dragging on the delivery of promised investments. The goal appears to be to begin to take market share from departed European and other firms while avoiding the risk of laying out large capital investments, at least until the nuclear crisis passes.[58]

China and the United States have recently begun to come into conflict on the issue of U.S. extraterritorial sanctions, particularly on foreign firms supplying refined petroleum products to Iran. This is a

---

[58] "Beyond Sanctions: Russia, China, and Iran Workshop," Brookings Institution, Washington, D.C., July 9, 2010, www.brookings.edu/events/2010/0709_sanctions.aspx.

market that Chinese firms have increasingly begun to fill in the wake of U.S. and European sanctions.[59] China, like most countries, does not recognize the legitimacy of U.S. extraterritorial sanctions. At the same time, pressure from Congress is moving the United States closer to imposing sanctions on Chinese firms doing business with Iran. This risks creating a counterproductive result, and ultimately undermining China's existing support for U.S. nonproliferation efforts.

International Nonproliferation Regime

The United States will need to reconcile its Iran policy with its broader interest in preventing the spread of nuclear weapons, and its need to uphold the international nonproliferation regime and the international laws and institutions that support it. This could involve difficult trade-offs. Although the non-nuclear weapons states (NNWS) that are signatories of the NPT have pledged to forgo nuclear weapons, they maintain a "right" to civilian nuclear technology.[60] This includes dual-use technologies such as elements of the fuel cycle that can be used as legitimate components of a civilian program or to make a bomb. Iran's uranium enrichment, by itself, does not violate the NPT. Nor does enrichment to 20% violate the treaty. Iran did violate the NPT in a number of ways, including several failures to report nuclear activities that it was required to declare to the IAEA. Iran also is subject to UNSC resolutions that have ordered the state to cease all sensitive fuel-cycle activities. However, in terms of the treaty's text, the operation of a large enrichment program that in theory could be used to make bombs is perfectly within the rules. This allows Iran to cover its nuclear program in a veneer of legitimacy, and forces the United States to adopt

---

[59] Park, in Wright, ed., 2010; LeMiere, 2009.

[60] The NPT asserts that all members have an "inalienable right" to "nuclear energy for peaceful purposes," and promises NNWS in good standing "the fullest possible exchange of equipment, materials, and scientific and technological information on the peaceful uses of nuclear energy." "Treaty on the Non-Proliferation of Nuclear Weapons," signed at Washington, London, and Moscow, July 1, 1968. Text available at www.fas.org/nuke/control/npt/text/npt2.htm.

positions and put forward demands that in key ways might appear to be in contradiction with the treaty it purports to uphold.

There are three ways in which the United States' Iran policy could negatively affect the international nonproliferation regime. First, U.S. policies could fail, and Iran could develop nuclear weapons. Such an outcome could undermine international respect and support for the NPT, and—more importantly—weaken U.S. credibility and the credibility of its counter-proliferation efforts. The United States has already strongly committed itself to preventing Iran from acquiring nuclear weapons, and has made a point not to take any options off the table in order to do so.[61] If Iran crosses that red line and the United States fails to act, other states could well conclude that the U.S. commitment to stopping the spread of nuclear weapons is a paper tiger, and that the United States is not willing to risk expending blood and treasure to prevent an adversary from acquiring a nuclear arsenal. Indeed, the United States has already found itself in this position with North Korea, which has twice tested nuclear weapons despite similar opposition from the United States.

Second, the United States could potentially undermine the international regime by holding Iran to demands that go beyond its treaty obligations under the NPT and its IAEA safeguards agreement, or beyond the requirements of lawfully passed Security Council resolutions. The United States' stated policies under the Obama administration are consistent with Iran's treaty obligations. The United States recognizes Iran's right to peaceful civilian nuclear technology and similarly recognizes that this includes a right to enrich uranium for nuclear energy purposes. The United States also points to the NPT's stipulation that this "right" applies only to states whose programs are peaceful in nature, and the fact that the IAEA has determined that it is not satisfied this is the case.[62] However, it is possible that in the future Iran

---

[61] Statements of U.S. policy have referred to an Iranian nuclear weapon as "unacceptable." See, for example, "Clinton: Nuclear-Armed Iran 'Unacceptable,'" Associated Press, March 22, 2010.

[62] For a statement of U.S. policy, see Secretary of State Clinton's December 2010 interview with the BBC. Clinton stated, "We told [the Iranians] that they are entitled to the peaceful use of civil nuclear energy . . . [b]ut they haven't yet restored the confidence of the interna-

could take actions on this front that satisfy the IAEA about its peaceful intentions, but not the United States. This could, for example, be the case were Iran agrees to tighter and more invasive inspections and safeguards, and to provide answers that satisfy the IAEA's outstanding questions about its past behaviors and possible military dimensions of its program. The United States and its partners would then either have to accept commercial-scale enrichment in Iran, or continue to demand a suspension of enrichment activities in apparent contradiction of the NPT's guarantee of civilian nuclear technology to member states in good standing. Such a stance could lend greater credibility to Iran's argument that the nuclear crisis is simply an American-led effort to weaken Iran's international influence and undermine the Islamic Republic.

Third, if the United States were to strike a negotiated bargain with Iran that conceded possession of the fuel cycle, at least in some limited form, there would also be a risk of weakening the international nonproliferation regime. This could send a signal to other states that were they, too, to begin a nuclear program, they might expect a similar settlement from the United States. The lesson from the Iran case could potentially be that if you hold out long enough and unerringly defy the United States and its allies, eventually they will accommodate you.

Although these are all legitimate concerns for U.S. policymakers, they should not draw attention away from the objective of denying Iran nuclear weapons. Of the three possibilities above, clearly the worst—not only for the international nonproliferation regime but for the United States itself—is the first one, because this would leave the United States facing a nuclear-armed Iran *and* weakened credibility. Either of the other two outcomes would be preferable. The North Korean case may be instructive on this point. Critics attacked the 1994 Agreed Framework because, among other things, it appeared to accept (some critics would say *reward*) North Korea's violations of the NPT. In retrospect, however, the damage to the international regime was

---

tional community, to the extent where the international community would feel comfortable allowing them to enrich." Kim Ghattas, "Clinton Urges Iran to Fully Engage in Nuclear Talks," BBC News, December 3, 2010.

likely greater from the two nuclear weapons tests, which came after the Agreed Framework had been terminated, and after the Bush administration had adopted a more confrontational stance than the previous administration. Furthermore, in practice, the NPT has proved to be less fragile than some have feared. The United States has in the past adopted positions toward North Korea, Pakistan, Israel, India, and others that either went further than the international regime or tacitly tolerated the violation of its spirit. Yet no obvious breakdown of the treaty has occurred as a result, nor has there been a sudden wave of states violating it.

CHAPTER FIVE

U.S. Policy Options

Current U.S. policy on the Iran nuclear issue draws on all of the available levers of U.S. statecraft: military, economic, and diplomatic. In the military arena, the United States actively reaffirms its commitments to defend regional allies, provides these allies with the means of defending themselves and deterring Iranian aggression through arms sales and military cooperation, and maintains a substantial troop presence in the region. Should it choose to do so, the United States could bring its military power to bear by conducting air strikes against Iranian nuclear targets. While U.S. leaders have stated their preference to avoid such an outcome, the United States has repeatedly affirmed its readiness to use military force if necessary to protect U.S. interests. Aside from its conventional military forces, the United States has also relied on special operations against Iran's nuclear program, including sabotage.

Economically, the United States has adopted tough unilateral sanctions against Iran, and has achieved increasingly tight sanctions through the UN Security Council. U.S. trade and financial sanctions have undermined the willingness of foreign firms to do business in Iran or with Iranian financial interests. The United States also has passed extraterritorial sanctions that can impose penalties on third-country firms that do business with Iran. Sanctions serve a dual purpose. They are coercive measures that are intended to positively influence Iranian decisionmaking. They also are intended to directly deny Iran access to the materials, resources, assistance, and finances it needs to pursue its nuclear objectives.

Diplomatically, the United States has joined with the other four permanent members of the Security Council and Germany (the P5+1) in an effort to negotiate a mutually agreeable settlement to the nuclear issue. This effort has involved the offer of packages of positive inducements in return for Iran meeting a set of demands regarding its nuclear activities. The P5+1 position is that Iran must suspend its sensitive nuclear fuel-cycle activities until it demonstrates to the international community that its nuclear activities are peaceful in nature. The P5+1 is prepared to offer a package of positive inducements that includes civilian nuclear cooperation, security assurances, the lifting of economic sanctions and the development of trade, and the restoration of diplomatic contacts. Negotiation of such a package is conditional upon Iran suspending its uranium enrichment.

As of January 2012, these efforts have been unsuccessful, and Iran continues to make progress with its nuclear program. Although sanctions and sabotage efforts have slowed Iran's progress, they have not reversed it. Tehran continues to be defiant in the face of four UN sanctions resolutions. Iran also is unyielding in its insistence that it will not trade away or even suspend its enrichment program and has ultimately rejected every diplomatic offer the P5+1 has presented.

This chapter considers the broad spectrum of U.S. policy options on the Iranian nuclear issue. The first section of the chapter presents an analytical framework to guide the subsequent policy evaluation. This framework categorizes U.S. policy tools along two dimensions: the nature of the policy instrument (military, economic, diplomatic), and its mechanism of action (as a means of *influence*, or a means of *force*). The subsequent sections of the chapter then outline the policy options available to the United States and consider their relative costs, benefits, and chances of success.

Framework of Analysis

The United States can draw from a substantial array of policy tools in its effort to prevent Iran from developing nuclear weapons or, failing that, to mitigate the negative consequences of a nuclear-armed

Iran. These tools include the use of preventive air strikes, arms sales to regional allies, offers of positive inducements in negotiations, economic sanctions, export controls, sabotage, and naval blockade. Each has its costs and benefits, and each may be more or less appropriate depending on the specific circumstances in which it is employed, or the exact way in which policies are designed. These tools of statecraft are rarely used in isolation, and instead are generally part of an overall policy strategy that involves mixture of coercion, inducements, and defensive strategies, using military, economic, and diplomatic statecraft.

Available policy tools can usefully be sorted along two dimensions: the form of U.S. power employed (military, economic, or diplomatic), and the mechanism by which it can change Iran's behavior. For the latter, U.S. policy choices may either *influence* Iranian decision-making by changing the perceptions of costs and benefits of Iranian leaders—or their relative influence over the policy process—or directly change or restrict Iran's behaviors through *brute force*.[1]

Tools of influence work by changing an adversary's calculus of costs and benefits. This can involve either the use of threats (negative sanctions) or the promise of reward (positive inducements). In either case, the threat or promise is linked to a set of explicit or implicit demands.[2] A threat may be stated, or implied by a demonstration of force. Limited air strikes, for example, may be intended to convince an adversary to yield. Similarly, economic sanctions may be imposed in the aim of convincing an adversary to agree to terms. In either case, the intent is to coerce by giving the enemy a taste of punishment, with

---

1 Much of the typology and conceptual basis for state influence and coercion is from Schelling's work on deterrence. See Thomas Schelling, *Arms and Influence*, New Haven, Conn.: Yale University Press, 1966. It also is consistent with George's concept of "coercive diplomacy," which he describes as "forceful persuasion." Alexander L. George, David K. Hall, and William E. Simons, *The Limits of Coercive Diplomacy: Laos, Cuba, Vietnam*, Boston: Little, Brown, 1971. The categorization of tools of statecraft is taken from David A. Baldwin, *Economic Statecraft*, Princeton, N.J.: Princeton University Press, 1985.

2 The analytical framework presented here is from Robert J. Reardon, *Nuclear Bargaining: Using Carrots and Sticks in Nuclear Counter-Proliferation*. Ph.D. dissertation, Massachusetts Institute of Technology, 2010. Also relevant is Kenneth A. Oye, *Economic Discrimination and Political Exchange: World Political Economy in the 1930s and 1980s*, Princeton, N.J.: Princeton University Press, 1992.

the implication that if it does not give in to demands, more pain will be forthcoming.

Influence, either through coercion or by promising rewards for good behavior, stands in contrast to the direct imposition of will through brute force. When brute force is used, the adversary's decisions are irrelevant. Positive results are achieved by simply presenting the enemy with the desired outcome. Territory is seized. Armies are defeated. Regimes are overthrown. Needed finances and resources are denied. Whether the adversary's cost-benefit calculus changes or stays the same, the outcome is the same. Table 5.1 illustrates how tools of statecraft can be sorted according to these two dimensions.

It is important to note that many tools of statecraft can operate through *both* mechanisms. Economic sanctions, for example, both affect the Iranian decisionmaking process and directly limit the state's ability to pursue its nuclear goals. Similarly, the limited use of military

Table 5.1
Analytical Categories of U.S. Statecraft Tools, with Examples Relevant to the Iranian Nuclear Issue

	Military	Economic	Diplomatic
Influence (negative): sanctions/coercion	Military threats Demonstration of force Force deployments Third-party arms sales Arms embargo	Trade/financial sanctions Naval blockade	Sever diplomatic ties Censure through international organization
Influence (positive): inducement/reward	Security guarantee	Aid or assistance Technology transfers Enhanced or restored trade/ access to markets	Enhanced or restored diplomatic ties High-level meeting/state visit
Brute force	Sabotage Special Ops Air strikes against nuclear program	Sanctions against nuclear-related entities Export controls on nuclear-related technology/ materials	Build international support for tighter export controls

force can directly degrade capabilities while also serving as a threat of future punishment to Iran's leaders. Thus, a given policy choice could fail to achieve positive results along one causal mechanism but succeed in another. Economic sanctions, for example, may fail to convince Iran's leadership to change their behavior, but could succeed by directly limiting access to needed resources and usefully delaying progress on the nuclear program.

Finally, the nature of any given U.S. policy choice—whether it is a means of influence or a tool of brute force—is often a perceptual distinction rather than an objective one. Often, the target of the policy will interpret any given move quite differently than the United States intends it. This is most important in the case of military force, as nearly any major deployment of U.S. military forces in the region is likely to be interpreted by Iran as a threat, regardless of U.S. intentions. U.S. efforts to provide adequate defenses for regional interests or allies could be interpreted by Iran as a form of coercive threat, or as preparations for an attack. This creates a substantial risk of miscalculation.[3]

The following sections examine the policy choices that are available to the United States. These choices may involve the use of one or more tools of statecraft. They also may have more than one effect on outcomes, and may both impose brute-force outcomes on Iran and at the same time influence Iranian decisionmaking. The analytical framework presented here, by clarifying these distinctions, allows for a fine-grained and insightful assessment of policy choices.

Military Force

Air Strikes

Both the United States and Israel possess the military capability to conduct successful air strikes against a number of key Iranian nuclear targets. The United States has the ability to broaden such an attack to

---

[3] This is related to the security dilemma, which describes how efforts to improve one's security through defensive measures can be viewed as threatening by an adversary, prompting efforts to meet that threat with defensive improvements of their own. This can, paradoxically, leave both sides less secure than they were before. See Robert Jervis, *Perception and Misperception in International Politics*, Princeton, N.J.: Princeton University Press, 1976.

include a wide set of regime-related targets that could either seriously degrade Iran's nuclear and conventional capabilities or potentially weaken the regime's hold on power. Israel's capabilities are less certain. Israel Defense Forces (IDF) is likely capable of destroying the main facilities of the Iranian program, but it would face a greater risk of operation failure than would the United States.[4] Both U.S. and Israeli decisionmakers have indicated that they do not believe that air strikes could definitively destroy Iran's nuclear program. Several have stated, however, that air strikes could set the Iranian program back by several years.[5]

Air strikes would affect both Iran's *capabilities* as well as its *decisionmaking process*. They would operate as both a brute-force instrument to directly degrade or destroy capabilities and an instrument of influence that alters the decisionmaking calculus of the Iranian leadership. Both of these effects are important. Air strikes can successfully destroy nuclear infrastructure and degrade capabilities over the near term. Under certain circumstances, they could effectively forestall a breakout dash once Iran has initiated one. However, it is unlikely that they can destroy Iran's ability to reconstitute its program should it choose to do so. They could also risk creating *political* effects that make nuclear weaponization more likely over the longer term by convincing Iran that it needs nuclear weapons more than ever, and leading it to redouble its efforts to acquire them.

The United States could choose to use air strikes against Iran if it were to conclude that an Iranian breakout dash were under way, or was

---

[4] Raas and Long, 2007; Long, 2011; Kenneth M. Pollack, Daniel M. Byman, Martin Indyk, Suzanne Maloney, Michael E. O'Hanlon, and Bruce Riedel, *Which Path to Persia? Options for a New American Strategy Toward Iran*, Washington, D.C.: Brookings Institution Press, 2009, pp. 103–139; Abdullah Toukhan and Anthony H. Cordesman, *Study on a Possible Israeli Strike on Iran's Nuclear Development Facilities*, Washington, D.C.: Center for Strategic and International Studies, 2009; Allin and Simon, 2010.

[5] Allin and Simon, 2010, pp. 53–54. Some Israeli officials have suggested that an attack could successfully delay Iran's nuclear progress for an extended period of time, and that air strikes could be repeated should Iran seek to reconstitute its program. Simon cites one Israeli official referring to this as "mowing the lawn." See Steve Simon, "An Israeli Strike on Iran," Contingency Planning Memorandum No. 5, Carnegie Endowment for International Peace, November 2009. Also see Goldberg, 2010; and Isabel Kershner, "Israeli Ex-Spy Predicts Delay for Iran's Nuclear Ambitions," *New York Times*, January 7, 2011.

imminent. The United States would be most likely to choose this path if it had "smoking-gun" evidence of a breakout. This could include evidence from inspectors that Iran had begun enriching uranium beyond the 20% threshold, clear evidence of intent in intelligence reports, or revelations of a secret weapons program or large-scale parallel enrichment program.

The United States also could consider air strikes under conditions of more ambiguous evidence of a breakout. Iran could orchestrate a crisis in order to provide itself with an excuse to expel inspectors or withdraw from the NPT, while still claiming it has no intention of weaponizing. There could also be less-than-solid intelligence indicating that the regime is working to produce weapons-grade HEU.

The United States' chances of successfully stopping an Iranian breakout dash using air strikes would depend on whether Iran were using a secret facility to enrich HEU. If Iran possessed such a facility, and its location were truly secret, it could divert its existing stocks of UF6 and leave the United States without an opportunity to react. The United States would be aware that a breakout had begun very quickly, but without knowing where enrichment was taking place, it could not use air strikes to stop it. Under such circumstances, however, the United States would likely be able to command substantial international support in an effort to enact severe economic sanctions against Iran. Nonetheless, the absence of an effective military response in this case highlights the importance for the United States to make the prevention and detection of Iranian secret nuclear facilities a policy priority.

Without the availability of hidden enrichment facilities, any Iranian attempt at breakout, given its technical capabilities and resources in early 2012, would have a high likelihood of being stopped by U.S. air strikes. As of January 2012, the only known site where Iran could enrich HEU is the FEP at Natanz. A breakout attempt at this site would require a minimum of months, and possibly well over a year. In this case, the FEP would present a vulnerable target, because the Iranians would be dependent upon this fixed site for the enrichment process.

On an operational level, the United States would have little trouble destroying the Natanz site before Iran could complete the enrichment of sufficient HEU for a bomb. Additionally, an Iranian breakout dash, especially if the United States could present convincing public evidence that it had begun, would offer conditions of maximum legitimacy for U.S. air strikes against Iran, as well as the least risk of political fallout in its aftermath. Evidence that Iran had begun enriching uranium to 90% purity, especially if that evidence were presented by the IAEA, would make it unlikely that Russia or China would oppose the use of military force.

Air strikes against Natanz would end a breakout dash, but it would not destroy the Iranian nuclear program. The United States would need to decide whether to limit air strikes to Natanz or to strike at a broader set of targets. The advantage of expanding the target list would be that a breakout attempt would offer a rare opportunity to destroy these targets with the least risk of political fallout, and when Iran's defenses would already have been suppressed. Also, if the United States were to forgo these targets, the Iranians would likely seek to move them to hidden locations with improved defenses, and do so after IAEA inspectors had been expelled. Yet even if the United States were to strike a broad target set, this would still likely not bring Iran's nuclear ambitions to an end, because Iran could build new facilities and reconstitute its program.

While such a breakout would be a greatly alarming event, it is also unlikely to occur, at least over the near term. Iran has little to gain at present by initiating an activity that could invite an attack, particularly at a time when its capabilities are so limited that it could take years for a breakout to produce even one bomb. Iran also appears content to work toward improving its program while remaining within the NPT.

A likelier development to trigger such a crisis would be for Iran to take steps that could greatly reduce or eliminate the warning time the United States would receive about an Iranian breakout dash. There are different ways in which Iran could cross such a red line. One would be for it to produce and stockpile enough 20% LEUF6 to fuel a weapon, and in excess of what it would need to fuel the TNRR.[6] Another would

---

[6] As of November 2011, Iran had produced 76.8 kg of 20% LEUF6. The 2010 "fuel-swap" deal proposed by the Vienna Group would have provided 120 kg of 20% LEU fuel, which corresponds to roughly 150 kg of 20% LEUF6. Taking the IAEA's 25 kg HEU "significant quantity" as a benchmark, given that 25 kg of 93% HEU is mathematically equivalent to

be for Iran to rapidly increase the rate of its 20% LEU production, either by significantly increasing the number of cascades dedicated to the task, or by deploying more advanced centrifuge models. This could present the United States with a quickly closing window of time during which air strikes would be most likely to forestall such a development. Once Iran produced enough 20% LEU to make one or more weapons, its breakout time would be substantially shortened. The United States also would have an incentive to destroy Iran's stocks of LEU before they could be diverted and hidden.

If Iran were to take any of these steps, the United States would face a difficult choice. Because none of these steps would rise to the same level of provocation as a more overt breakout dash, U.S. air strikes under these circumstances would likely not enjoy much international legitimacy. However, the United States also would feel pressure to act, both domestically and from regional allies, especially Israel.

Air strikes can successfully end a breakout dash that is in progress, but they are unlikely to successfully undermine Iranian technical progress, particularly over the long term. A broader preventive military strike with the objective of destroying or substantially degrading Iran's capacity to produce nuclear weapons over a longer term would require successfully targeting a number of hardened, dispersed, and hidden facilities around the country. The target list would likely include Iran's uranium enrichment facilities at Natanz and Fordow, the INTC near Isfahan (especially the UCF), and the unfinished HWR and heavy water production facility near Arak.[7] It also would involve locating and destroying any secret enrichment facilities.

---

172 kg of 20% LEUF6 (a figure that assumes zero wastage and perfect efficiency), the production of 20% LEUF6 in excess of the 150–180 kg range would be alarming, and could trigger an international crisis. According to the ISIS, 120 kg of 20% LEU fuel could supply the TNRR for 6–21 years, depending on operating power and capacity factor. See IAEA, GOV/2011/65, para. 8; IISS, 2011, p. 74; and David Albright, "Technical Note: Annual Future Low-Enriched Uranium Fuel Requirements for the Tehran Research Reactor," ISIS, October 7, 2009. Also see Chapter Two of this monograph. Note also that a substantial portion of the 20% LEUF6 that Iran has produced has been converted to fuel plates.

[7] The HWR and heavy water production plant at Arak are less critical targets than those related to uranium enrichment. The plutonium route to a bomb is more difficult to conceal, and at present much more challenging for the Iranians. The Arak reactor is not finished and

Also, to prevent Iran from quickly reconstituting its program, an attack would have to destroy the facilities where centrifuge parts are manufactured, stored, and assembled. This would be a more difficult objective to achieve. These facilities are not under IAEA safeguards, and identifying and locating them would require good intelligence and involve significant uncertainty.[8] Sites that have been identified, or ones that were known in the past, have typically been small, easily concealed from reconnaissance satellites, and located in densely populated urban areas. Failure to destroy these sites would allow the Iranians to rebuild their enrichment program, because the machines could be manufactured relatively quickly. After an attack, the United States would not be able to have confidence that it successfully destroyed all of these sites, and there would be uncertainty about Iran's ability to reconstitute its program.

It is also likely that, anticipating such an attack, Iran has already taken measures to make its program more survivable. This could include the construction of redundant facilities—especially for the manufacture of centrifuges—and the hardening of sites, such as by burying them underground. The existence and nature of the Fordow site, which is hardened against air attack, suggests that Iran has already been working along these lines.

Air strikes would likely invite Iranian retaliatory attacks against U.S. regional interests and U.S. allies. This could take several forms. Iran could harass shipping in the Persian Gulf, and has threatened to retaliate against an attack on its nuclear program by closing the Strait of Hormuz and destroying Gulf oil facilities.[9] Either on their own initia-

---

it is unclear when (or whether) it will be. Iran will also encounter challenges in fueling the reactor, and does not have any known reprocessing facilities that could be used to produce enough weapons-grade plutonium for a bomb. It is possible for Iran to overcome all of these challenges, but the time scale involved, and the difficulty in hiding its plutonium-related facilities, make air strikes against these targets far less critical.

8 Little is publicly known about where Iran's centrifuges are produced. IISS, 2011; David Albright et al., 2008.

9 Smith, 2007. For an examination of Iran's ability to close the Strait of Hormuz, see Caitlin Talmadge, "Closing Time: Assessing the Iranian Threat to the Strait of Hormuz," *International Security*, Vol. 33, No. 1, Summer 2008. For an analysis of a potential Iranian missile

tive or under direction from Tehran, Iranian-supported terrorist organizations in the Levant could conduct attacks on Israel. Iran also could increase its support for anti-U.S. groups in Iraq and Afghanistan. Such retaliatory attacks could potentially lead to a wider regional conflict involving the United States. They also could be a destabilizing influence in an already uncertain political situation in the Middle East.[10]

Air strikes of any magnitude risk producing perverse domestic political effects in Iran. They could reinforce Iran's commitment to develop its nuclear capabilities. If it had not done so already, Iran could use such an attack as a pretext to expel IAEA inspectors and withdraw from the NPT. As a result, a military strike aimed at destroying the country's nuclear program could have the paradoxical effect of making the development of nuclear weapons easier for Iran over the long term by allowing it to work toward a bomb without any pretense of peaceful intentions. Also, if an attack were to take place without clear evidence that Iran had initiated a breakout, it could turn out that no decision had in fact been made to weaponize. Air strikes, however, would almost certainly change that.

Air strikes could rally the population around the regime, and strengthen the domestic legitimacy and standing of regime hardliners. This could facilitate crackdowns against more pragmatic domestic opponents, and greatly weaken regime opponents. It could play directly into the hands of the most hardline elements of the regime and ultimately further their interests at the expense of both more moderate domestic political factions as well as the United States.

An attack would also likely undermine international support for U.S. nonproliferation policy and rally regional popular support for Iran. It would be especially difficult for the United States to maintain Russian and Chinese support for continued UN pressure on Iran. Both Russia and China have been ambivalent about sanctions, and their sup-

attack on GCC oil assets, see Joshua R. Itzkowitz Shifrinson and Miranda Priebe, "A Crude Threat: The Limits of an Iranian Missile Campaign Against Saudi Arabian Oil," *International Security*, Vol. 36, No. 1, Summer 2011.

[10] Allin and Simon, 2010, pp. 98–106. The authors describe worst-case scenarios in which tit-for-tat attacks, either in the Levant or the Gulf, escalate into a larger conflict.

port for four rounds of UN sanctions resolutions has required extensive U.S. effort and political capital. Both states also have a strong interest against the use of U.S. military force in the region, and a chief concern for both in referring the Iran nuclear dossier to the UNSC has been the possibility of the United States using the Security Council as cover for military force as it did in Iraq.

Ultimately, it is unlikely that air strikes would be able to do more than delay Iran's progress over the short term. It will be most tempting to use force should Iran begin a breakout dash. Under that circumstance, air strikes could halt the dash to a weapon, but could facilitate eventual acquisition of weapons by shoring up Iranian domestic support for the regime and undermining international support for the United States. It could also sow further suspicion and hostility between the United States and Iran—a dangerous situation should Iran actually acquire nuclear weapons. U.S. decisionmakers would be presented with a Hobson's choice between regional instability and the risk of conflict on the one hand, and a nuclear-armed Iran on the other.

Any U.S. decision on air strikes will have to take possible Israeli action into account. The United States' ability to persuade Israel not to conduct an attack on its own will diminish should evidence arise that Iran has begun a breakout run. Similarly, should Iran begin to rapidly increase its stocks of 20% LEU beyond an amount justifiable by a civilian nuclear program, Israel could decide to act. The United States has a strong interest in avoiding an Israeli attack on Iran, as it would bring no benefits over a U.S. attack, and potentially greater costs. Israel's military capabilities are more limited than those of the United States, and the risk of operational failure would be greater. An Israeli attack also would require Israeli planes to overfly Arab states in order to reach targets in Iran, which could have negative diplomatic consequences. Similarly, an attack on Iran by Israel would be more likely to produce regional political instability and to rally both domestic and regional popular support for the regime in Tehran. It would run the same risks of retaliatory attacks and the loss of international support for nonproliferation efforts as would an attack by the United States. Finally, the United States would not be able to avoid the perception of complicity, as it would widely be assumed that the United States either directed the attack or acquiesced to it. If faced with such a situation, the United States may be forced to conduct air strikes on its own in order to preempt Israeli action.

Non-Kinetic Force: Special Operations and Cyberwarfare

The United States also has non-kinetic options to slow Iranian nuclear progress. These include sabotage, cyberwarfare, and other intelligence operations designed to degrade Iran's nuclear capabilities and deny Iran the resources necessary to produce a weapon. Like kinetic military options, these measures will likely only delay Iran. However, because their use entails lower costs and risks, they are more attractive policy tools.

U.S. efforts in these areas are unsurprisingly secretive, and the full nature and extent of past and present U.S. covert operations in Iran is not publicly known. Nonetheless, there have been a number of important revelations about the use of offensive cyberweapons by the United States and Israel against Iran, including the Stuxnet attack on Iran's uranium enrichment program.[11] These cyberattacks destroyed as many as 1,000 IR-1 centrifuges at Iran's Natanz enrichment facility.[12] It is also not certain that Iran has successfully mitigated all of the effects of the Stuxnet attack, and the virus (or other viruses) may still infect the software that operates many of Iran's gas centrifuges.[13] Furthermore,

---

[11] Shuster, 2011. As this monograph was going to press, a number of significant revelations about the extent and nature of the American and Israeli cyberwarfare efforts against Iran's nuclear program came to light. These efforts were part of a larger U.S. special operations program called Olympic Games. See David E. Sanger, *Confront and Conceal: Obama's Secret Wars and Surprising Use of American Power*, New York: Crown Publishers, 2012; and David E. Sanger, "Obama Ordered Sped-Up Wave of Cyberattacks Against Iran," *New York Times*, June 1, 2012. Among other things, it was revealed that Stuxnet was only one element of a long-running cyberwarfare program that had begun during the George W. Bush administration.

[12] See Albright et al., February 15, 2011.

[13] New information about the Duqu and Flame computer worms were becoming available as this monograph was going to press. See Nicole Perlroth, "Researchers Find Clues in Malware," *New York Times*, May 30, 2012; Ellen Nakashima, Greg Miller, and Julie Tate, "U.S., Israel Developed Flame Computer Virus to Slow Iranian Nuclear Efforts, Officials Say," *Washington Post*, June 19, 2012.

assassinations of Iranian nuclear scientists by unknown attackers, in which the United States has strongly denied involvement, have both reduced the already limited pool of top-echelon nuclear experts available to Iran, and may have an impact on the motivation of others working on the program.[14]

Non-kinetic attacks on the program can influence Iran's nuclear decisionmaking by raising the costs and risks of nuclear breakout. Attacks such as Stuxnet, or the turning of Iranian nuclear scientists, can lead Tehran to question its ability to defend its program, the reliability of its equipment and facilities, the loyalty of its nuclear workers, and its ability to conceal its actions and intentions. All of these present the leadership with a higher risk premium in its nuclear efforts. It also forces the regime to take costly defensive measures that divert resources that could otherwise be put into the nuclear program.

Importantly, non-kinetic operations do not run the same risks of escalation, loss of international support, or paradoxical domestic political effects that kinetic attacks do. By their very nature, their sponsorship is ambiguous and deniable. Their direct effects are less spectacular and less visible, and they are likely to fall below the threshold that would trigger retaliation. Iran's retaliatory options are limited. Iran lacks the technical capability to respond in kind, and the retaliatory options it does possess would appear disproportionate. It also may be more difficult for the regime to portray itself as a beleaguered victim when attacks against it succeed through domestic disloyalty or ruse. In fact, in many cases, the regime will have as much incentive to deny the existence of an attack as will the United States.

Although covert operations against Iran run a lower risk of escalation, this is not to say that they carry *no* escalatory risk. The assassination of Iranian nuclear scientists, for example, has raised the possibility of an escalating spiral of retaliation. Iran publicly linked the assassinations to Israel and the United States, and some analysts have described similar attacks against Israeli diplomats in February 2012 as

---

[14] Alexander Marquardt, "U.S. Denies Role in Iranian Nuclear Scientist's Assassination," ABC News, January 11, 2012.

Iranian retaliation.[15] Recent revelations about the cyberwarfare campaign against Iran's nuclear program also suggest that it may be difficult to maintain secrecy and anonymity. It is also unclear whether such covert operations have led to strategic gains that outweigh these risks.

Economic Sanctions

Although analysts and policymakers tend to focus on the coercive use of sanctions—their ability to convince an adversary to change its behavior—they can also operate through brute force by directly degrading capabilities. U.S. and U.S-supported multilateral sanctions against Iran have been designed to serve several purposes, using both coercion and brute force. Former U.S. ambassador James Dobbins, who is among a small number of American diplomats to have participated in direct talks with Iranian officials, has identified four distinct goals of economic sanctions against Iran: to influence Iran's nuclear decisionmaking, to degrade Iran's military and nuclear capabilities, to "promote positive political change in the nature of the Iranian regime," and to deter other potential proliferants through example.[16]

As an instrument of influence, economic sanctions seek to change the calculus of Iranian decisionmakers by raising the costs of continued defiance of international demands. Although the mechanism is an economic one—the economic pain of sanctions is the coercive instrument—the ultimate effect must be *political*, as policy change can only

---

15 This is not to say, however, that covert operations carry *no* escalatory risk. The assassination of Iranian nuclear scientists in particular has raised the possibility of an escalating spiral of retaliation. Iran publicly linked the assassinations to Israel and the United States, and some analysts have described similar attacks against Israeli diplomats in February 2012 as Iranian retaliation. John Walcott, "Diplomat Attacks Raise Specter of Escalating Israel-Iran War," Bloomberg News, February 14, 2012. The United States has strongly denied involvement in the assassination of Iranian nuclear scientists. Alexander Marquardt, "U.S. Denies Role in Iranian Nuclear Scientist's Assassination," ABC News, January 11, 2012.

16 James Dobbins, "Iran Sanctions: Options, Opportunities, and Consequences," Testimony Before the Committee on Oversight and Government Reform, Subcommittee on National Security and Foreign Affairs, United States House of Representatives, December 15, 2009.

be achieved when economic restrictions create the appropriate political pressure to influence the decisionmaking process.[17]

This distinction is critical, because the economic hardship created by sanctions may in fact not result in political pressure for positive change. Instead, sanctions can have a perverse political effect. They can strengthen the hand of elites that oppose compromise, rally public support for continued defiance, and undermine the very groups that most support the policy changes the sanctions are intended to produce. Sanctions also can trigger effective efforts to adapt by shifting trade patterns or diverting finances, or can even provide rents to regime elements by increasing their control over a scarce good, which they can then preferentially dole out to domestic supporters. Overall, economic pain does not always lead to effective political pressure on the regime.

In many ways, Iran is an unlikely candidate for the successful use of sanctions as a coercive tool. Economic sanctions in general are a blunt and uncertain instrument. Even the most optimistic studies suggest that sanctions will usually fail to achieve their desired coercive goals.[18] This is particularly the case with authoritarian adversaries. Sanctions have an especially poor track record in matters of "high politics" related to state security. Regime survival will always trump economic pain, and existing UN sanctions—or any sanctions regime the United States is likely to achieve given existing political realities—are not nearly enough to threaten the current regime's existence.

---

[17] There is extensive literature on economic sanctions and their mechanisms of influence on the target state's decisionmaking process. The ideas presented here can be found in Johan Galtung, "On the Effects of International Economic Sanctions: With Examples from the Case of Rhodesia," *World Politics*, Vol. 19, No. 3, 1967; Jean-Marc F. Blanchard and Norrin M. Ripsman, "Asking the Right Question: *When* do Economic Sanctions Work Best?" in Jean-Marc F. Blanchard, Edward D. Mansfield, and Norrin M. Ripsman, eds., *Power and the Purse: Economic Statecraft, Interdependence, and National Security*, London: F. Cass, 2000; and Jonathan Kirshner, "The Microfoundations of Economic Sanctions," *Security Studies*, Vol. 6, No. 3, 1997.

[18] The most widely cited study, whose findings are generally considered to be optimistic, finds a 3-in-10 chance of success for economic sanctions overall. Gary C. Hufbauer, Jeffrey J. Schott, Kimberly Ann Elliott, and Barbara Oegg, *Economic Sanctions Reconsidered*, 3rd ed., Washington, D.C.: Peterson Institute for International Economics, 2007.

The United States has pursued coercive sanctions against Iran for three decades, with few positive results.[19] Starting with the Reagan administration, the United States implemented a steadily tightening sanctions regime against Iran. These began with restriction of arms sales and foreign aid, and eventually came to include a comprehensive set of financial and trade sanctions. By 1997, the United States had banned essentially all economic activity with Iran.[20]

To put pressure on other states to join U.S. efforts, in 1996, the United States for the first time enacted secondary sanctions that threatened to impose penalties on third-country firms doing business with Iran.[21] These sanctions were passed by Congress over objections from the White House. They immediately provoked an outcry from European states that charged that extraterritorial sanctions violated international law. The most important extraterritorial sanctions were passed under the Iran and Libya Sanctions Act (ILSA), a law that, while consistently unenforced by the President, has caused tensions between the United States and its allies since its inception.[22] ILSA was greatly strengthened by the passage of the Comprehensive Iran Sanctions, Accountability, and Divestment Act (CISADA) of 2010, which

---

[19] Unilateral U.S. sanctions against Iran have been used for multiple objectives, not just to coerce Iran into changing its behaviors. A possible exception to the ineffectiveness of sanctions against Iran is the Carter administration's freezing of Iranian assets and trade embargo imposed after the taking of U.S. hostages. These sanctions likely contributed to Iran's eventual release of the hostages in 1981 under the Algiers Accord. Meghan L. O'Sullivan, *Shrewd Sanctions: Statecraft and State Sponsors of Terrorism*, Washington, D.C.: Brookings Institution Press, 2003, pp. 48–49.

[20] Some of these restrictions were later modified to allow for exceptions such as the sale of certain goods necessary for the safe operation of civilian aircraft, and for some foods and medicine. In 2000, as a confidence-building measure, the Clinton administration lifted the U.S. ban on imports for pistachios, dried fruits, carpets, and caviar. The ban was later restored under CISADA. Katzman, *Iran Sanctions*, 2011.

[21] During the 1990s, as the United States passed increasingly strict unilateral sanctions, the U.S.'s European allies initiated a policy of "critical dialogue" in which they sought to use expanding diplomatic and economic ties with Iran as positive inducements for improved behavior. O'Sullivan, 2003.

[22] ILSA became less controversial after President Clinton made it clear that he intended to use his authority to waive sanctions against foreign firms.

expanded ILSA's provision to include firms selling refined petroleum products to Iran. CISADA also sought to reduce the President's ability to use discretion in the implementation of sanctions on foreign firms.

During the George W. Bush administration, the United States also began to use the power of the U.S. Treasury Department to restrict Iranian access to the international financial system. The objective of this campaign has been to deter foreign banks from doing business with Iranian entities. This policy, which was continued and strengthened by the Obama administration, has successfully cut Iran's financial sector off from much of the world financial system.

UN multilateral sanctions are not nearly as comprehensive as the unilateral sanctions that have been adopted by the United States. However, they have put important restrictions on Iran's trade and access to the international financial system, and are built on an impressive degree of international consensus. Between 2006 and 2010, mostly through the United States' initiative, the UN Security Council has passed four increasingly tougher multilateral sanctions resolutions against Iran: Resolutions 1737, 1747, 1803, and 1929. UNSCR 1929, adopted in June 2010, is the toughest. It greatly expanded the set of affected Iranian entities, strengthened implementation, and imposed important restrictions on trade, shipping, travel, banking, and arms. The resolutions do not forbid trade and investment in Iran's energy sector, but they provide a hook for states to impose such restrictions unilaterally.

UN sanctions on Iran have focused on Iranian individuals and organizations that are connected to the country's nuclear program, while avoiding comprehensive measures that would impose substantial economic pain on the civilian population as a whole. Despite support from the United States, the sanctions do not forbid trade and investment related to Iran's energy sector. Given the particular interests of Security Council permanent members Russia and China in this sector, and a broader interest in avoiding measures that could disrupt the global oil supply and raise energy prices at a time when the world's major economies are already weak, it is unlikely that the United States would be able to win support for such measures in the Security Council.

The United States did succeed, however, in both persuading the Council members to accept language in the text of Resolution 1929 that supports tougher voluntary sanctions by UN member states and convincing important allies such as the EU and Japan to adopt unilateral sanctions that came close to matching the United States' sanctions against Iran. The EU, Japan, and South Korea passed sweeping new sanctions in 2010 that approximated the U.S. sanctions regime, with the major exception of the U.S. oil embargo. EU sanctions banned energy sector investment, enacted restrictions on banking and financing, and banned all arms sales.

The United States tightened sanctions against Iran in the wake of the November 2011 IAEA report, which detailed Iranian weapons-related activities. In November, the Obama administration issued Executive Order 13590, followed by a Treasury Department determination that the Iranian financial system, including its Central Bank, was "a jurisdiction of primary money laundering concern."[23] These measures extended existing U.S. sanctions to any firms supplying oil equipment or services to Iran, and further reduced Iran's access to the U.S. financial system. In concert with the new U.S. measures, Britain and Canada announced that they would sever all access to their financial systems by Iranian institutions.

U.S. extraterritorial sanctions were significantly expanded with the passage of the National Defense Authorization Act in December 2011. The law contained an amendment—passed despite objections from the Obama administration—that imposes sanctions on foreign firms that conduct business with Iran's Central Bank. The President may seek to waive sanctions for national security reasons, if the sanctions would adversely affect global oil supplies, or if a foreign state demonstrates that it has taken measures to significantly reduce its oil trade with Iran.[24] After the law's passage, the United States successfully pressured key allies—including Japan, South Korea, and the EU—to reduce oil purchases from Iran. In late January 2012, the EU went further by passing an oil embargo against Iran.

---

[23] Department of the Treasury, "Finding That the Islamic Republic of Iran Is a Jurisidiction of Primary Money Laundering Concern," *Federal Register*, Vol. 76, No. 227, November 25, 2011.

[24] David Nakamura, "Obama Signs Defense Bill, Pledges to Maintain the Rights of U.S. Citizens," *Washington Post*, December 31, 2011.

Overall, there have been signs that sanctions are beginning to impose real economic pain on Iran. The Iranian rial steadily lost value between 2009 and 2011, and after the United States began to push for tighter sanctions in late 2011, the value of Iran's currency began to fall steeply.[25] A growing number of international firms are becoming reluctant to do business, particularly business requiring longer-term investments, in Iran. Although Chinese firms have proved willing to fill some of the vacuum in the energy sector, this has often taken the form of making deals as a placeholding measure rather than actually committing financing and resources. It is not clear whether Chinese firms will continue to play this role in the wake of new sanctions against Iran's Central Bank and the U.S. effort to close global markets to Iranian oil. Rising oil prices have managed to offset some of the negative effects of sanctions. The EU oil embargo and sanctions against Iran's financial sector, however, will likely impose significant pain on the Iranian economy regardless of any changes in world oil prices. Pledges by the Gulf States to increase production in order to maintain stable oil supplies could help to keep oil prices steady.

The principal intent of these sanctions efforts has been to pressure Iran to come to the negotiating table. The four UN sanctions resolutions demand that Iran suspend its uranium-enrichment program and cease development of nuclear-capable ballistic missiles. There is, however, no evidence as of yet that sanctions have positively influenced Iran's decisionmakers. One round of sanctions were passed in the wake of the collapse of negotiations with Iran that took place in late 2009, when Iran first agreed in principle to, and later rejected, the U.S. fuel-swap proposal endorsed by the Vienna Group. Iran also announced its intention to enrich uranium to 20% during this period. After both UNSCR 1929 and EU sanctions were passed, Iran returned to the negotiating table briefly in late 2010 and again in early 2011 in Istanbul. These rounds of talks were unproductive. Although Iran began to signal its willingness to negotiate after new sanctions were enacted in late 2011 and early 2012, it continues to push forward with its nuclear

---

[25] Rick Gladstone, "In Reversal, Iran Allows Interest Rates to Increase," *New York Times*, January 26, 2012.

program, and its stated resolve to develop its enrichment capabilities has, if anything, hardened. Iran has also responded to the threat of an oil embargo with a threat to close the Strait of Hormuz.

Nor is there evidence that sanctions have begun to generate political pressure for positive change in Iranian domestic politics. Prominent opposition figures have sought to use sanctions as a basis for criticizing the regime leadership; however, the conservative leadership has been at least as successful at using rising tensions with the United States and the West as a way to brand the opposition's support for compromise as traitorous. The regime also has successfully begun to use sanctions as cover to pass economic reforms such as ending subsidies on gasoline.[26]

Economic sanctions also can be used as tools of brute force. They can directly degrade Iran's nuclear program and weaken its ability to develop nuclear weapons. UN multilateral sanctions have, in fact, been designed with this goal in mind. Export controls and trade bans on nuclear-related and dual-use technologies and expertise, and on important inputs such as maraging steel have been an important element of the international sanctions regime, and most effective. They have made it more difficult for Iran to acquire the materials and equipment it needs to expand its enrichment program and replace centrifuges as they break down. They also have starved Iran of much of the foreign assistance on which it had depended earlier to improve its nuclear and ballistic missile capabilities. The latest sanctions, UNSCR 1929, allowed for the interdiction of Iranian shipping if there is suspicion that the cargo is related to the nuclear and missile programs or arms trade.

Sanctions are not a foolproof way of starving the nuclear program, and Iran has long availed itself of the international black market and the existence of states and firms willing to break with the sanctions regime. While sanctions are unlikely to stop or reverse Iran's program, they can slow its progress and raise costs. Reliance on the black market makes it difficult to find steady suppliers for materials and technology, greatly raises the costs of these imports, and presents serious quality

---

[26] Suzanne Maloney, "The Economics of Influencing Iran," *Middle East Memo*, No. 16, Saban Center for Middle East Policy at the Brookings Institution, March 2010.

problems. One apparent effect of these measures has been to raise questions about Iran's ability to complete the IR-40 HWR at Arak, and to develop a parallel plutonium route to the bomb.[27] Efforts to deny access to inputs for the nuclear program can have a secondary coercive role as well. The nuclear program will likely become increasingly unattractive as further technological achievements are frustrated, the program becomes more costly, and it draws resources from other state objectives.

Sanctions also can work by promoting long-term political change in Iran. Their success in doing so will depend heavily on how sanctions are designed, as well as the U.S. ability to hold together a multilateral sanctions coalition over the long term. In this case, sanctions are most likely to promote positive political change in Iran if they are targeted at specific institutions and groups—particularly those who support the nuclear program—and put the burden of economic pain on powerful elites in the regime rather than on the general population. Many of the existing sanctions are designed this way, especially financial sanctions on nuclear-related firms and bureaucracies and on entities related to the IRGC. The travel ban is similarly targeted at key members of the elite. Sanctions of this type have a relatively successful track record in past cases, but have typically required long periods of time—generally years—before they begin to have an effect.[28] A principal challenge will be to successfully manage a broad international sanctions coalition over such a time period. This will be difficult given the potential payoffs from Iran's energy sector for defectors.

Another key challenge will be to prevent sanctions from triggering a domestic backlash in Iran. This is a particular risk with the use of sanctions instruments such as an oil embargo that could have broadly negative effects on the Iranian population as a whole. Although such measures would indeed impose significant economic pain on Iran, they would also risk rallying the population to the support of the regime, and undermining the political opposition. The risk is particularly great considering that Iran's enrichment program enjoys broad support

---

[27] IISS, 2011, p. 80.

[28] Meghan L. O'Sullivan, "Iran and the Great Sanctions Debate," *Washington Quarterly*, Vol. 33, No. 4, October 2010.

among both the public and the elites, and has been successfully linked in the popular discourse to Iranian national autonomy and pride. Tough trade sanctions could likely be portrayed as a U.S. attempt to extend its regional hegemony over Iran and to weaken a regional rival.

Sanctions will work best as part of a long-term containment strategy rather than as a short-term means of coercion. As a result, the United States will need to focus its efforts on maintaining broad international support for the long-term implementation of sanctions. U.S. secondary sanctions on foreign firms, such as those enacted under ILSA and CISADA, risk undermining that, while accomplishing little in terms of Iran's nuclear program. Tough or "crippling" measures such as an oil embargo risk escalation and counterproductive domestic political effects. Instead, the United States should focus its efforts in areas most likely to produce results with the least risk of creating perverse effects. Financial sanctions on key Iranian entities, maintaining broad international support for sanctions, export controls, and the interdiction of shipping are the most important. These measures can make it more difficult and costly for Iran to push forward with its nuclear program and provide incentives for long-term political change in Iran.

Positive Inducements

Positive inducements are rewards that are promised to another party in return for agreement to a set of demands. The United States has joined with the other members of the P5+1 to offer various packages of positive inducements to Iran in an effort to convince the Iranians to reverse their nuclear efforts. These have included economic, diplomatic, and security-related rewards. In return, the P5+1 has demanded that Iran suspend its enrichment of LEU, cease its development of nuclear-capable ballistic missiles, and agree to a more intensive IAEA inspections regime, including implementation of the Additional Protocol and continuous monitoring of nuclear-related sites. Different packages of positive inducements have been offered to Iran through a series of negotiations that have taken place intermittently since 2002.

Negotiations between the P5+1 and Iran have revolved around two tasks. The first task is to create a pause in the crisis to facilitate the negotiation of a more complete deal to resolve the nuclear question. However, the closest the two sides have come to agreeing to such a pause was during the 2006–2008 discussions of a "freeze-for-freeze" deal, in which the P5+1 would freeze additional sanctions deliberations in the UN in return for an Iranian freeze on any expansion of its enrichment program. The 2009–2010 fuel-swap negotiations were intended to play a similar role.[29]

The other task is to negotiate a more extensive settlement to resolve the crisis. Since Iran's enrichment freeze ended in 2005, the two sides have not engaged in formal negotiations toward such a settlement. Instead, they have engaged in a mostly public exchange of bargaining proposals. The P5+1 proposals have involved offers of civilian nuclear assistance such as the provision of LWRs and fuel-supply guarantees, increased trade opportunities and the lifting of sanctions, security guarantees, and regional security cooperation on issues such as Afghanistan and Iraq. In return, Iran would have to agree to suspend sensitive fuel-cycle activities until it could assure the international community that its nuclear intentions were peaceful.

There is little to show for the past eight years of bargaining initiatives. Between 2003 and 2005, Iran did agree to suspend its enrichment program and to implement the Additional Protocol, but these arrangements collapsed in 2005 with the election of Mahmoud Ahmadinejad.[30] Although the United States began a renewed push for engagement with Iran after the election of Barack Obama, the United States and its allies have increasingly turned toward coercive measures in the

---

[29] The freeze-for-freeze deal would have made room for "pre-negotiations" in which the two sides could settle on an arrangement for formal negotiations. For formal negotiations to begin, however, Iran still had to agree to suspend enrichment. The freeze-for-freeze initiative was ultimately rejected by Iran. The fuel swap would not in itself have led to an enrichment freeze, but could have slowed escalation of the crisis by temporarily limiting Iran's breakout options, as Iran would have had to ship the bulk of its LEU stockpile out of the country. This could have provided breathing room for discussions about formal negotiations.

[30] Iran also worked with the IAEA to resolve some outstanding questions about its past nuclear work, but over time Iran has restricted its cooperation with Vienna, and significant suspicions remain about whether Iran has worked, and perhaps continues to work, on weaponization.

wake of the 2009 post-election uprisings in Iran and the collapse of the fuel-swap deal in late 2009.

There are a number of reasons to believe that positive inducements will not be able to convince Iran's decisionmakers to give up its nuclear program. First, the conservatives that dominate the regime have few incentives to agree to any deal. Regime hardliners can benefit domestically from continued conflict with the United States. Conservatives have found tensions with the United States over the nuclear program as a useful means of painting pragmatists and reformists in the opposition as weak at best and traitorous at worst in their advocacy for a more conciliatory approach.[31] The West's coercive measures can provide cover for a crackdown on regime opponents, a scapegoat for domestic economic ills, and a rallying cry to build popular support.

Second, conservatives—including the Supreme Leader—may see many of the P5+1's inducements as more of a threat than a benefit.[32] Dialogue with the United States and greater integration into the international system are seen by conservatives as a threat to Iran's social and political order. Western civilian nuclear cooperation could reduce Iran's self-sufficiency and make the country dependent on the West for its domestic energy supply. Security guarantees and promises to provide a guaranteed supply of nuclear fuel are not credible to these elites.

Third, as long as the domestic political landscape in Iran remains uncertain and fractured, it is unlikely that any single group commands the influence that would be required to see a deal through. This dynamic was on display after Iranian negotiators agreed in principle to a fuel-swap proposal in 2009. In this case, it was—ironically—President Ahmadinejad who supported making a deal with the P5+1. The plan to ship Iran's nuclear fuel abroad in return for fuel rods for

---

31 Breffni O'Rourke, "Iran: Ahmadinejad's Threat to 'Traitors' Points to Widening Rift," *Radio Free Europe/Radio Liberty*, November 14, 2007.

32 Karim Sadjadpour, *Reading Khamenei: The World View of Iran's Most Powerful Leader*, Washington, D.C.: Carnegie Endowment for International Peace, 2008, pp. 16–17.

the TNRR fell apart after it met with opposition from rival political groups.[33]

Fourth, from the beginning, the two sides in the negotiation have stuck to mutually exclusive and unyielding positions on the issue of enrichment. The P5+1 has demanded that any negotiation of a deal include, at a minimum, a (likely long-term) suspension of enrichment. The Iranians have consistently refused to suspend enrichment.

Like sanctions, positive inducements can promote longer-term domestic political change. In fact, sanctions and positive inducements are best viewed as complementary components of a long-term containment strategy. On the one hand, sanctions can raise the costs of the nuclear program, and create incentives for domestic political transformation over time. On the other hand, positive inducements offer a clear—and potentially face-saving—exit ramp from the bite of sanctions. This is most likely to be successful when positive inducements are paired with a clearly articulated set of demands, and a package of rewards for meeting them.

A significant barrier to an agreement is the fact that the P5+1 and Iran have each committed itself to a bargaining position that is entirely contradictory to the other. It is very unlikely that Iran will agree to a suspension of its enrichment program. A possible way past this impasse could be to present a bargaining offer in which Iran can continue to enrich uranium, but accepts much stricter and more invasive safeguards.

There are reasons to recommend such a position. First, acceptance of some level of enrichment would undermine Iranian rhetoric about attacks on its "right" to civilian nuclear power both domestically and internationally. Demands for a full suspension allow Iran to exploit anti-Western and anti-colonial resentment both within Iran

---

33 The deal was attacked both by rivals such as Larijani from within the conservative factions as well as by leaders of the reformist faction such as Moussavi. The broad and vocal opposition to a negotiated deal championed by Ahmadinejad highlights the degree to which the nuclear issue has become politicized, and can serve as a domestic political football that is, in many ways, independent of actual policy considerations. The deal was not rejected on its merits as much as to prevent Ahmadinejad from reaping the domestic political cachet from striking an agreement.

and among other states in the Non-Aligned Movement (NAM) by claiming that efforts to deny Iran the ostensibly peaceful capability to enrich uranium for reactor fuel is part of a broader effort to deny Iran influence and independence, and to exert U.S. and Western hegemony. Iran also is able to point to states like Japan and Brazil that possess the full nuclear fuel cycle and use this as evidence of Western hypocrisy. However substantively empty these arguments may be, they resonate with their audiences and complicate U.S. diplomacy. By agreeing to limited enrichment under tight IAEA monitoring, the United States could weaken much of the appeal of these arguments and create greater domestic and international pressure on Tehran. It also could push the Russians and Chinese to be more cooperative with U.S. nonproliferation policies, as these states have been reluctant to acknowledge the United States' position on complete rollback.

Second, a willingness to accept enrichment, even in a circumscribed form, could create the necessary bargaining space to actually produce a long-term deal with the Iranians. Although there are a number of factors that would continue to make this unlikely—including the nature of the regime, the fact that Iran's enrichment capability is already quite advanced, and a host of current domestic political and regional conditions that create disincentives to negotiation—there are reasons to suggest that a deal would at least be possible. Not least of these is that the Iranians themselves have consistently put forward bargaining offers along these lines, have strongly sold the idea to their domestic audience that the West's failure to accept civilian enrichment is the *non-plus-ultra* barrier to a settlement, and could see such an offer as a last-chance opportunity to escape the spiral of sanctions and threats in which it finds itself. The regime also could see acceptance of a more limited civilian enrichment program as a way to save face with both its international and domestic audiences, because it could accept the deal and declare victory.

Third, acceptance of Iranian enrichment within specified limits in return for enhanced inspections and safeguards could help to address the possibility of Iran constructing clandestine enrichment facilities. As discussed in Chapter Two, the existing safeguards at Natanz make the FEP and PFEP unattractive settings for an Iranian breakout, because it would be difficult to use these facilities for that purpose without giving the United States and its allies weeks or months of warning. A single-minded focus on these declared facilities risks overlooking the possibly greater danger of Iran pursuing a breakout dash at a secret facility. Even if the United States and its allies were to succeed in winning a suspension of enrichment at declared facilities, this would do little about the problem of secret enrichment. However, enhanced access to undeclared sites and nuclear personnel could help to better prevent such a scenario, and improve the intelligence capabilities of the United States and its allies.

There are a number of potential costs to such a shift in U.S. policy. There would inevitably be a reputational cost to making a sudden policy shift to accept enrichment after years of staunchly opposing such a move under two consecutive administrations from different parties. There is also the risk that others would perceive such a change as a sign of U.S. weakness or, at a minimum, a lack of resolve. U.S. threats of further economic or military punishment could be less credible in the future as a result. However, at present, the United States is in the position of sticking to a demand that it likely cannot achieve and is apparently (and quite understandably) not willing to back up with military force. The United States is certainly paying reputational costs already by continuing to maintain that it will not accept Iranian enrichment while Iran continues to make yearly progress in doing just that. The costs could be dramatically greater should Iran eventually develop nuclear weapons.

There also would be a risk that legitimizing enrichment in Iran would undermine U.S. efforts to limit Iran's breakout capability. If the United States and its partners agreed to Iranian enrichment, efforts to restrict Iran's access to foreign sources of technical and material assistance for their nuclear program would be delegitimized, and Iran's ability to improve its breakout capabilities could be enhanced. As a result, the United States would likely demand that strict and verifiable limits be placed on Iran's enrichment program. It would be difficult to convince the Iranians to agree to any arrangement that imposed such limits, and it also would be difficult to design safeguards that provided convincing assurances that Iran was respecting them. However, these challenges must be considered in the light of the fact that, as of late 2011, Iran continues to improve its breakout options at any rate, however slowly.

Any U.S. offer to accept limited enrichment in Iran would necessarily have to be linked to substantial demands for improved monitoring and assurance provisions. Ratification of the Additional Protocol, acceptance of the revised Code 3.1, and continuous monitoring of all nuclear facilities by the IAEA would only be a starting point. Iran should be required to give up enrichment beyond 3.5% purity—something it has already signaled a willingness to do. Iran also could be required to limit the number of cascades used to enrich uranium, not to deploy next-generation centrifuge models, and to limit all of its uranium enrichment to the FEP at Natanz. Other measures could include the constant physical presence of IAEA inspectors at critical sites, improved surveillance capabilities such as real-time closed-circuit monitoring, and unfettered IAEA access to sites, equipment, and personnel—including undeclared ones. The United States could demand limits on the locations and amounts of UF6 that can be stockpiled, and other ways to make breakout more difficult for Iran. There would be real advantages for the United States under such an arrangement, and it could keep the enrichment program to a smaller scale than it otherwise would be.

It is important to note, however, that the optimal outcome for the United States is the verifiable end of Iran's enrichment program. The issue is whether or not this can be achieved, and if it cannot, whether the repeated attempt to do so will actually lead to a much worse outcome. The suggestion that the United States consider continued Iranian enrichment to 3.5% purity is premised on the conclusion that the continued insistence on an enrichment freeze will not succeed, and will lead the United States to forgo other acceptable solutions to the nuclear issue.

As politically difficult as it would be for the United States to make such an offer, it is also not likely that Iran would agree to it, at least in any form that imposed real restrictions on the scale and scope of the Iranian enrichment program. Yet, even if such an offer were rejected, it would be worth pursuing. If an offer fails to produce an agreement, it can still help build international support by demonstrating the willingness of the United States to compromise, and can create positive domestic political incentives in Iran by undermining conservatives' efforts to paint the United States as an aggressor, and by weakening the political effects of presenting the fuel cycle as a national "right" that the United States is trying to deny Iran. In fact, even if the United States cannot yield on its demand that Iran suspend enrichment, it can still benefit from a continued good-faith effort to negotiate.

Containment

Any effective containment strategy against Iran should meet the following two related objectives:

- mitigate potential negative regional and global effects of Iran's nuclear program
- prevent Iran from developing nuclear weapons

Although preventing Iran from acquiring weapons should be the primary goal, a forward-looking containment strategy also will anticipate the possibility of a nuclear-armed Iran, and begin to lay the foundation for effectively containing it. In particular, the strategy should focus on deterring nuclear use and denying Iran any political or military gains from its nuclear weapons.

There are potential trade-offs, however, between these two goals. Measures intended to deter a potentially nuclear-armed Iran could actually create greater incentives for Iran to weaponize in the first place. Specifically, efforts to improve the defensive capabilities of U.S. regional allies and deter Iranian aggression in the region may increase Iran's perception of regional threats, and trigger a security dilemma. Even measures that may be intended as purely defensive, such as the deployment of missile defenses, could increase Iran's perception of a threat. Iran could view efforts to improve the regional defenses of U.S. forces and U.S. allies as preparations for Iranian retaliation after an impending attack. Any negative shift in the regional balance of power risks providing Tehran with an incentive to weaponize.

The most appropriate model for a containment strategy against Iran is George Kennan's original vision for a containment strategy against the Soviet Union, which sought to prevent the expansion of Soviet power and influence into critical areas of the world. Rather than bringing the fight to the USSR itself, Kennan advocated using containment to promote long-term and non-violent regime change, and to moderate Soviet behavior.[34] A containment strategy against Iran should be considered in a similar light, bringing together the denial of gains through military means, weakening of ideological appeal through political reform and economic development, economic and diplomatic isolation, and non-violent political pressure for positive and stable regime transformation. Containment is most likely to succeed over the long term when all of these elements are brought to bear.

The previous sections of this chapter have shown how the prudent use of non-kinetic operations against Iran's nuclear infrastructure, further development of effective military defenses, economic sanctions, and offers of positive inducements can form the core elements of such a containment strategy. Although none of these tools is likely to resolve the nuclear issue in the short term, they can help to delay Iran's progress and raise its costs, reduce incentives for weaponization, and promote positive political change over time. Air strikes are unlikely to produce positive results, but intelligence operations such as cyberwarfare and sabotage can set back Iran's program without triggering escalation or provoking a crisis. These are tools that the United States should continue to develop, along with the intelligence capabilities that are necessary to carry them out.

Economic sanctions are effective at restricting Iran's access to materials, funds, technology, and expertise needed to advance its nuclear efforts. Such sanctions may not be able to stop Iran's progress, but they can delay it. The United States should continue to work with its allies and international partners to further restrict access to

[34] Kennan's original ideas on containment were outlined in the famous "X article" authored by Kennan under the pseudonym "X" in *Foreign Affairs*. X, "The Sources of Soviet Conduct," *Foreign Affairs*, Vol. 25, No. 4, 1947. Sadjadpour also calls for a U.S. containment strategy modeled on Kennan's ideas. Karim Sadjadpour, "The Sources of Soviet Iranian Conduct," *Foreign Policy*, November 2010.

technologies and resources related to nuclear weapons and ballistic missiles, and to achieve UNSC authorization for stricter controls on Iranian international cargo. Economic sanctions can provide an incentive for political change in Iran over the long term. This is most likely to be successful by setting clear conditions for lifting sanctions, and by pairing sanctions with offers of positive inducements for compliance with demands. Limited concessions by Iran should be encouraged by responding with limited concessions such as a partial lifting of sanctions.

Continued negotiations with Iran both through the P5+1 as well as other fora will be a critical element of both preventing Iran from developing weapons and preparing a containment strategy should this fail. Negotiations are unlikely to succeed in the near term, but the chances of reaching an agreement could be increased by offering to accept an Iranian enrichment capability in a limited form in return for improved verification measures and stricter inspection and safeguard provisions.

Even if the United States cannot agree to any level of Iranian enrichment in the near term, it should continue to pursue negotiations with Iran aimed at putting an end to Iran's enrichment of LEU to 20%. If Iran greatly increases its stocks of 20% LEU, which it has indicated it intends to do, it could trigger a crisis. The United States should continue to support efforts to develop a stop-gap arrangement along the lines of the 2010 fuel-swap proposal in order to forestall such a crisis and buy time for further negotiations.

Even if negotiations fail, they can be an effective way of promoting longer-term political change, and are therefore worth pursuing. The current regime in Iran builds it legitimacy from confrontation with the United States. Continued offers of positive inducements in good faith can help to undermine that narrative and to weaken the regime's ability to use it to its domestic political advantage.

Although the first-order objective of the United States should be to prevent weaponization, an effective strategy also should begin to lay the groundwork to deter a nuclear-armed Iran should these efforts fail. Such a strategy must take into consideration the following concerns:

- Nuclear weapons may embolden Iran to become more aggressive regionally.
- Iran may provide nuclear weapons or fissile material to others.
- Iran could lose control over one or more of its weapons.
- Iran could use nuclear blackmail against U.S. regional allies.
- Iran could attack the United States or its allies with nuclear weapons.
- U.S. regional allies might bandwagon—or at least hedge—with a nuclear Iran.
- Iranian development of a nuclear weapons capability could lead other states in the region to pursue their own nuclear arsenals—i.e., Iran could trigger the falling of nuclear "dominoes."
- Iranian nuclear capability could convince Israel that it must publicly declare its own nuclear capability in order to deter Iran.
- Iranian weaponization could undermine U.S. credibility and the legitimacy of the international nonproliferation regime.

Iran is not an irrational actor, and has demonstrated repeatedly in its foreign policy that it will behave pragmatically to further its own interests. If Iran were to develop nuclear weapons, its arsenal would be small, and its delivery capabilities would likely be limited and unreliable. The vastly superior nuclear and conventional forces of the United States and Israel would likely be sufficient to deter Iran from using a nuclear weapon. Israel possesses a credible second-strike capability, confronting Iran with the prospect of massive retaliation.[35] The U.S. military presence in the Gulf, along with existing U.S. security guar-

---

[35] Israel is one of a few states to possess all three pillars of the nuclear triad: the ability to deliver nuclear warheads from land, sea, and air. The triad, and the relatively large number of deployed warheads (estimated to be around 100), vastly improves the likelihood that Israel would retain the ability to retaliate after an Iranian first strike. Ultimately, a secure second strike would depend on Iran's nuclear capabilities as well, but it is unlikely Iran will develop an arsenal and delivery capability that could provide it with a first-strike counterforce capability. This is particularly unlikely to occur without an offsetting adjustment in Israeli nuclear forces. Cirincione et al., 2005, pp. 259–275; Douglas Frantz, "Israel Adds Fuel to Nuclear Dispute," *Los Angeles Times*, October 12, 2003.

antees to its Gulf allies, should be more than enough to deter Iranian nuclear forces from attacking the United States or its allies in the region.

Moreover, efforts to make that deterrent more credible by extending the U.S. nuclear umbrella to these states would be politically difficult and costly, while providing only marginal benefits at best. The extension of the nuclear umbrella would be a hard sell at home, and potentially unwelcomed by the GCC states. At a minimum, a defense umbrella would likely be a difficult sell politically to the GCC states under current circumstances, when Iran has not yet acquired weapons, and some of these states could be reluctant to be seen as strongly balancing against Iran and as direct parties to a U.S. containment strategy rather than as bystanders.[36] Nor is it clear that an explicit U.S. commitment to defend its Gulf allies with nuclear weapons would be a more credible deterrent to Tehran than existing U.S. and Gulf capabilities and security arrangements. While such arrangements could be considered in the future, they are unnecessary at present and could, in fact, escalate regional tensions if Iran interpreted a stronger U.S. commitment to its Gulf allies as a threat.

A more stable course would be for the United States to continue to encourage security cooperation among the GCC states, while continuing with arms sales that improve regional defensive capabilities. This could include existing U.S. efforts to expand the region's missile defense capabilities, which will both help deter Iranian aggression and protect the Gulf States against conventional missile attacks and an accidental or unintended attack by Iran.

Rather than an Iranian preemptive nuclear strike, a likelier possibility is that Iran would misjudge the political utility of its nuclear arsenal. The established nuclear powers have discovered that the possession of nuclear weapons does not easily translate into improved political influence or coercive power. Nuclear weapons can effectively deter attacks on one's territory and vital interests, but have not proved to be useful for much else. However, emerging nuclear powers have

---

36 Shahram Chubin, "Extended Deterrence in Iran," *Strategic Insights*, Vol. 8, No. 5, Winter 2009; Davis et al., 2011, pp. 60–61.

often discovered this only after first trying to use nuclear weapons for coercive purposes and encountering a crisis.[37] This was the case with the United States and the USSR during the Cold War, as well as with India and Pakistan in their nuclear rivalry. It is a mistake that Iran could repeat should it develop nuclear weapons.

Iran could seek to use its nuclear weapons as cover for non-nuclear regional aggression in several ways. It could encourage proxy attacks on Israel by Hezbollah or other terrorist groups, believing that its nuclear arsenal would provide these groups with an effective extended deterrent. Although this could trigger a conflict, it would be one that Israel would be well capable of handling. Israel is more than capable of meeting any challenge from regional proxies with its conventional forces, and Iran would discover quickly that its nuclear arsenal would have no influence on Israel's willingness to take action against its adversaries.

Iran also could adopt a more aggressive posture toward the Gulf States, believing that the nuclear shadow will encourage bandwagoning. Here again, however, Iran's options would be limited. Iran does not possess the conventional military capabilities to challenge the GCC states on the battlefield, and an attack could be adequately met by technologically superior Gulf military forces as well as existing U.S. military assets in the region. It is unlikely that Iran would risk a direct conventional military confrontation with the United States in the Gulf and, in fact, Iran has consistently avoided such a confrontation in the past.[38] Even during the Iran-Iraq War, after the United States accidentally shot down an Iranian airliner, Tehran exercised restraint.

Iran could support domestic sedition in the Gulf States, or sponsor attacks on oil infrastructure. It also could harass shipping in the Persian Gulf or seek to close the Strait of Hormuz. However, Iran would again find that its nuclear arsenal provides little advantage. U.S. naval forces in the Gulf can successfully prevent a closing of the Strait

---

[37] Marc Trachtenberg, "A 'Wasting Asset': American Strategy and the Shifting Nuclear Balance, 1949–1954," *International Security*, Vol. 13, No. 3, 1989; Forrest E. Morgan, Karl P. Mueller, Evan S. Medeiros, Kevin S. Pollpeter, and Roger Cliff, *Dangerous Thresholds: Managing Escalation in the 21st Century*, Santa Monica, Calif.: RAND Corporation, MG-614-AF, 2008.

[38] Chubin, 2009.

and protect Gulf shipping, just as the United States did toward the end of the Iran-Iraq War.[39] Iranian efforts to sow sedition among Gulf Shias would not be greatly aided by an Iranian nuclear arsenal. Iranian-sponsored proxy attacks on Gulf infrastructure such as port facilities or pipelines could be costly, but they can be defended against.[40] Most importantly, because the United States and its regional allies can meet all of these challenges without the need to attack Iranian territory, an Iranian nuclear arsenal would not fundamentally change the U.S. ability to pursue these missions using existing capabilities and security arrangements.

The United States can, however, pursue several policies that could help to both deter an Iranian attack and defend U.S. interests in the Gulf. The United States should continue to support domestic political reform and democratization in the region. Greater political pluralism and the enfranchisement of Shia minorities in the Gulf can help to reduce Iran's potential appeal to these groups and improve domestic stability. The United States should continue to approach this issue with caution, and in dialogue with its regional partners, to avoid disruptive and destabilizing political change. The United States also should work to improve defenses of critical infrastructure in the region to reduce the possibility of an attack on oil facilities affecting the world's oil supply or the stability of world petroleum prices. Missile defenses are an important component of this effort, as is the construction of pipelines and other new infrastructure to reduce the dependence on existing facilities. The United States should continue its efforts to reassure Gulf allies of its commitment to their security, while promoting greater security dialogue among the GCC states. As long as the United States continues its security partnerships with these states, bandwagoning with Iran will be unlikely. Although the Gulf States may seek to build more stable relations with Iran and diversify their security relationships, they do not wish for Iranian hegemony in the region, and Iran's efforts to

---

[39] Talmadge, 2008.

[40] Shifrinson and Priebe, 2011.

achieve such a position are more likely to encourage tighter alliances with the United States than appeasement.[41]

More concerning than the possibility of bandwagoning is the risk of the Gulf States—particularly Saudi Arabia—seeking to balance against a nuclear-armed Iran by developing nuclear weapons of their own. The Saudis have, in fact, suggested that they would seek to acquire nuclear weapons should Iran do so.[42] The further spread of nuclear weapons in the Middle East would be regionally destabilizing, would pose a threat to Israel as well as the United States, and could undermine the international nonproliferation regime. The United States would need to address this concern with a mix of reassurances that it will stand by its allies and warnings that a Saudi nuclear program would be detrimental to U.S. interests and disruptive for U.S. relations in the region. The United States also could offer civilian nuclear cooperation and other economic inducements in return for strong nonproliferation guarantees. The United States has already developed such an arrangement with the UAE, which agreed to strict IAEA safeguards in return for American nuclear assistance.[43] The United States has used similar leverage with South Korea in the past to discourage the ROK from developing the nuclear fuel cycle or a weapons program.[44]

The United States would need to work closely with Israel to build a coordinated approach to containment. U.S.-Israeli solidarity will be important in maintaining a credible deterrent against Iran, and necessary to prevent regional instability. The United States would have to convince Israel to allow the United States to take the lead in containment, and to maintain its current policy of nuclear ambiguity. This too, will require strong reassurances from the United States, which should include continued arms sales, particularly state-of-the-art missile defenses.

---

[41] Chubin, 2009.

[42] Moseley, 2011.

[43] The United States has, in fact, been pursuing this course. See Jay Solomon, "U.S., Saudis to Discuss Nuclear Agreement," *Wall Street Journal*, July 29, 2011.

[44] For a summary of U.S. nonproliferation efforts with the ROK, see Reardon, 2010.

The United States can work to reduce Iranian misjudgment and miscalculation by seeking to build stronger lines of communication with Iran. One lesson from U.S. containment strategies during the Cold War that can be extended to Iran is that stable deterrence depends upon the ability to send and receive clear and credible signals to and from an adversary. This was the logical basis for the Washington-Moscow hotline and other efforts to improve transparency and clarity.

One way the United States can improve its lines of communication with Iran is to open formal military-to-military contacts in the Gulf. U.S. and Iranian naval forces have already benefited from the establishment of informal contacts, which have had some success in reducing the chances of inadvertent conflict and improved stability.[45] The United States could model such a relationship on similar contacts with the Soviet Union during the Cold War, and on military communication channels between UN and North Korean forces at the DMZ in Korea. Another possibility would be to open a U.S. liaison office in Tehran. It has become politically contentious in the United States for the U.S. government to maintain open diplomatic channels with America's adversaries; however, this attitude is both counterproductive and dangerous. Diplomatic contacts are not rewards and do not confer legitimacy.[46] They can be used to communicate clear threats, establish essential red lines, and coordinate military activities to avoid unintended conflict or escalation. They also can be an important source of information about an adversary's intentions, preferences, capabilities, and domestic political constraints. If Iran were to acquire nuclear weapons, some form of communication channel would be essential to maintaining stable deterrence.

---

[45] Daniel Goure and Rebecca Grant, "U.S. Naval Options for Influencing Iran," *Naval War College Review*, Vol. 62, No. 4, Autumn 2009.

[46] Robert J. Reardon, "Should We Talk to Our Adversaries?" Paper presented at the International Studies Association 2011 Annual Convention, Montreal, Canada, March 19, 2011; and Tara Maller, "Diplomacy Derailed: The Consequences of Diplomatic Sanctions," *Washington Quarterly*, Vol. 33, No. 3, July 2010.

CHAPTER SIX

Conclusion

The previous chapters of this study have examined Iran's nuclear program, the forces and processes that shape Iran's nuclear decisions, and the international context in which the Iranian nuclear crisis is set. They identified possible future trajectories of the Iranian program, the range of U.S. policy options, and the potential costs and benefits of these policies. This conclusion summarizes the key policy implications of the research.

Iran likely seeks to continue to improve its breakout options—shortening the time required to make weapons, increasing the number of weapons it could produce, and improving its delivery vehicles. It is unlikely Iran has already decided to weaponize. If Iran initiated a breakout dash now, it would still likely take it more than a year to produce a single bomb, and possibly longer. It would be difficult for Iran to begin such a dash to a bomb without providing the United States with ample warning.

Iran's behavior to date is consistent with the goal of acquiring all of the necessary elements to make nuclear weapons, while deferring the question of whether or not to cross the nuclear threshold. As long as that decision is not made, the United States will have opportunities to convince Iran not to weaponize. In many ways, Iran's program is poorly suited for the cost-effective production of energy. Iran also faces a number of resource and technical challenges that could prevent it from ever developing an indigenous nuclear energy program. The hurdles to making a bomb, however, are fewer, and Iran has already cleared many of them.

Iran has both the technical capability to make nuclear weapons and enough LEU stockpiled that, if it were further enriched, would be sufficient to produce at least one nuclear weapon. Iran's ballistic missiles are likely advanced enough to deliver a weapon to targets throughout the Middle East, including Israel. It also likely has the ability to overcome the technical challenges of building a warhead suitable for mating to its missiles. However, its existing breakout options are all unattractive. It is unlikely that Iran would be able to make a deliverable weapon in under a year and it could require significantly longer, even if Iran were to decide to dedicate all of its efforts to doing so today. It also is unlikely that Iran would be able to initiate a dash for a bomb without quickly alerting the United States. At least over the near term, Iranian weaponization will likely be deterred by these challenges. It is to Iran's advantage to continue to improve its breakout options while remaining within the NPT and publicly claiming that its program is for peaceful purposes. Despite the best efforts of the United States and its allies, Iran continues to make progress with its nuclear program.

The United States should continue to pursue efforts to prevent Iran from weaponizing. At the same time, the United States should start to put into place the elements of an effective containment strategy.

A prudent policy course for the United States would be to continue to focus its primary efforts on preventing Iran from acquiring weapons, while simultaneously putting into place the requisite capabilities to effectively contain a nuclear Iran. A key challenge to achieving this will be to avoid any commitment of forces to the region that Iran would interpret as a threat to the regime. Such a threat could make weaponization more likely by convincing the regime that it needs nuclear weapons to deter the United States. A strategy that is built on drawing down U.S. forces in Iraq and Afghanistan, continued weapons transfers to the GCC centered on missile and air defenses, economic sanctions aimed at starving the Iranian nuclear program, and continued offers of positive inducements through negotiations is most likely to accomplish these goals.

Air strikes are unlikely to destroy Iran's nuclear program, and could have the paradoxical effect of making it easier for Iran to acquire weapons in the long run.

A U.S. preventive strike against Iran's nuclear program is unlikely to accomplish more than delay the program. Over the longer term, an attack could reinforce Iran's resolve to acquire weapons, undermine international support for nonproliferation efforts, rally international and domestic audiences to the regime's side, reinforce the domestic political power of conservative factions, and ultimately make it easier for Iran to reconstitute its program without the need to maintain the pretense of a civilian energy program or the presence of IAEA inspectors. However, a unilateral strike by Israel would risk even greater costs, with less chance of success. The United States may need to carry out limited strikes—particularly if Iran initiates a breakout run—if the only available alternative is Israeli unilateral action.

Economic sanctions, as a means of influence on Iranian decisionmaking, are unlikely to succeed in the near term. They can, however, effectively slow Iran's nuclear progress, which in turn could dissuade Iran from weaponizing. They can also help to promote long-term positive political change in Iran.

Iran's current political conditions, among other factors, make it unlikely that economic sanctions will convince the regime to change its position on enrichment. However, sanctions have been successful in denying Iran resources and funds required for the continued progress of the nuclear program, which has raised the costs of weaponization and delayed the program's progress. The United States also has effectively built a broad international coalition against Iran through its sanctions efforts in the UN Security Council. Sanctions that are targeted at the nuclear program and the financial assets of Iranian entities related to the program can provide incentives for political change in Tehran over the long term. This will be most effective if they are paired with offers of positive inducements for compliance and linked to clearly articulated conditions for their removal. Small concessions by Iran should similarly be met with minor concessions on sanctions.

The current U.S. bargaining strategy with Iran is unlikely to succeed. Negotiating efforts could be improved if the United States were to support a bargaining position through the P5+1 that accepted some level of Iranian enrichment in return for substantially more restrictive safeguards and a more intrusive inspections regime. Continued negotiations, even if they do not succeed in

producing an agreement, can promote long-term political change in Iran.

It is unlikely that Iran will agree to any offer of positive inducements the United States is prepared to deliver as long as the United States insists that Iran suspend all of its sensitive fuel cycle activities. Negotiations should still, however, be pursued in good faith. They help build international support for other U.S. policies. They can also positively influence Iran's decisionmaking over the long term. By engaging diplomatically with Iran and identifying clear and credible rewards for compliance with the international nonproliferation regime, the United States can effectively disarm the regime's ability to use the nuclear issue as a cudgel against domestic opponents. The regime has created a legitimizing narrative that depends on U.S. hostility and coercion. Consistent offers of rewards and negotiations in good faith help neutralize that narrative and undermine its political legitimacy.

The United States could also consider supporting a bargaining offer from the P5+1 that accepts some limited enrichment capability in Iran, provided Iran agrees to strict safeguards and an invasive inspections regime. It is unlikely that the United States will convince Iran to give up enrichment. Such a bargaining position would simply be recognizing an existing reality. Such a shift in the United States' bargaining stance could bring risks and weaken U.S. credibility. However, this needs to be weighed against the blow to U.S. credibility and security that could result from the continued expansion of Iran's enrichment program or from Iran's acquisition of a weapon.

A nuclear-armed Iran would be a threat to U.S. interests and could destabilize the Middle East. A nuclear Iran could seek to use its weapons to expand its regional influence and establish hegemony in the Persian Gulf. Iranian miscalculation also could trigger crisis or even a regionwide conflict. It is strongly in the United States' interest to prevent Iran from developing a nuclear arsenal.

Although Iran's nuclear program continues to make progress, it is likely that Iran has not yet decided to weaponize. Furthermore, the United States possesses military, economic, and diplomatic tools that can be used to effectively reduce the chances of Iran acquiring nuclear weapons. To achieve this goal, the United States needs to continue to maintain broad international support for its nonproliferation policies and adopt a patient but firm strategy that simultaneously works toward a negotiated settlement while encouraging long-term political change in Tehran.

The success of such a strategy is not certain. As a result, it is prudent for the United States to begin to lay the groundwork for a containment strategy that anticipates a nuclear-armed Iran. This can be done effectively without sacrificing strategies aimed at preventing weaponization. A containment strategy should focus on the defense of regional allies, the establishment of stable and clear lines of communication with Tehran, the development of strong intelligence capabilities, and policy coordination with regional partners, especially Israel. Economic sanctions, continued negotiations through the P5+1, and offers of positive inducements for Iranian compliance are all important elements of both the effort to prevent weaponization and the development of an effective containment strategy.

Bibliography

"70 kg of 20% Enriched Uranium Produced in Iran," Fars News Agency, October 18, 2011. As of July 23, 2012: http://english.farsnews.com/newstext.php?nn=9007161339

Abdo, Genieve, and Jasim Husain Ali, "Misunderstanding Bahrain's Shia Protestors," al Jazeera, April 3, 2011. As of July 23, 2012: http://www.aljazeera.com/indepth/opinion/2011/03/201132982742988712.html

Addis, Casey L., Christopher M. Blanchard, Kenneth Katzman, Carol Migdalovitz, Jim Nicol, Jeremy M. Sharp, and Jim Zanotti, *Iran: Regional Perspectives and U.S. Policy*, Washington, D.C.: Congressional Research Service, R40849, January 13, 2010. As of July 23, 2012: http://assets.opencrs.com/rpts/R40849_20100113.pdf

"Ahmadinejad v Ayatollah: Who Will Win Iran Dust-Up?" BBC News, July 8, 2011. As of July 23, 2012: http://www.bbc.co.uk/news/world-middle-east-14061556

Albright, David, "Annual Future Low-Enriched Uranium Fuel Requirements for the Tehran Research Reactor," ISIS, October 7, 2009. As of July 23, 2012: http://isis-online.org/isis-reports/detail/technical-note-annual-future-low-enriched-uranium-fuel-requirements-for-the/

Albright, David, Paul Brannan, and Christina Walrond, "Stuxnet Malware and Natanz: Update of ISIS December 22, 2010 Report," ISIS, February 15, 2011. As of July 23, 2012: http://isis-online.org/uploads/isis-reports/documents/stuxnet_update_15Feb2011.pdf

Albright, David, and Jacqueline Shire, "Iran's Uranium Stockpile Dwindling," ISIS, December 30, 2009. As of July 23, 2012: http://isis-online.org/uploads/isis-reports/documents/Iran_uranium_30Dec2009.pdf

Albright, David, Jacqueline Shire, and Paul Brannan, "IAEA Safeguards Report on Iran: Iran Making Progress but Not Yet Reliably Operating an Enrichment Plant," ISIS, May 25, 2007. As of July 23, 2012:
http://www.isis-online.org/publications/iran/IranSafeguards25May2007.pdf

Albright, David A., Jacqueline Shire, and Paul Brannan, "Can Military Strikes Destroy Iran's Gas Centrifuge Program? Probably Not," ISIS, August 7, 2008. As of July 23, 2012:
http://www.isis-online.org/publications/iran/Centrifuge_Manufacturing_7August2008.pdf

Albright, David, Jacqueline Shire, Paul Brannan, and Andrea Scheel, "Nuclear Iran: Not Inevitable," ISIS, January 21, 2009. As of July 23, 2012:
http://www.isisnucleariran.org/assets/pdf/Iran_paper_final_2.pdf

Albright, David, Jacqueline Shire, and Paul Brannan, "Is Iran Running Out of Yellowcake?" ISIS, February 11, 2009. As of July 23, 2012:
http://www.isisnucleariran.org/assets/pdf/Iran_Yellowcake.pdf/

Albright, David, Jacqueline Shire, and Paul Brannan, "Iran's New Centrifuge: What Do We Know About It?" ISIS, April 13, 2010. As of July 23, 2012:
http://www.isisnucleariran.org/assets/pdf/Irans_new_centrifuge_13April2010.pdf

Albright, David, and Andrea Stricker, "Iran's Nuclear Program," in Robin Wright, ed., *Iran Primer: Power, Politics, and U.S. Policy*, Washington, D.C.: United States Institute of Peace, 2010, pp. 77–81.

Albright, David, and Christina Walrond, *Iran's Gas Centrifuge Program: Taking Stock*, ISIS, February 11, 2010. As of July 23, 2012:
http://isis-online.org/uploads/isis-reports/documents/Natanz_Operation_11Feb2010.pdf

Albright, David, and Christina Walrond, "Iran's Advanced Centrifuges," ISIS, October 18, 2011. As of July 23, 2012:
http://isis-online.org/uploads/isis-reports/documents/Iran_Advanced_Centrifuges_18October2011.pdf

Allin, Dana H., and Steven Simon, *The Sixth Crisis: Iran, Israel, America, and the Rumors of War*, New York: Oxford University Press, 2010.

Alterman, Jon B., "China's Hard Choices on Iran," *Middle East Notes and Comment*, Washington, D.C.: Center for Strategic and International Studies, October 2009.

Ansari, Ali M., *Iran Under Ahmadinejad: The Politics of Confrontation*, IISS Adelphi Paper No. 393, New York: Routledge, 2007.

Aras, Bulent, and Fatih Ozbay, "Dances with Wolves: Russia, Iran, and the Nuclear Issue," *Middle East Policy*, Vol. 13, No. 4, 2006.

Aslund, Anders, "Gazprom: Challenged Giant in Need of Reform," in Anders Aslund, Sergei Guriev, and Andrew Kuchins, eds., *Russia After the Global Economic Crisis*, Washington, D.C.: Peterson Institute for International Economics, 2010, pp. 151–168.

Bakri, Nada, "Torture Used on Protesters in Bahrain, Report Says," *New York Times*, November 23, 2011.

Baldwin, David A., *Economic Statecraft*. Princeton, NJ: Princeton University Press, 1985.

Barry, Ellen, "Russia Dismisses Calls for New UN Sanctions," *New York Times*, November 9, 2011.

Barzashka, Ivanka, "Using Enrichment Capacity to Estimate Iran's Breakout Potential," FAS Issue Brief, January 21, 2011. As of July 23, 2012: http://www.fas.org/pubs/_docs/IssueBrief_Jan2011_Iran.pdf

Barzashka, Ivanka, and Ivan Oelrich, "Increased Safeguards at Natanz: What Does It All Mean?" FAS Strategic Security Blog, August 28, 2009. As of July 23, 2012:
http://www.fas.org/blog/ssp/2009/08/increased-safeguards-at-natanz-what-does-it-all-mean.php

Beehner, Lionel, "Russia's Nuclear Deal with Iran," *Council on Foreign Relations Backgrounder*, February 28, 2006. As of July 23, 2012: www.cfr.org/iran/russias-nuclear-deal-iran/p9985

Belopolsky, Helen, *Russia and the Challengers: Russian Alignment with China, Iran, and Iraq in the Unipolar Era*, New York: Palgrave Macmillan, 2009.

Ben-Meir, Alon, "Israel's Response to a Nuclear Iran," *International Journal on World Peace*, Vol. 27, No. 1, March 2010.

"Beyond Sanctions: Russia, China, and Iran Workshop," Brookings Institution, Washington, D.C., July 9, 2010. As of July 23, 2012: www.brookings.edu/events/2010/0709_sanctions.aspx

Blanchard, Jean-Marc F., Edward D. Mansfield, and Norrin M. Ripsman, eds., *Power and the Purse: Economic Statecraft, Interdependence, and National Security*, London: F. Cass, 2000.

Bowley, Graham, "Despite Call to Halt, Iran Says It Will Continue Its Nuclear Program," *New York Times*, July 31, 2008.

Broad, William J., and David E. Sanger, "Vienna Meeting on Arms Data Reignites Iran Nuclear Debate," *New York Times*, March 3, 2008.

Broad, William J., John Markoff, and David E. Sanger, "Israeli Test on Worm Called Crucial in Iran Nuclear Delay," *New York Times*, January 15, 2011.

Burr, William, "A Brief History of U.S.-Iranian Nuclear Negotiations," *Bulletin of the Atomic Scientists*, Vol. 65, No. 1, January/February 2009.

Cambanis, Thanassis, "Stronger Hezbollah Emboldened for Fights Ahead," *New York Times*, October 6, 2010.

"China Passes E.U. in Trade with Iran," UPI, February 9, 2010.

"China, Russia on Board in Sweetened Offer to Iran," CNN, June 5, 2006. As of July 23, 2012:
http://www.cnn.com/2006/WORLD/meast/06/01/us.iran/index.html?iref=all search

Chinoy, Mike, *Meltdown: The Inside Story of the North Korea Nuclear Crisis*, New York: St. Martin's, 2008.

Chubin, Shahram, *Iran's Nuclear Ambitions*, Washington, D.C.: Carnegie Endowment for International Peace, 2006.

Chubin, Shahram, "Extended Deterrence in Iran," *Strategic Insights*, Vol. 8, No. 5, Winter 2009.

Chubin, Shahram, "The Domestic Politics of the Nuclear Question in Iran," in Joachim Krause and Charles King Mallory IV, eds., *The Strategic Implications of the Iranian Nuclear Program*, Berlin: Aspen Institute, 2010, pp. 84–93.

Cirincione, Joseph, Jon B. Wolfsthal, and Miriam Rajkumar, *Deadly Arsenals: Nuclear, Biological, and Chemical Threats*, 2nd ed., Washington, D.C.: Carnegie Endowment for International Peace, 2005.

Clapper, James, Testimony Before the Senate Committee on Armed Services, "Hearing to Receive Testimony on the Current and Future Worldwide Threat to the National Security of the United States," March 10, 2011. As of July 23, 2012:
http://www.armed-services.senate.gov/Transcripts/2011/03%20March/11-11%20-%203-10-11.pdf

"Clinton: Nuclear-Armed Iran 'Unacceptable,'" Associated Press, March 22, 2010.

Cohen, Craig, ed., *Capacity and Resolve: Foreign Assessments of U.S. Power*, Washington, D.C.: Center for Strategic and International Studies, 2011.

Commission to Assess the Ballistic Missile Threat to the United States, "Executive Summary of the Report of the Commission to Assess the Ballistic Missile Threat to the United States," July 15, 1998. As of July 23, 2012:
http://www.fas.org/irp/threat/bm-threat.htm

Cordesman, Anthony H., and Martin Kleiber, *Iran's Military Forces and Warfighting Capabilities: The Threat in the Northern Gulf*, Washington, D.C.: Center for Strategic and International Studies, 2007.

Cordesman, Anthony H., and Adam C. Seitz, *Iranian Weapons of Mass Destruction: The Birth of a Regional Nuclear Arms Race?* Santa Barbara, Calif.: Greenwood, 2009.

Corera, Gordon, *Shopping for Bombs: Nuclear Proliferation, Global Insecurity, and the Rise and Fall of the A.Q. Khan Network*, New York: Oxford University Press, 2006.

Cowell, Alan, "Iran Won't Retreat on Nuclear Program," *New York Times*, July 24, 2008.

Cowell, Alan, "Iran to Build More Enrichment Plants," *New York Times*, February 22, 2010.

Crail, Peter, "Iran Raising Uranium-Enrichment Level," *Arms Control Today*, Vol. 40, No. 2, March 2010.

Crail, Peter, "Iran's First Power Reactor Goes Critical," *Arms Control Today*, Vol. 41, No. 5, June 2011.

Currier, Carrie Liu, and Manochehr Dorraj, "In Arms We Trust: The Economic and Strategic Factors Motivating China-Iran Relations," *Journal of Chinese Political Science*, Vol. 15, 2010.

Davis, Lynn E., Jeffrey Martini, Alireza Nader, Dalia Dassa Kaye, James T. Quinlivan, and Paul Steinberg, *Iran's Nuclear Future: Critical U.S. Policy Choices*, Santa Monica, Calif.: RAND Corporation, MG-1087-AF, 2011. As of July 23, 2012:
http://www.rand.org/pubs/monographs/MG1087.html

Dehghan, Saeed Kamali, "Ahmadinejad Fights to Preserve His Dwindling Power," *Guardian*, May 9, 2011.

deLeon, Rudy, Brian Katulis, and Peter Juul, *Strengthening America's Options on Iran: 10 Key Questions to Inform Debate*, Washington, D.C.: Center for American Progress, 2012.

Department of Defense, "Unclassified Report on Military Power in Iran," April 2010. As of July 23, 2012:
http://www.fas.org/man/eprint/dod-iran.pdf

Department of the Treasury, "Finding That the Islamic Republic of Iran Is a Jurisidiction of Primary Money Laundering Concern," *Federal Register*, Vol. 76, No. 227, November 25, 2011.

Devenny, Patrick, "Hezbollah's Strategic Threat to Israel," *Middle East Quarterly*, Vol. 13, No. 1, Winter 2006.

Dobbins, James, "Iran Sanctions: Options, Opportunities, and Consequences," Testimony Before the Committee on Oversight and Government Reform, Subcommittee on National Security and Foreign Affairs, United States House of Representatives, December 15, 2009, As of July 23, 2012:
http://www.rand.org/pubs/testimonies/2009/RAND_CT337.pdf

Dougherty, Jill, "Clinton: Sanctions Against Iran Helping Delay Its Nuclear Program," CNN, January 10, 2011. As of July 23, 2012: http://articles.cnn.com/2011-01-10/world/iran.clinton.remarks_1_nuclear-program-nuclear-weapons-iran?_s=PM:WORLD

Downs, Erica, "Beijing's Tehran Temptation," *Foreign Policy*, July 30, 2009. As of July 23, 2012: http://www.foreignpolicy.com/articles/2009/07/30/chinas_tehran_temptation

Einhorn, Robert J., and Gary Samore, "Ending Russian Assistance to Iran's Nuclear Bomb," *Survival*, Vol. 44, No. 2, 2002.

Elson, Sarah Beth, and Alireza Nader, *What Do Iranians Think: A Survey of Attitudes on the United States, the Nuclear Program, and the Economy*, Santa Monica, Calif.: RAND Corporation, TR-910-OSD, 2011. As of July 23, 2012: http://www.rand.org/pubs/technical_reports/TR910.html

"Europe 'Rock-Solid' That Iran Cease Enrichment Ahead of New Talks," Agence France Presse, April 16, 2005.

Farhi, Farideh, "Iran's Deepening Internal Battle," *Frontline*, June 7, 2011. As of July 23, 2012: http://www.pbs.org/wgbh/pages/frontline/tehranbureau/2011/06/irans-deepening-internal-battle.html

Feldman, Shai, *Nuclear Weapons and Arms Control in the Middle East*, Cambridge, Mass.: Center for Science and International Affairs, Harvard University, 1997.

Felgenhauer, Pavel, "The 'Unraveling Relationship' Between Russia and Iran," BBC News, July 24, 2010. As of July 23, 2012: http://www.bbc.co.uk/news/world-europe-10684110

Fitzpatrick, Mark, *The Iranian Nuclear Crisis: Avoiding Worst-Case Outcomes*, Oxford: Routledge, 2008.

Fitzpatrick, Mark, "Iran: The Fragile Promise of the Fuel-Swap Plan," *Survival*, Vol. 52, No. 3, June/July 2010.

Frantz, Douglas, "Israel Adds Fuel to Nuclear Dispute," *Los Angeles Times*, October 12, 2003.

Freilich, Chuck, *Speaking About the Unspeakable: U.S.-Israeli Dialogue on Iran's Nuclear Program*, Washington, D.C.: The Washington Institute for Near East Policy, 2007.

Galtung, Johan, "On the Effects of International Economic Sanctions: With Examples from the Case of Rhodesia," *World Politics*, Vol. 19, No. 3, 1967.

Garver, John W., "Is China Playing a Dual Game in Iran?" *Washington Quarterly*, Vol. 34, No. 1, Winter 2011.

George, Alexander L., David K. Hall, and William E. Simons, *The Limits of Coercive Diplomacy: Laos, Cuba, Vietnam*, Boston: Little, Brown, 1971.

Ghattas, Kim, "Clinton Urges Iran to Fully Engage in Nuclear Talks," BBC News, December 3, 2010. As of July 23, 2012:
http://www.bbc.co.uk/news/world-us-canada-11917186

Gladstone, Rick, "Iran Signals Revenge over Killing of Scientist," *New York Times*, January 12, 2012.

Gladstone, Rick, "In Reversal, Iran Allows Interest Rates to Increase," *New York Times*, January 26, 2012.

Glaser, Alexander, "Characteristics of the Gas Centrifuge for Uranium Enrichment and Their Relevance for Nuclear Weapon Proliferation," *Science & Global Security*, Vol. 16, No. 1, 2008.

Goldberg, Jeffrey, "Point of No Return," *Atlantic Monthly*, Vol. 306, No. 2, September 2010.

Gordon, Michael R., and Eric Schmitt, "U.S. Says Exercise by Israel Seemed Directed at Iran," *New York Times*, June 20, 2008.

Goure, Daniel, and Rebecca Grant, "U.S. Naval Options for Influencing Iran," *Naval War College Review*, Vol. 62, No. 4, Autumn 2009.

Green, Jerrold D., Frederic Wehrey, and Charles Wolf, Jr., *Understanding Iran*, Santa Monica, Calif.: RAND Corporation, MG-771-SRF, 2009. As of July 23, 2012:
http://www.rand.org/pubs/monographs/MG771.html

Greenhouse, Steven, "U.S. Says Russia Promised Nuclear Gear to Iran," *New York Times*, April 29, 1995.

Grier, Peter, "Why Does Iran Need More Potent Uranium? Medical Care," *Christian Science Monitor*, October 21, 2009.

Gutterman, Steve, and Lidia Kelly, "Russia Hopes Its Proposal Can Revive Iran Nuclear Talk," Reuters, August 17, 2011.

Harrington, Mark, "Evidence Emerges of Iran's Continued Nuclear Weapons Research," *Jane's International Defence Review*, March 13, 2008.

Heinonen, Olli, "The 20 Percent Solution," *Foreign Policy*, January 11, 2012. As of July 23, 2012:
http://www.foreignpolicy.com/articles/2012/01/11/the_20_percent_solution

Hildreth, Steven A., *Iran's Ballistic Missile Programs: An Overview*, Washington, D.C.: Congressional Research Service, RS22758, February 4, 2009. As of July 23, 2012:
http://www.fas.org/sgp/crs/nuke/RS22758.pdf

Hufbauer, Gary C., Jeffrey J. Schott, Kimberly Ann Elliott, and Barbara Oegg, *Economic Sanctions Reconsidered*, 3rd ed., Washington, D.C.: Peterson Institute for International Economics, 2007.

IAEA, "Islamic Republic of Iran," *IAEA Country Nuclear Power Profiles*, Vienna: International Atomic Energy Agency, December 2002. As of July 23, 2012: http://www-pub.iaea.org/mtcd/publications/pdf/cnpp2003/cnpp_webpage/PDF/2002/index.htm

IAEA, "Implementation of the NPT Safeguards Agreement in the Islamic Republic of Iran," Vienna: International Atomic Energy Agency, GOV/2003/40, June 6, 2003. As of July 23, 2012:
http://www.iaea.org/Publications/Documents/Board/2003/gov2003-40.pdf

IAEA, "Implementation of the NPT Safeguards Agreement in the Islamic Republic of Iran," Vienna: International Atomic Energy Agency, GOV/2003/75, November 10, 2003. As of July 23, 2012:
http://www.iaea.org/Publications/Documents/Board/2003/gov2003-75.pdf

IAEA, "Implementation of the NPT Safeguards Agreement in the Islamic Republic of Iran," Vienna: International Atomic Energy Agency, GOV/2004/83, November 15, 2004. As of July 23, 2012:
http://www.iaea.org/Publications/Documents/Board/2004/gov2004-83.pdf

IAEA, "Communication Dated 26 November 2004 Received from the Permanent Representatives of France, Germany, the Islamic Republic of Iran and the United Kingdom Concerning the Agreement Signed in Paris on 15 November 2004," Vienna: International Atomic Energy Agency, INFCIRC/637, November 26, 2004. As of July 23, 2012:
http://www.iaea.org/Publications/Documents/Infcircs/2004/infcirc637.pdf

IAEA, "Communication Dated 12 September 2005 from the Permanent Mission of the Islamic Republic of Iran to the Agency," Vienna: International Atomic Energy Agency, INFCIRC/657, September 15, 2005. As of July 23, 2012:
http://www.iaea.org/Publications/Documents/Infcircs/2005/infcirc657.pdf

IAEA, "Implementation of the NPT Safeguards Agreement and Relevant Provisions of Security Council Resolutions in the Islamic Republic of Iran," Vienna: International Atomic Energy Agency, GOV/2007/22, May 23, 2007. As of July 23, 2012:
http://www.iaea.org/Publications/Documents/Board/2007/gov2007-22.pdf

IAEA, "Implementation of the NPT Safeguards Agreement and Relevant Provisions of Security Council Resolutions 1737 (2006) and 1747 (2007) in the Islamic Republic of Iran," Vienna: International Atomic Energy Agency, GOV/2007/58, November 15, 2007. As of July 23, 2012:
http://www.iaea.org/Publications/Documents/Board/2007/gov2007-58.pdf

IAEA, "Implementation of the NPT Safeguards Agreement and Relevant Provisions of Security Council Resolutions 1737 (2006), 1747 (2007), and 1803 (2008) in the Islamic Republic of Iran," Vienna: International Atomic Energy Agency, GOV/2008/15, May 26, 2008. As of July 23, 2012:
http://www.iaea.org/Publications/Documents/Board/2008/gov2008-15.pdf

IAEA, "Implementation of the NPT Safeguards Agreement and Relevant Provisions of Security Council Resolutions 1737 (2006), 1747 (2007), 1803 (2008), and 1835 (2008) in the Islamic Republic of Iran," Vienna: International Atomic Energy Agency, GOV/2009/8, February 18, 2009. As of July 23, 2012: http://www.iaea.org/Publications/Documents/Board/2009/gov2009-8.pdf

IAEA, "Implementation of the NPT Safeguards Agreement and Relevant Provisions of Security Council Resolutions 1737 (2006), 1747 (2007), 1803 (2008), and 1835 (2008) in the Islamic Republic of Iran," Vienna: International Atomic Energy Agency, GOV/2010/10, February 18, 2010. As of July 23, 2012: http://www.iaea.org/Publications/Documents/Board/2010/gov2010-10.pdf

IAEA, "Implementation of the NPT Safeguards Agreement and Relevant Provisions of Security Council Resolutions in the Islamic Republic of Iran," Vienna: International Atomic Energy Agency, GOV/2010/62, November 23, 2010. As of July 23, 2012:
http://www.iaea.org/Publications/Documents/Board/2010/gov2010-62.pdf

IAEA, "Implementation of the NPT Safeguards Agreement and Relevant Provisions of Security Council Resolutions in the Islamic Republic of Iran," Vienna: International Atomic Energy Agency, GOV/2011/29, May 24, 2011. As of July 23, 2012:
http://www.iaea.org/Publications/Documents/Board/2011/gov2011-29.pdf

IAEA, "Implementation of the NPT Safeguards Agreement and Relevant Provisions of Security Council Resolutions in the Islamic Republic of Iran," Vienna: International Atomic Energy Agency, GOV/2011/54, September 2, 2011. As of July 23, 2012:
http://www.iaea.org/Publications/Documents/Board/2011/gov2011-54.pdf

IAEA, "Implementation of the NPT Safeguards Agreement and Relevant Provisions of Security Council Resolutions in the Islamic Republic of Iran," Vienna: International Atomic Energy Agency, GOV/2011/65, November 8, 2011. As of July 23, 2012:
http://www.iaea.org/Publications/Documents/Board/2011/gov2011-65.pdf

IAEA, "Implementation of the NPT Safeguards Agreement and Relevant Provisions of United Nations Security Council Resolutions in the Islamic Republic of Iran," Vienna: International Atomic Energy Agency, GOV/2011/69, November 18, 2011. As of July 23, 2012:
http://www.iaea.org/Publications/Documents/Board/2011/gov2011-69.pdf

IAEA, "Implementation of the NPT Safeguards Agreement and Relevant Provisions of Security Council Resolutions in the Islamic Republic of Iran," Vienna: International Atomic Energy Agency, GOV/2012/23, May 25, 2012. As of July 23, 2012:
http://www.iaea.org/Publications/Documents/Board/2012/gov2012-23.pdf

Institute for Science and International Security, "Update on the Arak Reactor in Iran," Washington, D.C.: ISIS, August 25, 2009. As of July 23, 2012: http://isis-online.org/uploads/isis-reports/documents/Arak_Update_25_August2009.pdf

International Institute for Strategic Studies, *Nuclear Programs in the Middle East: In the Shadow of Iran*, London: IISS, 2008.

International Institute for Strategic Studies, *Iran's Ballistic Missile Capabilities: A Net Assessment*, London: IISS, 2010.

International Institute for Strategic Studies, *Iran's Nuclear, Chemical and Biological Capabilities: A Net Assessment*, London: IISS, 2011.

"Iran and the West, Part 3: Nuclear Confrontation," BBC News, first broadcast February 21, 2009. As of July 23, 2012:
youtube.com at http://www.youtube.com/watch?v=3hHfV19kXcQ

"Iran, Defiant, Approves Plan for 10 Enrichment Sites," Associated Press, November 29, 2009.

"Iran Rejects 'Unacceptable' EU Nuclear Offer," Agence France Presse, August 5, 2005.

"Iran Says It Has Produced Its First Nuclear Fuel Rod," Associated Press, January 1, 2012.

"Iran Says Turkey Best Place for Future Talks with World Powers About Nuclear Program," Associated Press, January 5, 2012.

"Iran Vows Not to Halt Its Nuclear Program Despite Western Pressure," Associated Press, May 5, 2008.

"Iran Vows to Resist Pressure to Drop Nuclear Fuel Program," Reuters, March 13, 2005.

"Iranian Nuclear Power Station 'Begins Generating Electricity,'" Reuters, September 4, 2011.

Jervis, Robert, *Perception and Misperception in International Politics*, Princeton, N.J.: Princeton University Press, 1976.

Jervis, Robert, *The Illogic of American Nuclear Strategy*, Ithaca, N.Y.: Cornell University Press, 1984.

Johnson, Ed, "Europe Offers Iran Civilian Nuke Support," Associated Press, August 5, 2005.

Kamrava, Mehran, "The 2009 Elections and Iran's Changing Political Landscape," *Orbis*, Vol. 54, No. 3, Summer 2010.

Kan, Shirley A., *China and Proliferation of Weapons of Mass Destruction and Missiles: Policy Issues*, Washington, D.C.: Congressional Research Service, RL31555, December 13, 2007. As of July 23, 2012:
http://assets.opencrs.com/rpts/RL31555_20071213.pdf

Kan, Shirley A., *China and Proliferation of Weapons of Mass Destruction: Policy Issues*, Washington, D.C.: Congressional Research Service, RL31555, May 26, 2011. As of July 23, 2012:
http://digital.library.unt.edu/ark:/67531/metadc84036/m1/1/high_res_d/RL31555_2011May26.pdf

Kapur, S. Paul, *Dangerous Deterrent: Nuclear Weapons Proliferation and Conflict in South Asia*, Stanford, Calif.: Stanford University Press, 2007.

Katzman, Kenneth, *Iran Sanctions*, Washington, D.C.: Congressional Research Service, RS20871, March 1, 2011. As of July 23, 2012:
http://assets.opencrs.com/rpts/RS20871_20110301.pdf

Katzman, Kenneth, *Iran: U.S. Concerns and Policy Responses*, Washington, D.C.: Congressional Research Service, RL32048, March 4, 2011. As of July 23, 2012:
https://opencrs.com/document/RL32048/2011-03-04/

Kemp, R. Scott, and Alexander Glaser, "Statement on Iran's Ability to Make a Nuclear Weapon and the Significance of the 19 February 2009 IAEA Report on Iran's Uranium Enrichment Program," March 2, 2009, As of July 23, 2012:
http://www.princeton.edu/~aglaser/2009aglaser_iran.pdf

Kerr, Paul, "Questions Surround Iran's Nuclear Program," *Arms Control Today*, Vol. 36, No. 2, March 2006.

Kerr, Paul, "U.S., Allies Await Iran's Response to Nuclear Offer," *Arms Control Today*, Vol. 36, No. 6, July/August 2006.

Kershner, Isabel, "Israeli Ex-Spy Predicts Delay for Iran's Nuclear Ambitions," *New York Times*, January 7, 2011.

Kershner, Isabel, and Rick Gladstone, "Decision to Attack Iran Is 'Far Off,' Israel Says," *New York Times*, January 18, 2012.

Kessler, Glenn, "Early October New Deadline for Iran," *Washington Post*, September 21, 2006.

Khalaf, Roula, James Blitz, Daniel Dombey, Tobias Buck, and Najmeh Bozorgmehr, "The Sabotaging of Iran," *Financial Times*, February 11, 2011.

Khlopkov, Anton, "Iran Breakthrough for Russian Nuclear Industry," *Moscow Defense Brief*, Vol. 1, No. 19, 2010.

Kirshner, Jonathan, "The Microfoundations of Economic Sanctions," *Security Studies*, Vol. 6, No. 3, 1997.

Krauss, Clifford, "OPEC Agrees to Raise Its Production Target," *New York Times*, December 15, 2011.

Landler, Mark, "U.S. Says Sanctions Hurt Iran Nuclear Program," *New York Times*, January 10, 2011.

Landler, Mark, and Nazila Fathi, "United States to Join Nuclear Talks with Iran," *New York Times*, April 9, 2009.

Landler, Mark, and Clifford Krauss, "Gulf Nations Aid U.S. Effort to Choke Off Iran Oil Sales," *New York Times*, January 13, 2012.

LeMiere, Christian, "Tighter Bonds—China Strengthens Ties with Iran," *Jane's Intelligence Review*, November 11, 2009.

Levy, Adrian, and Cathy Scott-Clark, *Deception: Pakistan, the United States, and the Secret Trade in Nuclear Weapons*, New York: Walker, 2007.

Lewis, Jeffrey, "Uranium Deuteride Initiators Redux," *Arms Control Wonk*, May 25, 2011. As of July 23, 2012:
http://lewis.armscontrolwonk.com/archive/4032/uranium-deuteride-initiatiors-redux

Li Bin "Nuclear Missile Delivery Capabilities in Emerging Nuclear States," *Science & Global Security*, Vol. 6, No. 3, 1997.

Long, Austin, "Can They?" *Tablet*, November 18, 2011.

Lynch, Marc, *Upheaval: U.S. Policy Toward Iran in a Changing Middle East*, Washington, D.C.: Center for a New American Security, June 2011.

MacAskill, Ewen, and Robert Tait, "TV Diplomacy: Obama's Video Message to Iranians," *Guardian*, March 21, 2009.

Malek, Martin, "Russia, Iran, and the Conflict in Chechnya," *Caucasian Review of International Affairs*, Vol. 2, No. 1, 2008.

Maller, Tara, "Diplomacy Derailed: The Consequences of Diplomatic Sanctions," *Washington Quarterly*, Vol. 33, No. 3, July 2010.

Maloney, Suzanne, "Sanctioning Iran: If Only It Were So Simple," *Washington Quarterly*, Vol. 33, No. 1, January 2010.

Maloney, Suzanne, "The Economics of Influening Iran," *Middle East Memo*, No. 16, Saban Center for Middle East Policy at the Brookings Institution, March 2010.

Mark, J. Carson, "Explosive Properties of Reactor-Grade Plutonium," *Science & Global Security*, Vol. 4, No. 1, 1993.

Marquardt, Alexander, "U.S. Denies Role in Iranian Nuclear Scientist's Assassination," ABC News, January 11, 2012. As of July 23, 2012:
http://abcnews.go.com/Blotter/iranian-nuclear-scientist-killed-amid-heightened-tensions/story?id=15338086#.UA7VnGmXSY4

Medeiros, Evan S., *Reluctant Restraint: The Evolution of China's Nonproliferation Policies and Practices, 1980–2004*, Stanford, Calif.: Stanford University Press, 2007.

Meier, Oliver, "Iran and Foreign Enrichment: A Troubled Model," *Arms Control Today*, Vol. 36, No. 1, 2006.

Melman, Yossi, "Behind the Scene of UN Nuclear Inspection of Iran," *Ha'aretz*, October 22, 2010.

Miller, Greg, and Joby Warrick, "U.S. Report Finds Debate in Iran on Building Nuclear Bomb," *Washington Post*, February 19, 2011.

"Ministry 'Engineered' Parts of Iranian Nuclear Deal—Russian Ambassador to U.S.," Interfax, May 10, 1995 (BBC Monitoring).

Moore, Molly, "Iran Restarts Uranium Program," *Washington Post*, February 15, 2006.

Morgan, Forrest E., Karl P. Mueller, Evan S. Medeiros, Kevin S. Pollpeter, and Roger Cliff, *Dangerous Thresholds: Managing Escalation in the 21st Century*, Santa Monica, Calif.: RAND Corporation, MG-614-AF, 2008.

Moseley, Ray, "Saudi Prince Warns Iran on Nuclear Weapons," *al Arabiya*, June 30, 2011.

Moslem, Mehdi, *Factional Politics in Post-Khomeini Iran*, Syracuse, N.Y.: Syracuse University Press, 2002.

Mulrine, Anna, "Blockbuster U.S. Arms Sale to Saudi Arabia," *Christian Science Monitor*, September 21, 2010.

Nader, Alireza, "Ahmadinejad vs. the Revolutionary Guards," *Frontline*, July 11, 2011. As of July 23, 2012:
http://www.pbs.org/wgbh/pages/frontline/tehranbureau/2011/07/ahmadinejad-vs-the-revolutionary-guards.html

Nader, Alireza, David E. Thaler, and S.R. Bohandy, *The Next Supreme Leader: Succession in the Islamic Republic of Iran*, Santa Monica, Calif.: RAND Corporation, MG-1052-OSD, 2011.

Nakamura, David, "Obama Signs Defense Bill, Pledges to Maintain the Rights of U.S. Citizens," *Washington Post*, December 31, 2011.

Obama, Barack, Prepared Remarks at Cairo University, June 4, 2009. As of July 23, 2012:
www.whitehouse.gov/the-press-office/remarks-president-cairo-university-6-04-09

"Obama Prods Netanyahu, Iran in Mideast Foray," Associated Press, May 19, 2009.

"Obama Reaches Out to Muslim World," BBC News, January 27, 2009. As of July 23, 2012:
http://news.bbc.co.uk/2/hi/middle_east/8082676.stm

Office of the Director of National Intelligence, *Iran: Nuclear Intentions and Capabilities*, National Intelligence Estimate, November 2007. As of July 23, 2012:
http://www.dni.gov/press_releases/20071203_release.pdf

O'Rourke, Breffni, "Iran: Ahmadinejad's Threat to 'Traitors' Points to Widening Rift," *Radio Free Europe/Radio Liberty*, November 14, 2007. As of July 23, 2012:
http://www.rferl.org/content/article/1079131.html

O'Sullivan, Meghan L., *Shrewd Sanctions: Statecraft and State Sponsors of Terrorism*, Washington, D.C.: Brookings Institution Press, 2003.

O'Sullivan, Meghan L., "Iran and the Great Sanctions Debate," *Washington Quarterly*, Vol. 33, No. 4, October 2010.

Ottaway, Marina, "Iran, the United States, and the Gulf: The Elusive Regional Policy," *Carnegie Paper No. 105*, Washington, D.C.: Carnegie Endowment for International Peace, November 2009.

Oye, Kenneth A., *Economic Discrimination and Political Exchange: World Political Economy in the 1930s and 1980s*, Princeton, N.J.: Princeton University Press, 1992.

"Panetta: Iran Is Seeking Capability to Build Nuclear Weapon but Hasn't Decided to Develop One," Associated Press, January 8, 2012.

Park, John S., "Iran and China," in Robin Wright, ed., *The Iran Primer: Power, Politics, and U.S. Policy*, Washington, D.C.: United States Institute of Peace, 2010, pp. 182–185.

Parker, John W., *Persian Dreams: Moscow and Tehran Since the Fall of the Shah*, Washington, D.C.: Potomac Books, 2009.

Pollack, Kenneth M., Daniel M. Byman, Martin Indyk, Suzanne Maloney, Michael E. O'Hanlon, and Bruce Riedel, *Which Path to Persia? Options for a New American Strategy Toward Iran*, Washington, D.C.: Brookings Institution Press, 2009.

"Putin: Russia Opposes Force, Sanctions on Iran," Associated Press, June 21, 2011.

"Quds Day Speech by Chairman of Expediency Council Akbar Hashemi Rafsanjani," Voice of the Islamic Republic of Tehran, December 14, 2001 (BBC Monitoring).

Raas, Whitney, and Austin Long, "Osirak Redux? Assessing Israeli Capabilities to Destroy Iranian Nuclear Facilities," *International Security*, Vol. 31, No. 4, 2007.

Reardon, Robert J., *Nuclear Bargaining: Using Carrots and Sticks in Nuclear Counter-Proliferation*, dissertation, Cambridge, Mass.: Massachusetts Institute of Technology, 2010.

Reardon, Robert J., "Should We Talk to Our Adversaries?" paper presented at the International Studies Association 2011 Annual Convention, Montreal, Canada, March 19, 2011.

Reardon, Robert J., "Russia, Iran, and the Nuclear Nonproliferation Regime," paper presented at the International Security Studies Section (ISA)/International Security and Arms Control Section (APSA) Joint Annual Conference, Irvine, Calif., October 13, 2011.

Richelson, Jeffrey T., *Spying on the Bomb*, New York: W.W. Norton & Co., 2007.

Rubin, Uzi, "Showcase of Missile Proliferation: Iran's Missile and Space Program," *Arms Control Today*, Vol. 42, No. 1, January/February 2012.

"Russia, China Set to Sell Iran Reactors," Associated Press, September 11, 1992.

Sadjadpour, Karim, *Reading Khamenei: The World View of Iran's Most Powerful Leader*, Washington, D.C.: Carnegie Endowment for International Peace, 2008.

Sadjadpour, Karim, "The Sources of Soviet Iranian Conduct," *Foreign Policy*, November 2010. As of July 23, 2012:
http://www.foreignpolicy.com/articles/2010/10/11/the_sources_of_ssoviets_iranian_conduct

Sadjadpour, Karim, "The Rise and Fall of Iran's Ahmadinejad," *Washington Post*, July 13, 2011.

Sahimi, Muhammad, "Khamenei versus Khamenei: Will Ahmadinejad Be Impeached?" *Frontline*, July 10, 2011. As of July 23, 2012:
http://www.pbs.org/wgbh/pages/frontline/tehranbureau/2011/07/khamenei-versus-khamenei-will-ahmadinejad-be-impeached.html

Sanger, David E., and Steven R. Weisman, "U.S. and European Allies Agree on Steps in Iran Dispute," *New York Times*, March 11, 2005.

Sanger, David E., *Confront and Conceal: Obama's Secret Wars and Surprising Use of American Power*, New York: Crown Publishers, 2012.

Sanger, David E., "Obama Ordered Sped Up Wave of Cyberattacks Against Iran," *New York Times*, June 1, 2012.

Schelling, Thomas, *Arms and Influence*, New Haven, Conn.: Yale University Press, 1966.

Sciolino, Elaine, "Europeans Say Iran Agrees to Freeze Uranium Enrichment," *New York Times*, November 16, 2004.

Segal, Adam, "Segal: China Hoping to Avoid Confrontation over Iran's Nuclear Program," interview conducted by Bernard Gwertzman, Council on Foreign Relations, January 24, 2006. As of July 23, 2012:
http://www.cfr.org/china/segal-china-hoping-avoid-confrontation-over-irans-nuclear-program/p9652

"Sejil (Ashoura)," *Jane's Strategic Weapon Systems*, July 20, 2010.

Shaffer, Brenda, *Partners in Need: The Strategic Relationship of Russia and Iran*, Washington, D.C.: Washington Institute for Near East Policy, 2001.

"Shahab-3/4 (Ghadr-1)," *Jane's Strategic Weapon Systems*, July 20, 2010.

Shanker, Thom, "Aides Qualify Panetta's Comments on Iran," *New York Times*, December 20, 2011.

Shifrinson, Joshua R. Itzkowitz, and Miranda Priebe, "A Crude Threat: The Limits of an Iranian Missile Campaign Against Saudi Arabian Oil," *International Security*, Vol. 36, No. 1, Summer 2011.

Shleifer, Andrei, and Daniel Treisman, "Why Moscow Says No," *Foreign Affairs*, Vol. 90, No. 1, 2011.

Shuster, Mike, "Inside the United States' Secret Sabotage of Iran," NPR, May 9, 2011. As of July 23, 2012:
http://www.npr.org/2011/05/09/135854490/inside-the-united-states-secret-sabotage-of-iran

Simon, Steven, "An Israeli Strike on Iran," Contingency Planning Memorandum No. 5, Washington, D.C.: Carnegie Endowment for International Peace, November 2009. As of July 23, 2012:
http://www.cfr.org/israel/israeli-strike-iran/p20637

Smith, Michael, "Iran Threatens Gulf Blitz If U.S. Hits Nuclear Plants," *Sunday Times*, June 10, 2007.

Snyder, Glenn H., *The Balance of Power and the Balance of Terror*, San Francisco: Chandler, 1965.

Solingen, Etel, *Nuclear Logics: Contrasting Paths in East Asia and the Middle East*, Princeton, N.J.: Princeton University Press, 2007.

Solomon, Jay, "U.S., Saudis to Discuss Nuclear Agreement," *Wall Street Journal*, July 29, 2011.

Spector, Leonard, *Going Nuclear: The Spread of Nuclear Weapons, 1986–1987*, Cambridge, Mass.: Ballinger, 1987.

Taghavi, Roshanak, "Iran's Power Struggle Is Set to Escalate," *Guardian*, July 15, 2011.

Tait, Robert, "TV Diplomacy: Obama's Video Message to Iranians," *Guardian*, March 21, 2009.

Takeyh, Ray, "It's Not Israel That's Driving Tehran to Nukes," *International Herald Tribune*, August 27, 2005.

Takeyh, Ray, *Hidden Iran: Paradox and Power in the Islamic Republic*, New York: Holt, 2006.

Takeyh, Ray, *Guardians of the Revolution: Iran and the World in the Age of the Ayatollahs*, New York: Oxford University Press, 2009.

Talmadge, Caitlin, "Closing Time: Assessing the Iranian Threat to the Strait of Hormuz," *International Security*, Vol. 33, No. 1, Summer 2008.

Thaler, David E., Alireza Nader, Shahram Chubin, Jerrold D. Green, Charlotte Lynch, and Frederic Wehrey, *Mullahs, Guards, and* Bonyads*: An Exploration of Iranian Leadership Dynamics*, Santa Monica, Calif.: RAND Corporation, MG-878-OSD, 2010. As of July 23, 2012:
http://www.rand.org/pubs/monographs/MG878.html

Tirone, Jonathan, "Iran Raises Uranium Output as Photos Show Need for Wider Checks," Bloomberg News, November 3, 2009. As of July 23, 2012: http://www.bloomberg.com/apps/news?pid=newsarchive&sid=aMtzNb9WS83I

Toukhan, Abdullah, and Anthony H. Cordesman, *Study on a Possible Israeli Strike on Iran's Nuclear Development Facilities*, Washington, D.C.: Center for Strategic and International Studies, 2009. As of July 23, 2012: http://csis.org/files/media/csis/pubs/090316_israelistrikeiran.pdf

Trachtenberg, Marc, "A 'Wasting Asset': American Strategy and the Shifting Nuclear Balance, 1949–1954," *International Security*, Vol. 13, No. 3, 1989.

Trenin, Dmitri, and Alexey Malashenko, *Iran: A View from Moscow*, Washington, D.C.: Carnegie Endowment for International Peace, 2010.

United Nations Security Council Resolution 1737 (2006), S/RES/1737(2006), adopted December 23, 2006. As of July 23, 2012: http://www.securitycouncilreport.org/atf/cf/%7B65BFCF9B-6D27-4E9C-8CD3-CF6E4FF96FF9%7D/Iran%20SRES%201737.pdf

United Nations Security Council Resolution 1747 (2007), S/RES/1747(2007), adopted March 24, 2007. As of July 23, 2012: http://daccess-dds-ny.un.org/doc/UNDOC/GEN/N07/281/40/PDF/N0728140.pdf?OpenElement

"U.S.: Iran Faces 'Crippling' Sanctions If Nuclear Talks Fail," Reuters, April 22, 2009.

Vaez, Ali, and Charles D. Ferguson, "An Iranian Offer Worth Considering," *New York Times*, September 29, 2011.

Vinocur, John, "Clock Ticking for West to Act on Iranian Nuclear Program," *New York Times*, December 29, 2011.

Walcott, John, "Diplomat Attacks Raise Specter of Escalating Israel-Iran War," Bloomberg News, February 14, 2012. As of July 23, 2012: http://www.bloomberg.com/news/2012-02-13/delhi-blast-hurts-two-in-israeli-embassy-car-as-georgia-bomb-is-made-safe.html

Wallander, Celeste, "Russia's Interest in Trading with the 'Axis of Evil,'" PONARS Policy Memo 248, Washington, D.C.: Center for Strategic and International Studies, October 2002. As of July 23, 2012: http://csis.org/files/media/csis/pubs/pm_0248.pdf

Walt, Stephen M., *The Origins of Alliances*, Ithaca, N.Y.: Cornell University Press, 1987.

Wehrey, Frederic, Jerrold D. Green, Brian Nichiporuk, Alireza Nader, Lydia Hansell, Rasool Nafisi, and S.R. Bohandy, *The Rise of the Pasdaran: Assessing the Domestic Roles of Iran's Islamic Revolutionary Guards Corps*, Santa Monica, Calif.: RAND Corporation, MG-821-OSD, 2009. As of July 23, 2012: http://www.rand.org/pubs/monographs/MG821.html

Wehrey, Frederic, Theodore W. Karasik, Alireza Nader, Jeremy J. Ghelz, Lydia Hansell, and Robert A. Guffey, *Saudi-Iranian Relations Since the Fall of Saddam: Rivalry, Cooperation, and Implications for U.S. Policy*, Santa Monica, Calif.: RAND Corporation, MG-840-SRF, 2009. As of July 23, 2012: http://www.rand.org/pubs/monographs/MG840.html

Wines, Michael, "Middle East Trip Suggests Change in Policy by China," *New York Times*, January 13, 2012.

X (George Kennan), "The Sources of Soviet Conduct," *Foreign Affairs*, Vol. 25, No. 4, 1947.

Zanotti, Jim, Kenneth Katzman, Jeremiah Gertler, and Steven A. Hildreth, *Israel: Possible Military Strike Against Iran's Nuclear Facilities*, Washington, D.C.: Congressional Research Service, R42443, March 28, 2012. As of July 23, 2012: http://www.fas.org/sgp/crs/mideast/R42443.pdf